Nature's Colors

Nature's Colors:
Dyes from Plants
Ida Grae

Photography
DANIEL GRAE

ROBIN & RUSS HANDWEAVERS
533 North Adams Street
McMinnville, Oregon 97128

Republished in 1991 by Robin & Russ, Handweavers,
533 North Adams Street, McMinnville, Oregon 97128

Library of Congress Cataloging in Publication Data
Grae, Ida.
    Nature's colors.
    Bibliography: p.
    1. Dyes and dyeing.   2. Dye plants.   I. Title.
TP919.G7   667".26   73-11836
ISBN 1-56659-002-7

Acknowledgments

In this presentation of the ancient craft of dyeing I am indebted to the craftsmen who came before, and to my students—now colleagues—who are a constant inspiration and joy. I am particularly indebted to my natural dye seminar group, The Cabala, whose members gave unstintingly of their time, ingenuity, and devotion. They are Noel Brenner, Ruth Friend, Mary Mihal, Christine Nielson, Pat Todd, and Jessie Wold.

I am especially indebted to Dr. Elizabeth McClintock, Curator and Chairman, Department of Botany at the California Academy of Sciences, Golden Gate Park, San Francisco. She has acted as botanical consultant and has been most helpful with information and critique of the botanical material in this book.

I wish also to thank the following people for making plant specimens available to me for experimentation: Mr. Wayne Roderick, Museum Scientist, University of California Botanical Gardens, Berkeley, California; and Mr. John Kipping, Naturalist, Strybing Arboretum, Golden Gate Park, San Francisco.

Special appreciation goes to Mrs. Elizabeth Bates, Head, Engineering Library, Stanford University, for reading and critique of the manuscript, and to Carol Potter Hansen who helped arrange and type the manuscript. The beautiful drawings are the work of Constance Goddard.

My principal thanks are to my lovable daughter, Bettina, and to my husband, Daniel, whose encouragement has been vital to me. I also offer appreciation for the effort and fine results obtained by him in the photography for this book.

Contents

Introduction

Having practiced and taught textile art for many years, it is not surprising that color is one of my major preoccupations. Since my workshop is in the middle of a weedy meadow, it is also to be expected that nature became very important to me. Sometimes nature was there as a reminder of chores undone: too many weeds. Or again, it was planting time.

Other times the natural setting became a lure. I wondered: What is that plant? What would it do? Could one eat it? Would it yield a color? Then I made the plunge: I boiled up a bit of clean cloth and a plant and got a dyed sample! Thus began the fascination.

This is natural dyeing. It can be for anyone, and the dyes are present in many plants around us. Weeds, garden subjects, clay, and kitchen leftovers are possibilities. You need only learn a method of working. Kitchen tools and measurements and a shelf or two are more than adequate for a dyer's corner.

Once interested, it is possible to color-prospect endlessly. There are special methods of working which are directed toward discovery, rather than depending on recipes. One of these methods involves rotting rather than cooking. It is especially useful for achieving sensitive colors such as roses and reds. This is an ancient way and perhaps represents one of the earliest dyeing procedures.

Practicing early ways of dyeing can be rewarding. It is exciting to begin an experiment hoping for the unexpected. Perhaps it may lead to finding the ever-elusive blue. Or then again one might discover a magenta for cotton.

There are other rewards in this craft. It is satisfying to know that our way of getting color from nature was practiced for thousands of years. Following an ancient method or recipe gives one a feeling of continuity with the past. (One recipe for brown stains my fingernails. It must have had the same effect in 500 B.C.!)

At this point the reader may well say:

Fine. I would like to experience the excitement of discovery; the feeling of kinship; the sharpening of artistic perception. *But where am I going to find my dye stuff?*
From wild plants, flowers, and foods around you.

Are there recipes in this book?
Yes, more than 200.

What can I dye?
Yarn, cloth, macrame objects, crochet work, tie-dyed fabric, wood, and many other items.

Will the colors be fast?
Some will, others less so.

Can I expect to repeat a color?
Yes, but not exactly. Plants vary and results vary. Even commercial dyers have dye lot problems.

Can I do quantity dyeing?

Yes, if large enough quantities of
natural dyestuffs are available.
(What else might you ask?)
Why use natural dyes?

Because they are so beautiful. The
subtle range of color, the variation
within a color is to be found nowhere except in nature's own
abundant storehouse. And, because of the wonderful feeling of
"I did it!"

1

Let us discover dyeing as the ancients did

This chapter introduces the reader to direct, primitive ways of coloring. Many of the processes are still valid for us. First of all, we can find out that natural materials yield color, perhaps dye. We can also learn other uses for natural color beside textile dyeing: body painting, plant rubbings on different materials, cosmetic uses, picture painting, color testing. At the end of the chapter there are three recipes which can more accurately be called textile dyeing rather than painting. They represent true dyeing in its earliest stages. The ingredients are readily available and directions are simple. The techniques and recipes presented are not intended as substitutes for more developed methods. The reader is referred to other chapters for basic information and recipes. We begin by experiencing (which is the way dyeing began). Have you noticed that certain foods—such as beets and berries—color the fingers when being prepared? That some edibles—such as tea, wine, and fruit juice—stain your napkin or shirt or tablecloth and don't wash out? That some picnics leave us with unforgettable memories—such as grass or clay stains on clothing?

These are unsought experiences of coloration. They represent first-hand encounters with the fact that many plants and clays have dyes. We refer to such accidental effects as "stains," and we wish the colored spot would go away, or be "fugitive." Such would not be the case if we wanted dye in a fabric. We would want the fabric to remain dyed for a long time. We would wish for a permanent dye, rather than a fugitive one.

Anthropologists believe that early ways of coloring may have had their origin in accidental staining. It seems likely that the effects of colored juices from berries, nuts, and roots were noticed by primitive peoples and admired. To begin with, plants may have been applied directly on garments or on the body. Later, plants were crushed and the juices were utilized to paint the body and face. Colored clays were probably used in the same way as they are today. The painting of clothing and other objects was a natural next step. Color was also applied to the walls of caves, to baskets, to pottery, and to many other everyday objects.

With these early ways in mind, I am suggesting some color experiments. It is hoped that your spirit will be adventurous. Some of the results will be disappointing, but some of them will yield interesting color samples. It is even possible to achieve creative effects with these simple means. I promise this: you *may* get color on whatever you are marking, but for sure you will end up with color on something you are not intending to mark!

Following are several suggested experiments with plant rubbings. They will demonstrate the many coloring possibilities of natural material. The basic procedure is direct. It involves trying out various natural materials, for color, by *rubbing* them on paper, wood, porous ceramic ware, or fabric. *Any surface* that can be rubbed or marked on is fair game. It will be noticed that absorbent surfaces receive color better than dense, nonabsorbent surfaces.

Some plant materials, or foods, or clays do not have coloring power. Others will leave a deeply-colored mark. Surprisingly, a flower does not necessarily yield the color it so plainly shows. Red flowers do not always leave red marks, and white flowers are not always colorless on paper. Both red and purple petunias leave a purplish rubbing on paper and bisque ware (low-fired, unglazed ceramics). The purplish color of the red petunia has a greenish overtone. Red pentstemon yields a pale, magenta-pink on paper. Sunflower rubs off on wood and bisque ware as a deep yellow. There are many surprises.

Berries are full of color. We might say they have "tinctorial" qualities. As body stain, mulberries are more potent than blackberries. Perhaps in the spirit of fun (and some seriousness), I suggest using food materials as cosmetics. Pink your cheeks with strawberries or beets. Darken your eyelids with blackberries. Limn your eyes with blueberry juice. After all, these are natural, harmless substances, and it is fashionable to color the lips and eyelids.

WARNING: *Use only edibles and plants known to be nontoxic for cosmetics.*

The gourd and calabash present interesting possibilities for dyeing. Decorative utilitarian objects can be made from these dried vege-tables. Many West African peoples made their daily eating utensils from calabash. The design, usually geometric, was incised, or carved. Strongly colored plant juice can be used to rub into the incised pattern, or over the entire calabash. Juice from the mulberry is beautiful here.

Plant dyes can be used for sketching and painting. It is possible to utilize various plant juices as one would watercolors. The effect is similar because natural juices tend to be transparent. A leaf or flower, for example, can be rubbed directly on paper. Besides color, certain textural effects would result from the plant pulp. For instance, a blue iris, rubbed on paper, would leave a bluish area, and some fine bits of flower tissue for texture.

Sketches made in this way can be beautiful. However, some of the dyes are fugitive. I suggest several alternatives. One possibility is to make a book of paintings, and to let the paintings remain in book form. Thus the paintings are not exposed to light, as they would be hanging on a wall, and there will be no fading. Accordion-pleated, rice paper notebooks are inspiring to work in. They are also beautiful as completed objects.

The problem of fugitive color in natural painting can be avoided altogether. I recommend the use of clay and naturally occurring minerals. These pigments are usually lightfast, and are opaque, not transparent like plant juice.

Finally, a very practical use of plant rubbing must be mentioned— testing for dye possibilities. One can eventually find some correlation between the color rubbing and the dye potential of a plant. If a plant yields no color when used as a marker, it is not a good dye prospect. If a plant leaves a rich, deep color on paper, it is a good dye prospect. There is also some correlation between color as it appears on paper and after the dye process.

We have been describing primitive uses of dyes, primarily staining or painting. We have called our method painting rather than dyeing, because the colors were *applied to the surface* of various materials. The process of dyeing on the other hand involves penetration of the dye *into the substance*. Dyes can penetrate into a material when in solution. Heat helps dye penetration. Certain chemicals also help the process of dyeing.

When early man began heating dyestuff in water, a new phase of coloring began. Some of the dye used dissolved easily in water and penetrated materials very well. Whether or not the dye was permanent depended upon many factors. These are matters to be covered in later chapters.

Now, let us try some true dyeing. The three recipes which follow have a twofold purpose. They will serve as a kind of warm-up to demonstrate how direct natural dyeing can be. These recipes also represent types of dyestuff and methods which are relatively primitive. There will be a recipe using an ancient dyestuff that is also a spice: turmeric. Another recipe uses a chartreuse-colored lichen commonly known as staghorn moss. The third recipe uses tea and an iron pot. (In ancient times, a spring water which was rich in iron would have been used. We substitute the iron pot for the mineral springs.)

Some of the dye recipes have asterisks following the dye plant name. This means that the recipes use an unmordanted textile (fiber, yarn, or fabric). That is, the textile used will readily accept the dye without the aid of chemicals.

1 / TURMERIC SPICE*
(Curcuma longa)

BRIGHT GOLDEN ORANGE: ALL NATURAL FIBERS; POOR LIGHTFASTNESS.

Primarily a potent tinting method. Color will not fade in interior light. Accessories, such as scarves or turbans, can be dyed over if they fade.

TEXTILE
(or fiber types)

Wool, cotton, jute, linen, or silk—very clean and wet (I dyed 2 linen macrame wall hangings, 1 silk scarf, and 1 old linen towel—one at a time.) (10 ounces)

INGREDIENTS

Tin of turmeric spice (buy at grocery) (1½ ounces)
Lemon juice or vinegar (1 cup either)

WATER

Tap water will do, enough to cover and float articles to be dyed (4 quarts or more)

POT

Stainless steel, enameled (no chips), Pyrex, or ceramic (Absolutely clean! No grease!) (5-quart or larger)
Chopstick or stainless steel spoon for stirring

METHOD

1. Dissolve turmeric in hot water.
2. Add lemon juice or vinegar and stir.
3. Heat slowly. (This is the dye bath.)
4. Immerse textile and stir occasionally.
5. Simmer for 30 minutes (190°F or 83°–91°C).
6. Cool in dye bath.
7. Remove textile and rinse thoroughly in running water. (Do not use soap—it will color the textile red, fleetingly!)
8. Dry in shade.

Follow the same procedure for each additional textile, using same dye bath. If a very large pot is available, all pieces can be dyed at once, but more care in handling is necessary.

NOTE: Pots made of stainless steel, enameled, Pyrex, or ceramic ware will be referred to as "nonreacting" in following recipes.

2/STAGHORN MOSS LICHEN*
(Letharia vulpina)
GREENISH YELLOW: SILK OR WOOL; GOOD COLORFASTNESS.

Restricted to California. Canadian Cetraria, which is found in the northern United States and Canada, may be used in the same manner as staghorn moss. This lichen is rich in alum—one of the important mordant chemicals.

TEXTILE
(or fiber types)
Silk or wool—very clean and wet, soaked for 3 or 4 hours (I dyed two silk scarves and one skein of wool.) (4 ounces)

INGREDIENT
Staghorn moss (lichen), torn into small pieces (4 ounces)

WATER
Tap (4 quarts)

POT
Nonreacting (8-quart or larger)

METHOD
1. Soak moss in water overnight.
2. Enter yarn or fabric.
3. Boil for 1 hour, stirring occasionally.
4. Cool overnight in dye bath.
5. Rinse, pick out moss.
6. Dry in the shade.

3/BLACK TEA*
(Thea sinensis)
ROSE-TAN (STEP I): ALL NATURAL FIBERS; GOOD LIGHTFASTNESS.
GRAY OR BLACK (STEP II): ALL NATURAL FIBERS; GOOD WASHFASTNESS.

TEXTILE
Wool, silk, cotton, jute, or linen (very clean and wet) (3 ounces)

INGREDIENT
Fresh or used tea leaves (I used 20 tea bags) ($1\frac{1}{2}$ ounces, or 20 tea bags)
Vinegar (for Step II) (2 cups)

WATER
Tap (4 to 6 quarts, or as needed to cover)

POTS
Step I
Nonreacting (8-quart or larger)
Step II
Iron, absolutely without grease!

METHOD
Step I
1. Soak tea in boiling water for several hours.
2. Cool.
3. Enter cloth or yarn.
4. Simmer 30 minutes (190°F or 83°–91°C), stirring occasionally.
5. Cool overnight in dye bath.

For rose-tan: Rinse thoroughly and dry in shade.

For gray or black: Proceed to Step II.

Step II
1. Pour tea mixture (from Step I) into iron pot.
2. Add vinegar and simmer for 1 hour.
3 Cool.
4. Enter tea-dyed textile into iron pot.
5. Add water to cover if necessary.
6. Simmer for 30 minutes (190°F or 83°–91°C), moving textile around to prevent streaking.
7. Cool overnight in dye bath.
8. Rinse thoroughly.
9. Dry in shade.
10. Soap can be used.

NOTE: See Chapter IV for effect of special utensils.

Experimenter, please take note of the following:

1. The preceding recipes make use of the one-pot method. This means

the dye plant and the material to be dyed and the water are simmered together. The result is that plant particles will adhere to the fabric or yarn. When dyeing is completed these bits of plant material can be picked or shaken out. For more sophisticated methods see later chapters.

2. When you try these warm-up recipes, begin by testing small bits of yarn or fabric to see if you like the color and to find out if your fabric fiber will receive the dye. There are many mixtures of fibers and special fabric treatments that prevent a good dye result.

3. Recipe 1 is the easiest.

4. Recipe 2, staghorn moss, is a good one. However, not everyone will find this lichen. Try other lichens, and see what happens. Some work, some do not.

5. Good luck to you!

2

Types of natural dye-stuff; back-ground of selected exotic dyes

In this chapter, the three classes of natural dyes (direct, mordant, and vat) are defined. We then present briefly the story of the exotic imported dyes. These were the "commercial" dyes used from antiquity on into the nineteenth century. Their vital involvement in the track of history is indicated. Some contemporary uses of dye plants are mentioned, and dye recipes are included at the end of the chapter.

There are three classes of dyes from the point of view of how a textile receives dye. Were you tempted to try the turmeric recipe in Chapter I? Then you noticed how quickly both the dye bath and your textile became a brilliant orange-yellow. Similarly, with the greenish-yellow staghorn moss, as the dye bath began to simmer, color was taken up by the textile. These two dye substances belong to the class of dyes called "direct," or substantive. When a dye substance is soluble

in water and is taken up directly, it is a substantive dye. Turmeric, safflower, some lichens, and annatto are members of this group. All dyers wish there were many more like these.

The second class of dyes is called "mordant" dyes. Most natural dyes belong to this group. A dyestuff which *cannot be fixed* on the fiber without the use of chemical assistants is called a mordant dye. (A "mordant" is a chemical which combines with the dye within the fiber.) Most of the recipes in this book use mordant dyes. For this reason, it is important to learn how to use the fixing agents which hold the dye in the fiber. Examples of mordant chemicals are alum, chrome, iron, tin, and copper salts.

"Vat" dyes are the third class of dyestuff and the most rare in nature. The crude vat dye is insoluble. It must therefore be acted upon, either by bacteria or chemicals and reduced to solubility. When a textile is immersed in the solution and then exposed to air, the dye is oxidized and fixed permanently on the fiber. No wonder vat dyes are lightfast and washfast. The magnificent Tyrian purple and indigo blue are examples of this dye class. Even though vat dyeing is demanding, it is within the home dyer's capability.

We have discussed three dye classifications, divided according to the process by which the dye is fixed on the fiber. This is a useful grouping. We will actually be making use of these groupings in our recipes. Another helpful way of grouping dyes is by their origin, or source. From the point of view of source, dyes are either artificial or natural. Among the natural sources of dyes are plants, animals, and minerals. Our recipes make use mainly of plants. Examples of animal sources are Tyrian purple from mollusks and reds and scarlets from the female kermes, lac, and cochineal insects. Recipe 3 (Tea in an Iron Pot), and Recipes 4 and 5 (Iron Buff), demonstrate the use of mineral coloration.

HISTORICAL BACKGROUND

With the above information in mind, let us quickly survey a few of the great commercial dyes of antiquity. We do this partly to pay our respects, but mainly to gain knowledge.

Natural materials were the only source of dyes until 1856. At that time, Sir Henry Perkin, quite by accident, discovered a mauve-colored coal tar product which he named "mauveine." (He had been attempting to synthesize quinine.) This discovery proved to be the beginning of the artificial dye industry. Gradually, natural dyestuffs were discarded. Finally, with the synthesis of an indigo blue substitute in production in 1900, natural dyes became a part of the past.

It is important to point out the *accidental* aspect of Sir Henry's discovery. Natural dyes were doing the job. Recipes had been refined over thousands of years. The art of dyeing was highly developed. The colors were reasonably fast, as bright as one knew of, and cheap. Chemists were not concerned with textile colors because the old dyes were serving superbly. Besides, dyeing was not yet a science.

The point I am making is that the old dyes represented 6,000 years of trial, accidental discovery, and evolving refinement. All this was lost when the dye industry turned exclusively to the use of artificial dyes. Not only did we lose the technology of natural dyeing,

but we also lost contact with still another home art. And as a result, we lost a little more of our self-esteem. (It does give you self-esteem to know that you can go outdoors, collect a pot full of weeds, brew a dye, and color your shirt in the brew.)

It is recorded by ancient writers that there were at one time nearly a thousand different natural sources of dye. As trade in dyestuffs improved in the ancient world, there evolved a limited group of dyestuffs considered most desirable. When trade routes opened up in the sixteenth century, these dyes became available to European dyers.

The types of dyes in use in Europe until the discovery of the artificial mauveine were a highly selected group. They were all imported primarily from the Near East and South America. Let us henceforth refer to them as the "imported" or "exotic" dyes, as contrasted to dyes from local North American plants, which this book will concentrate on. The most efficient natural dyes were the exotic dyes. The professional or home dyer of the early 1800s had twenty or so dyestuffs which he could use. Of these, there were about nine colors considered the most practical. They were: indigo and woad blue; cochineal and madder red; logwood black; fustic, weld, safflower, and saffron yellow. Of these, logwood is the only dye still being used commercially. (It is used for black on silk and nylon.) The others are available in limited amounts and can usually be purchased from shops that sell handweaving and spinning supplies. A list of exotic dyestuff sources will be found in Appendix I.

Are the exotic dyes worthwhile? Indeed. They are our most efficient source of natural dye. However, they are costly. Furthermore, the art and sport of natural dyeing involves finding your own plant sources. I feel that gathering plants for dye is much more fun than simply buying a package of exotic dye.

Let us, nonetheless, look at some background history and practical use of the venerable four: indigo, woad, cochineal, and madder. The most important of the dyestuffs, and perhaps the most venerated, was indigo. In Asia, it had been known as a cosmetic and dye for more than 4,000 years. Dye from the leaves of this plant yielded a beautiful deep blue on wool and cotton. Furthermore, it was markedly fast to both light and water. Such double fastness is most unusual. Also, sources of blue dye are very scarce in nature.

On the other hand, a blue sky meets the eye everywhere! Can you imagine the great frustration of early dyers who were constantly being reminded of blue and yet never finding it? Little wonder that indigo, so blue and so colorfast, became a highly valued trade item. This dye belongs to the special class known as vat dyes, and was still being used commercially in the early part of the twentieth-century. It was the last to be replaced by synthetic dyes. Nowadays in India, the original home of indigo, its only use is for hair dye! A full circle— from body stain, to fabric stain, to vat dye *par excellence*, to hair dye. And then, whammo. Gone.

So venerable a dye plant deserves at least our knowledge of it. Let us go a step further. Why not grow a plant or two? Seed and growing instructions are available. (See Appendix I for addresses of seed dealers.) Because the process of preparing the dye from the leaves is tedious, odorous, and demanding, it is suggested that powdered or lump indigo be purchased for experiment. Ancient recipes for indigo blue dying will be described in Chapter VII.

Woad (*Isatis tinctoria*) was the source of blue in Europe until the seventeenth-century. The plant is a member of the mustard family and like mustard was accustomed to cold climates. The coloring principle derived from the leaves is *indigotin* as in the indigo plant, but is of much less concentration. Woad is also a vat dye and is very fast to light and washing.

Ovid tells us that the ancient Teutons darkened their gray hair with woad. Perhaps because I labored through Caesar's *Gallic War* the following quotation intrigues me:

All the Britons indeed dye themselves with woad, which produces a blue colour, and makes their appearance in the battle more terrible. (Book V paragraph 14. Translation by Henry J. Edwards)

Also, the name "Picts" was given the ancient Celts because it meant "painted people." They pierced their skin with flint tools and rubbed woad dye into the incised designs.

For centuries, woad was a crop of great economic importance in Europe. Indigo, though far superior, remained too costly a dye to compete with woad. Even after sea trade with India was established, woad interests fought the use of indigo. Local governments backed woad combines with decrees. In England, the use of indigo carried severe penalties as late as the seventeenth-century. In Germany, where woad was grown extensively, anti-indigo laws were common. In France, cloth dyers were not given full freedom to use indigo until 1737. Thus, the freedom to use indigo in Europe was delayed by about 250 years! (Wm. Legett, *Ancient and Medieval Dyes*).

May we close the circle? My heart is sad. No, woad is not even being used to blacken some aging artist's hair. In California, however, the once near-royal dye plant grows unbeknownst and abundantly. I discovered it listed as a pernicious weed (!) growing in a northern county. It is known as "Marlahan mustard" because of its common occurrence on this ranch. The plant is perennial and biennial and is a pretty garden subject. It can be grown easily. It is not practical to cultivate woad primarily for dye use, however, because the process of extraction, like that of indigo, is difficult.

Red plant dye sources are almost as scarce as blue. It is therefore no wonder that madder and cochineal have been esteemed for centuries. The brightest reds were of animal origin. Dyes were extracted from about four types of beetles *(Coccidae).* The kermes beetles live on oak and the cochineal beetles live on cactus and grass. The dyes are brilliant red and scarlet and are remarkably lasting. Pliny referred to reds (and also to Tyrian purple) as luxury colors. These were indeed costly dyes. Each insect furnished a droplet (the source is so tiny). Therefore only the rich could afford these dyes.

Of all the sources of red, cochineal, found on opuntia cactus, became the most used. This form had been discovered in great quantities by the Spanish con-

Figure 1   COCHINEAL (*Coccus cacti*)

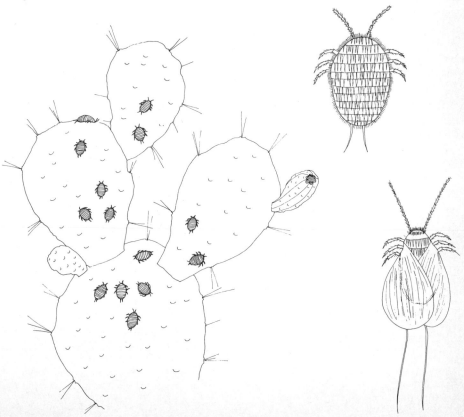

querors in Mexico who extorted and exported it to Europe. The Aztecs collected the mature female beetles by brushing or scraping them off the cactus. The beetles were killed by immersion in boiling water or vapor. Synthetic *alizarin* came into wide use in 1880 and thus completely replaced cochineal dye (for once I am not sorry). This dyestuff is still available and very much of a luxury. Its costliness (and feeling that it is cruel to kill so many insects for so little) leads me to suggest the use of a plant red, such as the madder root, or synthetic red dye!

The madder plant *(Rubia tinctorum)* is such an ancient and excellent source of red that its name means red in several languages. In Latin it is *rubia*, in German it is *rote*. Coffee, quinine, dyes, and medicines are all derived from this family. The dye, a mordant type, is obtained from the root of the plant, which is as slender as a pencil.

In Europe, madder became a plant of great economic importance. Charlemagne ordered it cultivated on his estates, hoping thereby to encourage farmers. In Holland, during the fifteenth, sixteenth and seventeenth centuries, it became the principal source of wealth. By 1782, France had become the top grower in Europe. We are told that the French Revolution ruined the madder farmers; they were later revived by a decree of Louis Philippe, which made red caps and trousers mandatory for his army.

In England, imported madder was used for dyeing the red British army uniforms (redcoats). Up to the time of the "1869 disaster," England's total madder imports came to one million pounds sterling! What happened in 1869? I call it the "Madder Disaster." Yes. It is

once again the end of a story. From a world production of 70,000 tons, madder declined to *nothing*, because in that year, 1869, artificial madder dye was synthesized. Historians speak of untilled and abandoned madder fields and of thousands of starving farmers. (See *The Cultivation of Madder* by G. Schaefer.)

Madder is gone, but it is not forgotten. Sweet woodruff, an herb, grows in many gardens. It is a member of the madder family, and its roots are said to make a fairly good red. Try substituting it in the madder recipe below. See illustrations of sweet woodruff and madder root (pages 23 and 189).

Following are some recipes that use mineral and exotic dyes. Indigo recipes are given in Chapter VII. It is recommended, however, that these be by-passed by the newcomer to dyeing. First of all, many imported dyes are expensive. Secondly, it is more confidence-inspiring to achieve dyes from the everyday, prosaic plants around us. Let us do it the way our early ancestors did—find our own! After you have experimented with plants of the countryside, try the mineral and exotic dyes.

4/COLONIAL IRON BUFF*
(Mineral Pigment from Scrap Iron)

ORANGE TO RUSTY RED: UNMORDANTED COTTON, LINEN, AND JUTE; REMARKABLY FAST TO LIGHT AND WASHING.

Mineral pigments have been used for fabric coloration for centuries. Before iron became a common metal, iron mineral springs were used for pigment dyeing. Iron rust is so permanent that sails were dyed with it. Manganese, chrome, and copper are also used as pigments. Metallic oxide coloration is lightfast and washfast but imparts stiffness to fabric. This is one difference between dye and pigment: dyes give utmost flexibility of fabric. Depth of color is achieved with pigments by successive dipping and airing (oxidizing) of the fabric. Indigo depends upon oxidation also, but it is a dye. The following method was practiced in American colonial times.

TEXTILE
Scoured, presoaked cotton, linen, or jute (3 or 4 ounces at a time)

INGREDIENTS
Scrap iron—nails, etc. (4 or 5 pounds)
Vinegar (1 gallon)
Water extract of wood ashes (enough to cover textile)

WATER
Tap (1 gallon)

POTS
Step I
Wood barrel

Step II
Nonreacting, used only for iron solutions or iron pot (large enough to accommodate rusty water and textile)

Step III
Basin or bucket used for wood ash extract

METHOD
Step I
Soak scrap iron in water and vinegar solution until water is deeply colored (2 months or more).

Step II
1. Heat iron liquor until just warm.
2. Enter textile and stir.
3. Lift out and wring.
4. Rinse textile lightly in plain water.
5. Wring out.

Step III
1. Dip textile in water extract of wood ashes.
2. Wring and shake out.
3. Hang in air to oxidize.
4. If deeper color is desired repeat Steps II and III.

5. Wash, rinse, and dry in shade.
NOTE: For wood ash extract: Place wood ashes on screen over a pan and pour hot water over them slowly. The water that drips through is strongly alkaline.
□ Henceforth, the word *textile* as it appears in a recipe can be understood to include fabric, yarn, loose fiber or garment to be dyed.

5/IRON BUFF*
(Mineral Pigment from Ferrous Sulfate)
ORANGE TO RUSTY RED: UNMORDANTED COTTON, LINEN, OR JUTE; REMARKABLY FAST TO LIGHT AND WASHING.

This recipe is a modern version of the preceding Colonial Iron Buff recipe.

TEXTILE
Scoured, presoaked cotton, linen, or jute (3 or 4 ounces at a time)

INGREDIENTS
Ferrous sulfate (4 tablespoons)
Washing soda (5% of weight of textile) (⅛ ounce)

WATER
Tap (2 gallons)

POTS
Step I
Any kind, even with chipped enamel. (You will not be able to use it for any other purpose.) (10-quart or larger)

Step II
Bowl, basin, or crock for the alkaline fixing bath. (10-quart or larger)

METHOD
Step I
1. Dissolve ferrous sulfate in 1 gallon of warm water.
2. Enter textile and stir.
3. Remove textile, wring, and rinse lightly.

Step II
1. Dissolve washing soda in 1 gallon of hot water.
2 Dip textile in washing soda bath.
3. Remove textile, wring, and shake out.

4. Hang in air to oxidize and turn orange.
5. Repeat Step I followed by Step II until desired depth of color is attained.
6. Wash, rinse, and dry in shade.

NOTES: Iron bath can be reused. □ Fixing bath gets dark and needs to be made afresh. □ Wear gloves. □ From this point on, a majority of the recipes do not include size of pot. It will be understood that the pot must be large enough to hold water, plant material, and the textile without crowding.

6/COCHINEAL
(Coccus cacti)
CRIMSON: ALUMED WOOL OR SILK; GOOD LIGHTFASTNESS.
ALSO CRIMSON:TANNIN-ALUMED COTTON; FAIR WASHFASTNESS.

One of the exotic dyes. Consists of the dried bodies of beetles which live on cactus. Main commercial source is from Mexico. Can be found in small amounts as an infestation on opuntia cactus growing in the United States.

TEXTILE
Scoured, presoaked, alum-mordanted, wool or silk; or cotton mordanted first in tannin and then with alum (8 ounces)

INGREDIENT
Cochineal (2½ ounces)

WATER
Distilled (3 gallons or enough to cover textile)

POT
Nonreacting

METHOD
1. Enter cochineal and a little water in dye pot.
2. Boil for a few minutes.
3. Add 3 gallons of water and the textile to the dye pot.
4. Boil for 30 minutes.
5. Cool and rinse.
6. Dry in shade.

NOTES: For silk use 3 ounces of cochineal and heat bath gradually to 212°F (100°C) for 30 minutes.
□ A pinch of tin crystals and cream of tartar added toward the end of dye period will yield a scarlet. (Remove textile from bath briefly while these ingredients are being added.)
□ Good results can be obtained by experimenting with various mordants. See Chapter V for mordanting directions.

7/CUTCH, CATECHU*
(Acacia catechu)
BROWN: COTTON AFTER-MORDANTED WITH CHROME; REMARKABLY FAST TO LIGHT AND WASHING.

Tree. Member of Pea Family. One of the exotic dyes and an unsurpassed cotton dye. Dye is extracted from the interior colored wood.

TEXTILE
Scoured, presoaked cotton (8 ounces)

INGREDIENTS
Cutch (1½ ounces)
Potassium dichromate (⅙ ounce)
Cream of tartar (⅙ ounce)

WATER
Distilled (enough to cover textile)

POT
Nonreacting

METHOD
1. Cover cutch with water in dye pot.
2. Soak several hours.
3. Enter cotton and heat to 200°F (93°C) for 1 hour.
4. Cool.
5. Prepare fresh water bath, adding chrome and cream of tartar dissolved in water.
6. Enter dyed cotton and heat to 140°F (60°C) for 30 minutes.
7. Cool, rinse with soap and water, and dry in shade.

NOTE: Additions of tin, iron, or copper to the dye bath will yield colors from yellow-brown to greenish to grayish to dark brown.

8/LOGWOOD CHIPS (Haematoxylon campechianum)

DARK TO MEDIUM BLUE: ALUMED COTTON, WOOL, OR JUTE; GOOD LIGHTFASTNESS.

One of the exotic dyes, imported from Central America. The only source of blue for cotton other than indigo. Not as colorfast as indigo, but potent, easier to use, and cheaper.

TEXTILE
Scoured, presoaked, alum-mordanted cotton, wool, linen, or jute (I dyed 2 ounces of yarn followed by a macrame hanging and a linen handkerchief and still the dye bath was not exhausted) (4 ounces)

INGREDIENTS
Logwood chips (1 ounce)
Cupric sulfate (2%) (1/8 ounce)

WATER
Distilled (1 gallon)

POT
Nonreacting

METHOD
1. Dissolve cupric sulfate in 1 gallon of water.
2. Add logwood chips and soak several hours.
3. Enter textile and heat to 122°F (50°C) slowly (takes about 20 minutes).
4. Keep at 122°F for 15 minutes.
5. Cool, rinse, and dry in shade.

NOTES: Try using an unlined copper pot instead of the cupric sulfate. If you can get blue, fine! □ Different mordants can be used before or with the dye bath for varying effect. Tin, for example, yields a purplish bloom.

9/LOGWOOD CHIPS (Haematoxylon campechianum)

BLUE: ALUMED WOOL; GOOD LIGHTFASTNESS.

TEXTILE
Scoured, presoaked alum-mordanted wool (8 ounces)

INGREDIENTS
Logwood chips (2 1/2 ounces)
Ground chalk (from pharmacy) (1/4 ounce)

WATER
Distilled (3 gallons)

POT
Nonreacting (5-gallon)

METHOD
1. Cover logwood chips with water and soak for several hours.
2. Mix chalk into dye bath.
3. Enter wool and simmer for 1 hour at 194°F (90°C).
4. Cool, rinse, and dry in shade.

NOTE: For a purplish bloom, add a pinch of tin crystals at end of dyeing.

10/LOGWOOD CHIPS, ONE-POT METHOD* (Haematoxylon campechianum)

BLACK TO GRAY: UNMORDANTED COTTON.

TEXTILE
Scoured, presoaked cotton (8 ounces)

INGREDIENTS
Logwood chips (4 ounces)
Ferrous sulfate (dissolved in 1 cup of hot water) (1/4 ounce)
Cream of tartar (dissolved in 1 cup of hot water) (1/2 ounce)

WATER
Tap (3 gallons)

POT
Nonreacting (5-gallon)

METHOD
1. Cover logwood chips with water and soak several hours.
2. Stir in the ferrous sulfate and cream of tartar solutions.
3. Enter cotton and slowly heat to 122°F (50°C) for 15 minutes.
4. Lift cotton out and expose to air for a few minutes.
5. Rinse and dry in shade.

NOTE: Less logwood and the addition of various tannin-rich substances will yield various gray colors.

11/LOGWOOD CHIPS
(Haematoxylon campechianum)

PURPLE: TIN-MORDANTED COTTON; GOOD LIGHTFASTNESS.

TEXTILE
Scoured, presoaked tin-mordanted cotton (8 ounces)

INGREDIENT
Logwood chips (4 ounces)

WATER
Distilled (3 gallons)

POT
Nonreacting (5-gallon)

METHOD
1. Cover logwood chips with water and soak for several hours.
2. Enter mordanted cotton and heat to 122°F (50°C) slowly for 15 minutes.
3. Cool, rinse, and dry in shade.

12/MADDER ROOTS
(Rubia tinctorum)

BRIGHT TO DULL RED: ALUMED WOOL OR SILK; FAST TO LIGHT.
ALSO BRIGHT TO DULL RED: TANNIN-ALUMED COTTON; FAST TO WASHING.

Madder Family. One of the exotic dyes. The red dye par excellence. Sweet woodruff is a member of this family, as is Northern bedstraw (Galium boreale), yellow bedstraw (Galium verum), cleavers (Galium aparine), and field madder (Sherardia arvensis L.) Please see the illustration of sweet woodruff (pages 23 and 189). Note the ring of leaves and the square stem. Roots of any member of the genus Galium probably yield a red dye. If you find any, follow the method indicated below for extracting dye.

TEXTILE
Scoured, presoaked alum-mordanted wool or silk (8 ounces)

INGREDIENTS
Madder (3½ ounces)
Ground chalk (⅙ ounce)

WATER
Hard or distilled (enough to cover textile)

POT
Nonreacting (5-gallon)

METHOD
1. Stir chopped-up roots into water.
2. Soak several hours.
3. Stir chalk into dye bath.
4. Raise temperature to 120°F (49°C).
5. Enter textile and heat to about 176°F (80°C) over a period of 1 hour.
6. Continue dyeing at this temperature for an hour longer. (Do not let dye bath cool off during the process.)
7. Cool, soap, rinse, and dry in shade.

13/WELD, ONE-POT METHOD*
(Reseda luteola)

YELLOW: SILK AND WOOL; REMARKABLY LIGHTFAST AND WASHFAST.
ALSO YELLOW: COTTON; LIGHTFAST BUT NOT WASHFAST.

Mignonette Family. Perennial garden subject. Has escaped into countryside in some parts of California. Has been used as a dye plant since antiquity. Said to be the best natural source of yellow of all time!

TEXTILE
Scoured, presoaked wool, or silk (8 ounces)

INGREDIENTS
Chopped up weld (dried or fresh, without roots) (4 ounces)
Alum (2 ounces)
Cream of tartar (½ ounce)
Ground chalk (¼ ounce)

WATER
Distilled (enough to cover textile)

POT
Nonreacting (5-gallon or larger)

METHOD
1. Combine all ingredients.
2. Enter textile.
3. Bring slowly to boil.
4. Boil 1 hour.
5. Cool in dye bath.
6. Rinse thoroughly and dry in shade.

NOTE: Previously mordanted textiles can be used: omit alum and cream of tartar in recipe and proceed as above.

3

Prospecting for dye plant material

Suggestions for plant observation and collecting are offered in this chapter. Some of the commonplace plants that contain dye, and several animal sources are mentioned. Places to find these are set forth, as well as ways to preserve and store plant materials. The possibility that plant relatives share tinctorial capability is proposed.

Many natural substances and plants contain dye. Once this fact is realized our attitude toward nature undergoes a change. A new kind of seeing occurs. One begins to notice more than just an occasional flower or a dramatic grouping of trees. The anonymity of greenness disappears. Individual plants stand out, the way a friend's face stands out in a crowd. An ordinary walk in the park can become a treasure hunt. *Every* plant becomes a lure and a promise.

What kinds of things yield dye? Almost anything. Foods, flowers, weeds, shrubs, wood, roots, bark, moss, beetles, snails, clay, iron. Several common foods are excellent dyes. Onions and tea are two examples. (See Chapter VI for a more detailed discussion of foods as dye sources.)

Home gardens can and do grow a number of dye subjects. Spring-blooming corms and bulbs have great possibilities. Faded hyacinth and crocus flower petals yield beautiful blues, turquoises, greens, and yellows. One variety, fall-blooming *Crocus sativus*, yields the ancient spice and dyestuff known as saffron. The orange-colored stigmas are used for saffron dye. Some of our old-fashioned perennial flower subjects are fine dye plants: marigold, coreopsis, dahlia and scabiosa are among these.

Those plants that are known as weeds have excellent dye possibilities. They represent our single most-ignored dye source. Weeds are simply unwanted or out-of-place plants. Unwanted, that is, by gardeners. Recently, I found that the so-called weed oxalis yields a neon orange and an almost-red dye! Since then, when referring to plants that others call weeds, I have said "so-called weeds."

Woad is an example of a plant that once had great economic importance and then lost favor. It

Figure 2 LADY'S PURSE
(*Calceolaria angustifolia*)

Figure 3   WILD GERANIUM (*Geranium* sp.)

was a source of blue dye in Europe until the trade routes were discovered. It is now considered a weed instead of an exotic dye plant. In the book *Weeds of California* (Robbins, Bellue, and Ball), *Isatis tinctoria* is listed as a pest of alfalfa fields in northern California. Some common weeds that yield dye are dock, nettle, wild mustard, yarrow, ragweed; burr clover, cheese weed, pickle weed, and sage.

Fresh and dried herbs should not be overlooked as dye sources. They are used in the same way that soft, nonwoody plants are used. Yellow or green might be the color expected. Many herbs are aromatic. Thus an added dimension can be achieved; maybe a sweet-smelling yellow, or a spicy gold, or a pungent green. It might be interesting to combine a sweet-smelling herb with an odorless plant that yields dye. A recipe for santolina will be found in the recipe section. Most herbs probably re-

quire four times as much plant as textile in an experiment. Since these are soft plants, they can be used whole or torn up.

Trees and shrubs are useful sources of dye. Walnut leaves and husks provide one of our best-known dyes. Plum leaves yield varying shades of purple, green, and yellow. Peach, pear, and cherry leaves contain yellow and beige coloring matter. Madrone, redwood, and oak bark are rich sources of tannin. Eucalyptus leaves yield brilliant orange and red dyes. Osage orange yields a rich yellow. The list is endless.

Algae, lichens, mosses, and ferns can furnish dye. Some of these produce substantive color, and all are beautiful. Large fungi-like mushrooms and shelf fungi are interesting dye subjects. (Be cautious: wear gloves; NEVER use dye pots for cooking food.) The Romans extracted a red dye from the seaweed *Fucus*. The brilliant chartreuse-colored staghorn moss produces a lime-yellow dye and a lasting, woodsy fragrance.

Animal sources of dye remain relatively unexplored. We have already mentioned the exotic red dye obtained from the cochineal scale. Other insects have been used for dye production, including other scales, mealybugs, and cynipid wasp galls. The following insects and insect groups are suggested as possible dye producers:

1. Cochineal scales (*Dactylopius* spp.) found on opuntia in the Southwest and in Florida (Gerber).

2. Lac scales (*Tachardiella* spp.) found on creosote bush (*Larrea*

sp.) and chamise (*Adenostoma* sp.) in desert areas of southern California.

3. Gall-like coccids (*Kermes* sp.) found on oaks in California.

4. Eriococcid scales (*Eriococcus* sp.), related to cochineal, found on many hosts (plants) near plant roots and top. The branches of elms are often infested in California.

5. Mealybugs, especially the red-bodied. Many garden plants are hosts to mealybugs.

For specialized information on insect dye sources, contact your local agricultural division and ask for a scale insect specialist. Try to find out which plants are hosts

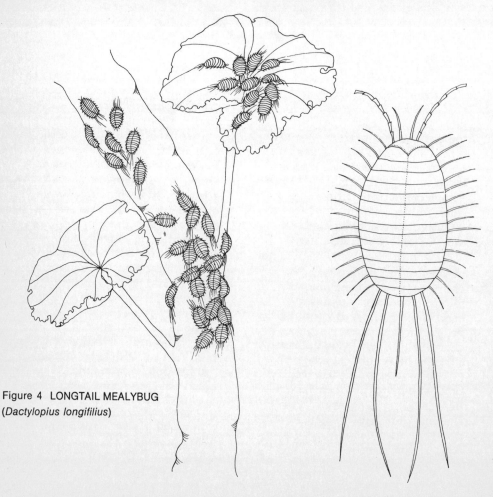

Figure 4 LONGTAIL MEALYBUG
(*Dactylopius longifilius*)

to scales in your area. Follow the cochineal recipe in Chapter II if you collect enough red-bodied insects. An experiment can be undertaken with a small amount of insects.

We have suggested groups of plants, and some insects, from which dyes have been extracted. One can see from the list that everyday, commonplace plants are potentially as useful as are some of the imported exotic dyes. The difference is that plants from next door or the backyard or cupboard are more accessible, and cheaper. And more fun to discover!

Now, a word about proportions of dye plant to yarn or textile. In general, at least twice as much plant (by weight) as textile is needed. A good three-parts plant to one-part textile by weight is usual, but it is not unusual to use six or eight times as much plant (by weight) as textile. There are exceptions: when using marigold flowers, three-fourths of a pound of fresh flowers will dye one pound of wool. Oxalis flowers are so potent that a one-to-one proportion is enough. Tannin-rich substances, such as tea, are also potent. Do not collect more plant material than you need. For an experiment, two to four cupfuls are enough. When following a recipe, use the amount needed for the weight of the textile.

What parts of plants are used for dyeing? The recipes that depend upon garden flowers use the whole flower head or separate petals from fruiting parts. Sometimes seed heads, after the flower is gone, can be used. A good recipe using petals can be parlayed into several recipes by using different stages of maturity or parts of the flower: bud, flower head, petals, or fruiting part. Each of these may yield a different shade or color. My coreop-

sis recipes (Recipes 99 and 100) demonstrate the above. I seldom use flowers until they begin to fade. In this way, the natural cycle can fulfill itself. It seems less destructive to pick a fading flower than to pluck a flower in its prime. Flower parts are prepared for dyeing by tearing them into bits. Proportions may vary a great deal. Some flowers are potent dye sources. Oxalis, for example, needs less than one-part flower to one-part textile by weight. Dahlias require the usual three-parts flower, to one-part textile by weight. When in doubt, err in favor of too much plant material rather than too little.

Leaves and stems are best used alone, without other parts of the plant. Stems are used together with leaves only if they are tender. Leaves and other green parts yield yellow, green, and sometimes red! (Remember eucalyptus.) Woody parts, such as old stems and twigs, can be used together. These are likely to be richer in tannin than young shoots and leaves. Usually beige and tan, and sometimes brown, result from old wood. For this reason, it is best to separate woody parts from tender parts. Tannin color is appreciated when you want it, but not when it masks or spoils another color.

Bark and wood can be excellent dye sources. In general, one can expect various beiges and browns from woody materials because of the tannin content. The bark of the oak is so rich in tannin that it has been a major source of this acid since antiquity. Some of the exotic woods used in furniture-making yield red dyes. Camwood and campeachy wood were used in earlier times. I have found that coralline and padauk wood yield magnificent shades of red (see Recipes 198, 217, 218). The wood or bark of any tree is prepared for dyeing by breaking it up into small bits or chips. For experimenting, try a proportion of one to one, or two parts wood to one part textile by weight.

Roots are not used as often for dyes as one might expect. Much mention has been made of the dandelion root yielding magenta. I have never found it so. One of my students from the East Coast says that a lavender-gray color is sometimes obtained from this root. Dock root yields a rich greenish gold and is substantive. Beets produce a deep magenta red which cannot be used on garments because of fading. Actually, our prime example of a dye extracted from roots is the beautiful madder red. Because our best red dye source is a root, one remains hopeful. Perhaps sooner or later another root dye will be discovered. The preliminary preparation of this plant part consists of grinding or chopping. Proportions of dye root to textile are usually about one to one, by weight.

Berries are an excellent source of dye. Elderberries, blueberries, and blackberries are well-known for their tinctorial qualities. There are also ornamental shrubs that produce useful berries. The privets are abundant berry producers, but rather difficult to work with. False hawthorn berries produce beautiful blues and purples. Mulberries yield violet, purple, or mauve, depending upon the dye procedures employed. Berries are generally encouraging dye subjects for several reasons: the colors are quite strong and fairly fast to light. Preparation consists of mashing the fruit. The proportion of berry to textile is about two to one, by weight.

Where does one go prospecting?

When? The answer to the second question is: anytime, especially if you are a nature buff, living near a green belt or rural area. However, if you are as far gone as I am on the subject of plants, it doesn't matter where you are. One night, while sitting in front of television, I suddenly found myself carefully studying the plants in a close-up shot. I had caught myself prospecting for dye plants on the television screen! What a sense of loss I experienced, realizing that those plants would never reach my dye pots!

The best source of plants for dyeing is your neighbor's garden. Seriously? Yes. The best source of plants for dyeing is any place where plant material is available. Since each dyer's circumstances will vary, I will mention general sources found to be useful. (City dweller, please see Chapter VI, The City Dweller and Natural Dyeing.

Figure 5 PIGWEED (*Amaranthus* sp.)

Figure 6 Three dye sources—lichens, madrone, and oak

Otherwise, I hope you may find the following information useful on your next vacation in the country.)

One can prospect for plants while driving around in a residential area. Even the driver can see unusual groupings of plants, or changes in color which might have meaning. Just today I saw a new patch of yellow beneath a stop sign.

It proved to be about two quarts of dandelion flowers after I stopped to pick them. Why is it that I see roadside plants so well, but pass by friends and stop signs?

Several days ago I noticed some unusual-looking, sprawling weeds growing near our local pharmacy. Later, when time permitted, I inspected the plants and found them to be of the amaranth family—possible dye subjects. Why were they growing there in a paved, city area, total strangers to downtown Mill Valley? Once, in the industrial area of a metropolis, I spotted a tomato plant growing out of a crack in the pavement!

Another, more appropriate kind of plant prospecting can be undertaken on nature hikes. In the country or in green, uninhabited areas, it is usually permissible to collect specimens. With this in mind, a hiker should carry along plastic bags and clippers. Half a pound of plant material is more than enough for one experiment. If the plant is to be identified, try preserving a specimen between two blotters. Prunings and weeds are sometimes free for the asking in parks and recreation areas.

Places where plants are displayed or sold are sources of material for dyeing. It is sometimes possible to collect leftover flowers from florists. (Beware of dyed flowers!) A great deal depends upon the attitude of the shopkeeper. I once tried to explain to a gimlet-eyed supermarket manager about the beauty of natural dyes and that his pile of faded carnations might produce an interesting color. It seemed to me that he suspected me of trying to cheat him out of something. Finally, with what appeared to be pity or suspicion, he decided. I also decided: *It isn't worth it.* A much friendlier way is to share your enthusiasm with a neighboring gardner. Tell him a dyer can use almost anything, including faded flowers. It is my experience that plant-lovers love plant-lovers. Your contacts will probably be more than pleased to share with you.

Collected plants sometimes need to be preserved unspoiled until dyeing time. We know that moldy or spoiled plants seldom yield color. Also, plant material which has faded or changed drastically is worthless. (The exception is material rich in tannin.) Some plants seem to retain tinctorial qualities if dried carefully. Marigolds, dahlias, chamomile, and sagebrush are such. Roots retain their dye capacity when dried. Dock root and madder root are examples. Dry mosses are as effective as fresh ones. Woody substances remain unchanged whether fresh or dry. Redwood, eucalyptus, walnut—the dyewoods—are examples. There are also many untried plant materials which would probably be effective dried or fresh. Experiments need to be carried out to prove the point. I can only say that slow, careful drying which does not greatly alter the original plant color

Figure 7 SAGEBRUSH
(*Artemisia tridentata*)

is worth trying. Dried material can be stored in a dry, cool, dark place, in jars, or in plastic bags.

Before leaving the subject of plant collecting, I would like to mention a rather interesting matter. It would appear that if a plant

Figure 8 Sweet woodruff and madder root (*Asperula odorata* and *Rubia tinctorum*)

yields dye, it is likely that other members of the same family, and especially the same genus, may yield dye also. It is an exciting hypothesis, because it suggests avenues of experimentation. For example, weld is the common name of a plant that yields a yellow dye. It is said to be the best natural yellow of all time. The botanical name of weld is *Reseda luteola.* Mignonette is the common name of the genus *Reseda*. It is also the name of a garden flower *Reseda odorata*, commonly available both in seed or as a seedling. Therefore, if you have a garden, plant mignonette! It is almost certain that you will obtain a superior yellow dye from it.

The madder root, used as a source of red dye since antiquity, belongs to a family which includes the herb, sweet woodruff (*Asperula odorata*), cleavers (*Galium aparine*), and bedstraw (*Galium*

verum). It is most likely that the roots of these yield a red dye. If one could collect enough roots, (they are very slim), it would be possible to obtain a good red dye. Sweet woodruff is easily grown. Cleavers and bedstraw are common weed members of this family.

There are at least thirty members of the genus *Galium* growing in the central and northeastern United States and adjacent Canada. There are thirty-eight members of this genus in California. To a dyer, these plants are worth their weight in gold. Learn how to recognize the distinctive features of this genus: the whorled arrangements of leaves in combination with a square stem; the flowers and seed capsules very small.

A good garden encyclopedia can be helpful in tracing plant relationships through family and genus. Visit your local arboretum. Find a botanist and ask for help. Exciting!

4

Basic information

What you will need, and what our ancestors used, in the way of pots, chemicals, and water, are described in this chapter. Preparation of the natural fibers—wool, silk, cotton, and linen—for dyeing, is discussed. Included is the scouring of wool, degumming of silk, and the cleaning and softening of linen and cotton. The importance of these preliminaries to a good dye job is set forth. None of the preliminaries is difficult, but they are important.

What equipment and materials does a home craftsman need for dyeing? I would like to answer this question by considering several selected life styles. Among nonindustrial peoples, dyeing was usually a home art. This means that production might be limited to a small group, with not many tools or objects used. If the group was not familiar with pottery, they could use any of the following: mollusk shells, calabash, cocoanut shells, bark objects, or possibly scooped-out tree parts. Sticks were used for stirring. Baskets or leaf parts could be used for strainers. Crushing and grinding implements might be stone or wood (*Primitive Dyeing Methods* by A. Bühler).

People who worked and fired clay had an added advantage. So far as dyeing goes, a pottery vessel allows greater freedom. It at once allows for the use of more heat, and removes the omnipresent tannin found in wooden vessels. (Pottery is also better than aluminum pots which adversely affect color.)

The Navajo used pottery. We are told that a Navajo dyer, early in this century, would need only an earthen pot, a frying pan, and a few sticks for his equipment (*Navajo Weaving* by C. A. Amsden). One thing such spare inventory denotes is *skill*. Only a practiced dyer could make do with so little.

Let us consider the utensils and apparatus necessary (in our culture) for a home dye workshop. We could do as the Navajo, and use only one pot. However, unlike the traditional Navajo, a new dyer is totally on his own. He is probably the first dyer in his family! Therefore, he should follow the suggestions below, tempered, of course, by considerations for space and economics.

UTENSILS AND EQUIPMENT

1. Several 3-gallon, enameled pails with lids.* (Diaper pails are inexpensive.) Be sure there are no chips in your enamel ware. One pail is reserved for alum mordanting. The 3-gallon size will serve up to ½ pound of textile stuff. A second pail is used for dyeing. (If the dyer intends to mordant with potassium dichromate also, then an additional pail is necessary.) Stainless steel pots are much more durable, but initially more expensive.

Pots used for mordanting and dyeing should be either stainless steel, enamel (no chips), Pyrex, or ceramic. Any other material affects the results. Larger pails are needed if the textile weight exceeds ½ pound per dye bath. (A 5-gallon

*Always keep dye pot covered when dyeing.

enameled canner is needed for mordanting one pound of yarn.)

2. Several 2- or 3-quart pots, enameled, Pyrex, or stainless steel, with lids. These are for preliminary dye experiments.

3. Assorted coffee tins, wide-mouth jelly and pickle jars.

4. Chopsticks or sticks or glass rods for stirring and lifting.

5. Plastic dishpan or bucket for soaking.

6. Plastic or stainless steel measuring-spoon set (1/4 teaspoon to 1 tablespoon).

7. Scale. A postal scale is the least expensive.

8. Thermometer. Candy thermometer is handy.

9. Glass measuring cup calibrated for ounces, tablespoons, and cubic centimeters.

Optional, but very useful

10. A large iron pot with lid, such as a Dutch oven. The older and rustier the better, but *no* greasy crust.

11. A large aluminum pot with lid.

12. A large unlined copper pot with lid. This is the most expensive and the least necessary.

It is possible, and more precise, to substitute chemicals for the effects of different metal pots. However, an earlier way of dyeing depended on the pot, rather than the chemical, for effect.

Remember, in every recipe in this book, the dye-pot requirements (as to composition) are specified. Many of the recipes require a *nonreacting* type of pot. This means: enamel, Pyrex, stainless steel, or ceramic. I have, therefore, referred to any one of the above pots as *nonreacting*, rather than listing all four kinds each time. *Reacting* pots are used for their particular metal

and are specifically named in the recipe. They are iron, unlined copper, tin, or aluminum. Also, the dye utensils and equipment *must not be used for any other purpose* than dyeing because dye plants might leave a poisonous residue in pots. And, any food grease in a vessel used for dyeing will interfere with dye penetration.

CHEMICALS NEEDED FOR NATURAL DYEING

The list of chemicals needed for a home dye workshop is small. Several can be purchased in the grocery store and are nonpoisonous. I refer to alum (for pickling) and cream of tartar (for meringue). (Pickling alum is not as effective as potassium alum.) A beginning dyer can decide to limit himself to this mordant pair and accept the limitations of color range and fastness. Why not? It has been my philosophy to encourage students to use simple, natural means. As experience is gained, more complex methods can be undertaken. It is also more economical to proceed cautiously.

Another commonly used mordant is chrome. It is very useful for wool. It is a poison and must be used with caution. However, it does add considerable fastness (as does copper) to light and washing. Therefore, its use is included for the sake of good dye practice.

Of the following list of ingredients, alum and cream of tartar are absolutely necessary:

1. *Alum* (potassium aluminum sulfate)—$KAl(SO_4)_2 \cdot 12H_2O$. Mordant. Nontoxic. Purchase at pharmacy or photographic supplier. Five pound jar.

2. *Copper* (anhydrous cupric sulfate)—$CuSO_4$. Mordant. Very toxic. Dangerous. If you can find

one, use an unlined (not tinned) copper pot instead of this chemical.

3. *Chrome* (potassium dichromate)—$K_2Cr_2O_7$. Mordant. Caustic and poisonous. Purchase from chemical supplier. Set one pot aside for chrome use *only*.

4. *Chrome-alum* (potassium chromium sulfate)—$KCr(SO_4)_2 \cdot 12H_2O$. Mordant. Purchase from chemical supplier or photo supplier. Poisonous.

5. *Iron* (ferrous sulfate)—$FeSO_4 \cdot 7H_2O$. Mordant. Nontoxic. Purchase from chemical supplier. I use an iron pot instead of this chemical.

6. *Tannin* (tannic acid)—$C_{14}H_{10}O_9$. Mordant. Purchase from chemical supplier.

7. *Tin crystals* (stannous chloride)—$SnCl_2$. Mordant. Moderately toxic. Purchase from chemical supplier. Keep tightly closed in a cool place. Two ounces will last a long time.

8. *White vinegar* (acetic acid, diluted)—$HC_2H_3O_2$. For acidity. Purchase at grocery.

9. *Chalk*, powdered (calcium carbonate)—$CaCO_3$. For alkalinity. Purchase at pharmacy.

10. *Cream of tartar* (potassium bitartrate)—$KHC_4H_4O_6$. Chemical assistant. Nontoxic. Purchase at grocery or chemical supplier. Keep lid tightly closed.

11. *Household ammonia*—NH_4OH. For alkalinity. Clear, nondetergent. Toxic. Purchase at grocery or pharmacy. (Do not use sudsy ammonia.)

12. *Salt* (sodium chloride)—$NaCl$. For leveling agent. Purchase at grocery.

13. *Baking soda* (sodium bicarbonate)—$NaHCO_3$. For alkalinity. Purchase at grocery.

14. *Washing soda* (sodium carbonate)—$Na_2CO_3 \cdot H_2O$. For alkalinity. Purchase at grocery.

NOTE: *The home dyer will, of course, scrupulously follow all the usual household precautions for keeping toxic substances labeled, sealed, and out of the reach of family, friends and pets.*

Figure 9 Mordant chemicals

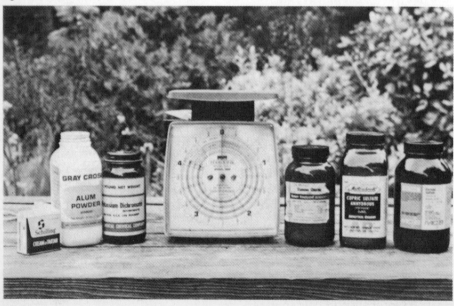

WATER

Water is indispensable in dyeing. It acts as a solvent—the dye dissolves in water. It also acts as the floating and heat-transmitting medium. Textile, dye, and mordant meet in the hot liquid under conditions of pressure. If we had no choice, any kind of water would be a godsend: puddle, slough, pond, spring, river, or ocean. So it was for early peoples. Whatever was at hand was used, including urine (with astonishing results)!

For dyeing purposes, the best water is rain water (only where the atmosphere is unpolluted), caught in clean, nonreacting vessels. This water is free of organic sediment, which is not true of pond and river water. It is also free of dissolved minerals, such as calcium, magnesium, and iron. Minerals like those commonly found in spring water interfere with color effects. Iron, for example, dulls (or *saddens*, as we say) color. In any event, dye results are unpredictable when spring or well water is used.

Calcium and magnesium commonly occur in city water supplies. When we speak of "hard" water we refer to the amount of calcium, magnesium, and iron in solution. Hard water is detrimental to dyeing, except in the special cases of madder, weld, and logwood. A phone call to your local water company can determine the degree of hardness of the city supply. There are other variable additions to public water supplies. Chlorine, for one, is a bleaching agent. There are also varying degrees of alkalinity in water, depending upon seasonal water levels and chemical additives.

Apropos of water differences, I remember being surprised by a Santa Barbara, California, dyer who routinely achieved green from onion skins with an alum mordant. Yellow or orange is the usual result on wool with onions in other parts of the United States. My friend was surprised to discover that I, in northern California, had to experiment and use special means to achieve a green from onions (see Recipe 248)!

It is advisable to use rain water or distilled water for experiments. Try out your tap water by following some of the recipes in this book. If the results are routinely good, then go on using your city supply. (Do not use rain water if you live in a smog area.)

TEXTILE MATERIALS

All natural fibers can be dyed with natural dyes. The animal fibers (wool and silk), are protein, and dye easily. The plant fibers (cotton, linen, jute, and others), are composed of cellulose. They are more difficult, but can be dyed with natural dyes. Each fiber type reacts in a specific way, and usually requires a different dye plant and process.

The man-made or synthetic fiber types are numerous and varied and, in general, cannot be naturally dyed. Several types of rayon do take natural dye but these types are seldom available. Let us leave the synthetics to the dye chemists and engineers who understand them and like them. Only the natural fibers, including pure wool, silk, cotton, linen, and jute are used in the experiments in this book.

Fiber, yarn, or fabric can be dyed. Spinners sometimes prefer dyeing the fiber or fleece. Producers of fabric, such as weavers, crocheters, and knitters prefer to dye the yarn rather than the finished textile. It is much easier to dye yarn than fabric, mainly because the yarn is directly exposed in a dye bath. It is also possible to work with smaller amounts of yarn. Fabric of more than a yard is bulky and requires much larger dye vessels. It is also more difficult to dye yardage and bulky items evenly.

Mass-produced yarn and fabric is increasingly being made of artificial fibers, and subjected to complex finishing processes, any one of which presents an almost insurmountable difficulty to the home craftsman. Unless the fabric or yarn to be dyed is *pure* cotton, wool, linen, and so forth, and otherwise unprocessed, it *cannot be dyed successfully* with natural dyes.

Natural white and bleached yarns are used for dyeing. Coarse, hard, firmly plied yarns are more difficult to dye than soft, fine or medium-weight, loosely plied yarns. Two-ply yarn is easier to dye than three or more plies. Very often, three-ply coarse wool dyes a pastel color in the same dye bath that a two-ply fine wool dyes a dark, rich color! Craftsmen, take heed: there is also a difference in yarns produced by different manufacturers as to sensitivity to natural dyes.

NOTE: Handspun yarn dyes beautifully *if it is thoroughly scoured.*

Try scouring the loose wool before it is spun.

Natural gray wool can be used for special effects in dyeing. For example, natural gray wool in a yellow dye bath looks more green than yellow. And natural black wool, which is really brown, makes a beautiful black if dyed with any of the recipes for black.

TEXTILE PREPARATION FOR DYEING

Textiles must be very clean and thoroughly wet before dyeing is begun. "Scouring" is the term used

for washing, and it is carried on with hot water and a pure neutral soap. The textile to be scoured might be a small garment, fabric, yarn, loose fleece, or fiber. The main object of wool scouring is to remove the grease called "lanolin." This fatty substance is natural to wool and may still be present in handwoven wool fabric. Cotton is scoured to remove natural waxes and to soften the fibers. Silk is scoured to remove gummy substances. Since dye cannot penetrate grease, wax, or gum, it is very important that the textile be thoroughly cleansed before being dyed.

SKEINING YARN

Before scouring, mordanting or dyeing have begun, it is important to prepare textile materials in order to avoid tangling. This is particularly true of yarn. Purchased skeins of four ounces or less are not too heavy for scouring or dyeing, however, the security ties *must be opened and retied loosely.* It is advisable to add two more evenly spaced ties to the skein. The usual

Figure 10 Making a skein of jute

Figure 11   A skein of jute

method of tying is to make a loose figure eight with cotton twine. Skeins that are prepared at home can be wound around the arm, from the hand and over the elbow. These are secured in the same manner as mentioned above. I prefer light-weight skeins of about one-fourth or one-half ounce for future experimenting with dye plants.

SCOURING WOOL YARN OR FLEECE

Some spinners like to dye their fleece (loose wool) before spinning. In this case, the fleece must be scoured before spinning into yarn. The fleece is prepared by picking out and discarding burrs and barn-yard matter, and opening it out by pulling gently.

For soaking and scouring I use either my kitchen sink, bathroom washbasin, a large dishpan, or even the washing machine. (Do not *agitate* materials in the washing machine; it is only used as a basin.)

SOAKING: Soak skeins or fleece overnight in unheated rainwater or distilled water. Pour water off. Soak again in fresh bath, if time allows. Lift skeins out with rods or chopsticks. Lift fleece out with hands. Drain water off.

NOTE: Presoaking is an *absolute must.*

SCOURING: Prepare soapy bath using strong soap and hot water to cover; (as hot as the hand can bear, or about 113°–122°F). Enter wool and allow to cool overnight. Rinse in lukewarm water. Repeat hot soapy bath if necessary, using slightly cooler water, (about 95°–101°F). Do not shock wool by sub-jecting it to sudden temperature changes. Allow cooling in bath. Rinse wool in lukewarm water until

Figure 12 Scouring the wool

water is clear. Squeeze or pat out excess water. Do not wring or twist. Hang skeins out to dry in shade or in bathroom. Use a wood rod and chopsticks through center of skein. Fleece is laid out on a towel to dry. Label all material to be stored.

Drying is not necessary if the textile—fleece, yarn, or fabric—is to be mordanted or dyed immediately. It can be kept damp for several days in plastic bags. During hot weather I store wet yarn in the refrigerator to prevent mildew.

SCOURING AND WETTING OF SILK

Raw silk contains up to twenty-five percent silk-glue or sericin. This substance must be removed so the silk will have luster, whiteness and suppleness. Silk-glue is best removed by boiling the yarn in soapy water. The scouring of silk is called "boiling off" or "degumming." Scouring can be partial or complete, depending on need. It is unlikely that the home craftsman will encounter unscoured silk. However, directions for scouring silk follow.

COMPLETE BOILING OFF: Use eight ounces of pure olive-oil soap per gallon of distilled water. Simmer skeined yarn for ninety minutes at 195°F or 90°C. Recook in a second soapy bath. Wash soap out thoroughly. Hang out to dry, or enter skeins into mordant bath. (Save first boil-off water for use in dye bath.)

WETTING: This process must be carried out on all silk yarn or fabric before mordanting or dyeing is begun. The skeined silk yarn or fabric is simmered at 195°F or 90°C for thirty minutes in a mildly soapy bath. Use a high-quality olive-oil soap or Lux soap and distilled water. Rinse thoroughly and mordant.

SCOURING OF PLANT FIBERS

Jute, cotton, and linen yarn or fabric benefit from a more vigorous

Soaking and Scouring the Textile (Fibre, Yarn or Fabric)

Action	Ingredients		Time
Soak	Yarn in Water 	together	24 hours or longer
Remove	Yarn and Water		
Mix	Soap and Hot Water 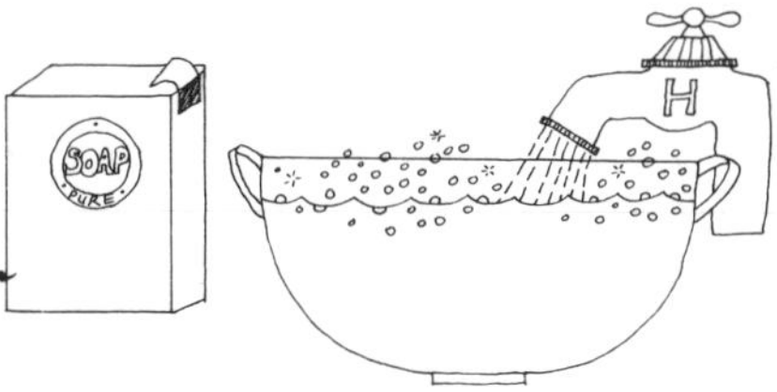		
Add	Textile		
Wash	Yarn Soap and Hot Water 	all together	Until Clean
Rinse	Yarn in Hot Water 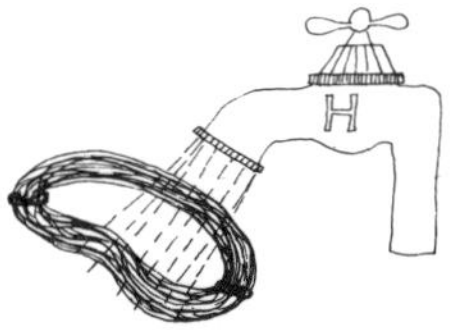		Until Clear
Proceed	to Pre-Mordanting or Dyeing or		
Store	Wet or Dry 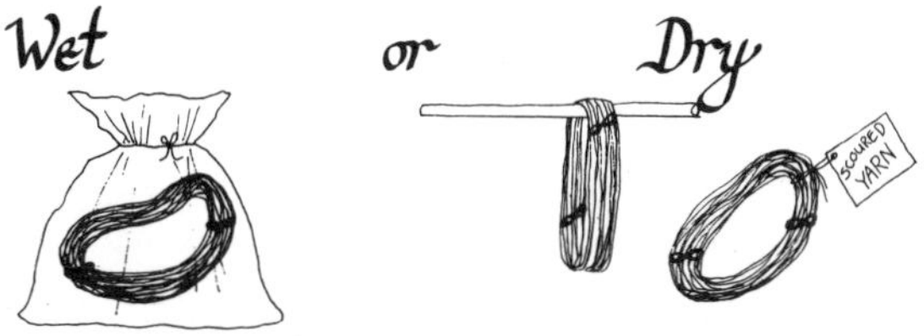		For Future use

Figure 13   Soaking and scouring the textile (fiber, yarn, or fabric)

processing. Skeins can be boiled in a solution of soapy water and a small amount of washing soda. One or two hours of boiling is necessary. The material can be left to soak overnight in the soap bath, and then rinsed in hot water. Jute and linen skeins can even be washed in the washing machine. The skeins must be tied in three places if tangling is to be avoided.

Straw, raffia, and reed are scoured very much like other plant fibers. They must first be tied into skeins or coiled into loose bundles and secured. After boiling in a soapy bath with a bit of washing soda, rinse thoroughly. Preliminary to dyeing, soak overnight or for several hours in boiling water.

Adequate scouring is the first hurdle a new dyer must clear. Often, poor dye results are directly traceable to insufficient scouring.

NOTE: For the one and only exception to this rule, see Recipe 21.

PRESOAKING THE TEXTILE

Textile stuff, whether it be fabric, yarn, or loose fiber, *must be thoroughly wet* before dyeing begins. This means wet through and through, not just on the surface. Such wetting can be achieved only by soaking for hours. It is even advisable to presoak materials before the scouring process. It is good practice to keep the textile wet from scouring, through mordanting, into dyeing! If this is not practical, remember to presoak the dry textile thoroughly before any dyeing procedure. *Only a thoroughly wet textile dyes well!* I cannot over-emphasize this point. Herein lies another much-neglected aid to dyeing success.

THE DYER'S CORNER

It is perhaps useful to conclude this chapter with a practical consideration. How and where will my dyeing equipment be stored? Two things are certain: all of it should be (1) kept together in a unit, readily accessible, and (2) not used for any other purpose.

There are various storage possibilities, depending upon the situation of the dyer. In my country kitchen, one lower cupboard shelf is devoted to dye pots. On the shelf above are chemicals and dried dye materials. Standing in the kitchen is a five-gallon distilled water dispenser. In the cooler, well below the fruits and vegetables, I keep several buckets with wet, mordanted yarns, waiting to be dyed. Some dyers keep an old-fashioned chest of drawers in the kitchen or bathroom as their dye corner. One of my students performed dyeing wonders in a dormitory room with only an electric plate, one dye pot, and a tiny shelf for chemicals. Let us get on with it!

WARNING: *Work in a well ventilated area and keep dye pot covered when dyeing.*

5
Dyeing procedures

Three different methods of dyeing, and noteworthy variations, are described in this chapter. They are: direct dyeing method, one pot (with mordant) method, and separate mordanting (before-or-after) dyeing. Results can be achieved with any one of these methods. However, each method has its advantages, depending on the dye plant used and personal preference. Directions are also written in chart form, for the sake of clarity. There are fourteen mordanting recipes in this chapter.

DIRECT DYEING METHOD

The direct dyes fulfill a dyer's dream. The dream can go like this: I found an abundance of green moss hanging from a tree. Because the tree was not in a restricted area, I gathered half a shopping bagful and brought it home to my dye pot. After simmering the moss, some skeins of wet wool, and water together for a while, the mixture was set out to cool. A day later the wool was ready to be rinsed and hung out. Was it green? No, orange. The color was lightfast and the fragrance reminded me of my black kitty who sleeps in apple trees (see Recipe 27).

It is a wonderful experience to work with the direct or substantive dyes. As we have mentioned, there

are not many dyes that belong to this class. As with all dyes, there is an affinity for certain fiber types and not for others. Following is a list of plants that yield direct dyes: walnut leaves and husks yield brown; staghorn moss, barberry, turmeric, dock, and safflower yield yellow and gold; certain lichens and annatto yield orange; fruit of the cactus yields magenta or orange; and petals of various delphiniums yield blue.

ONE-POT DYE AND MORDANT METHOD

Most of the natural dyes belong to the mordant class. This means that the dye requires the addition of a special chemical in order to penetrate and "fix" onto the textile. It is therefore not sufficient to use the direct method. For instance, yellow onion skins belong to the mordant class. If you simmer a bit of wool or cotton with a cupful of skins, the result is hardly worthwhile. However, if a teaspoon of alum and a pinch of cream of tartar are dissolved and added to the bath, the outcome is quite different. Preliminary tests are done this way. After simmering for fifteen or twenty minutes, the wool sample turns a beautiful deep yellow-orange. The cotton sample does not take the dye as well. (We are reminded here that fibers differ in their reaction to dyes and mordants.)

The one-pot dye and mordant method is similar to direct dyeing, with the addition of the mordant. This way is still a simple and pleasurable way to practice the art of dyeing. An impulsive dyer, or a person who likes to proceed with dispatch likes it. It is a practical method, particularly when the dyestuff is strong and the textile receptive. (Plant fibers such as linen and cotton do not respond well to this method. Therefore, more

One Pot Dye and Mordant Method

Action	Ingredients	Time
Soak Together	plant / scoured textile / water  — all together	Overnight
Simmer	All Together	15 Minutes
Remove	Textile from Pot	Temporarily
Add	Mordant Alum — A / Cream of Tartar 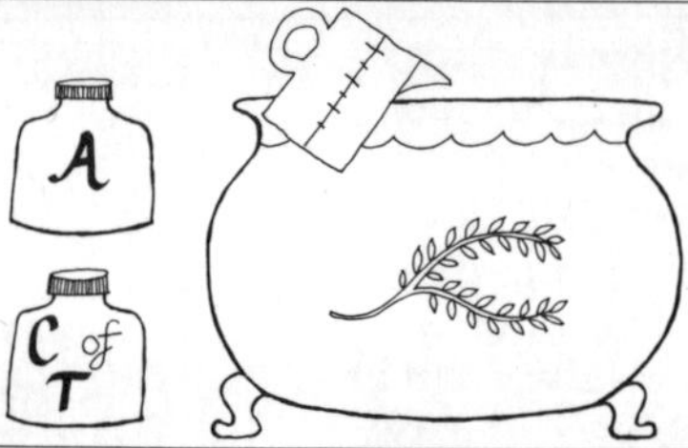 — C of T	
Return	Textile to Pot	
Simmer	 all together — A — C of T	30 Minutes
Cool	All Together	Overnight
Rinse	Textile 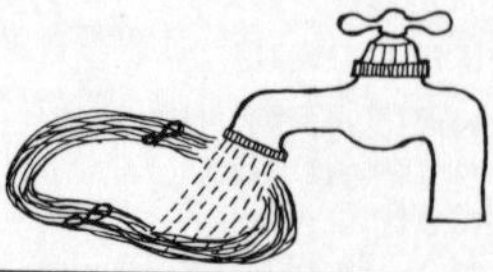	
Dry	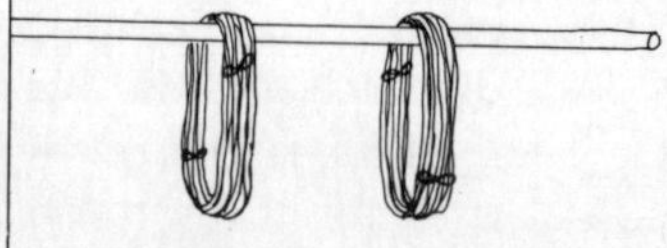	

Figure 14   One-pot dye and mordant method

elaborate preparations, known as preliminary mordanting, are necessary.)

Let us detail the one-pot dye and mordant method. When working without a recipe, try about three times as much new plant material as textile. (This rule does not apply to exotic dyes.) Example: for four ounces of wool, use twelve ounces of plant material, one ounce of alum, one-fourth ounce of cream of tartar, and four quarts of water (see Figure 14). Whenever feasible, use this method. Many dyers find it most useful for experimenting and for small projects.

There are certain limitations to the one-pot method, and these have led to *Variations*:

1. Some plants require long cooking before the dye is extracted. Long cooking, however, makes wool harsh and unmanageable. The natural answer to this dilemma is the perfect solution: *precook the plant material*, then strain it out and proceed with the addition of the mordant (see Figure 15).

NOTE: Precooking of plant material may precede dyeing in most recipes if plant material is tough, woody, or otherwise too bulky.

2. Plant material is too bulky and crowds the yarn. Here again, the answer to this problem is to precook the plant material, as above.

3. After dyeing is completed it is sometimes difficult to separate the dyestuff from the yarn or fleece. There are two solutions to this difficulty: (a) The plant material may be placed in gauze bags before the cooking begins, (b) Use Variation 1 above. Those dyers who are offended by the slightly mussed-up look of yarn cooked together with plant material may like the idea of using the gauze bags.

4. There is one real difficulty encountered with the one-pot method: some dyes require a *more intensively mordanted* textile or yarn. Yarns which are already mordanted before dyeing usually give better results. Regretfully, there is no way out of this difficulty except to change the method of mordanting. We must therefore consider *mordanting as a separate procedure.*

SEPARATE MORDANTING METHOD

We have said that mordant dyes need a special chemical, the mordant, in order to fix the dye onto the textile. In the one-pot method, the mordant was added *directly to the dye bath.* However, in many such instances, the yarn seems unable to hold dye. For this reason, mordanting is often done separately, either before, after, or before-and-after dyeing.

NOTE: Use nonreacting pots for all mordanting procedures.

PRE-MORDANTING METHODS: The procedure consists of adding the mordant and assistant, dissolved in a small amount of hot water, to a large pot of water. The scoured, wet yarn or textile is added and simmered, usually for one hour. After the mordanting is completed, one can proceed to dyeing, following any recipe that requires a pre-mordanted textile. It is also possible to store mordanted material for future dyeing. Mordanted yarn can be kept moist for several weeks, in cool weather, in plastic bags. Or, the yarn can be rinsed, dried, labeled, and stored for future dyeing projects.

Following are standard recipes for mordanting. Just as for dyeing, all goods must be presoaked and scoured. Yarn must be in skeins. The mordant recipes are written for

Preparing Dye Liquor Before Dyeing

Action	Ingredients	Time
Soak	Dye Plant in Water 	24 Hours
Simmer or Boil	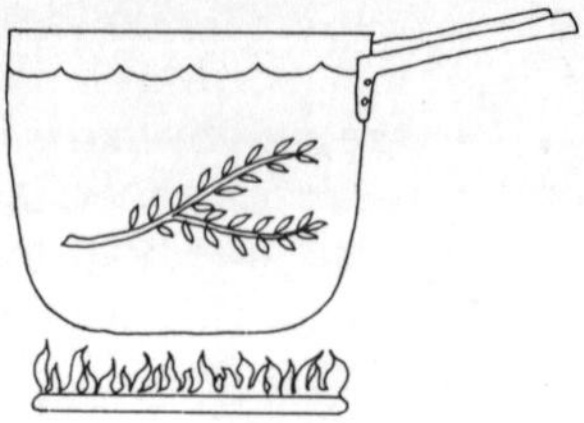 Dye Plant in Water	1 or 2 Hours
Cool	All Together	
Strain Out	Dye Plant from Dye Bath 	
Proceed	To Dyeing by Using Dye Liquor as Dye Bath	

Figure 15 Preparing dye liquor before dyeing

Figure 16 Pre-mordanting yarn

one pound (dry weight) of goods.
Use one-half the amount of mordant
for one-half pound of goods. (See
Table III in Appendix B: Chemicals
Used for Pre-Mordanting: Fixed
Percentages.)

ALUM PRE-MORDANTING RECIPE

TEXTILE
Wool or silk (1 pound)

MORDANT
Alum (4 ounces)

ASSISTANT
Cream of tartar (1 ounce)

WATER
Tap (4 gallons)

POT
Nonreacting (5-gallon, or large
enough for water to cover
and float textile)

METHOD
1. Dissolve alum and cream of
tartar in hot water.
2. Add to large pot of warm water.
3. Enter goods, cover pot.
4 Bring to simmer and simmer for 1
hour, turning occasionally.
5. Cool in mordant bath. Rinse.
6. Proceed directly to dyeing or cure
in mordant bath for several days,
or dry yarn and store for future use.

NOTES: The ageing or curing of
mordanted goods improves colorfastness and lightfastness. □ When
mordanting silk, do not simmer.
Keep bath at 160°F.

CHROME PRE-MORDANTING RECIPE

TEXTILE
Wool or silk (1 pound)

Pre-Mordanting the Textile (Fibre, Yarn or Fabric)

Action	Ingredients	Time
Measure	Mordant: Chrome (C) / Cream of Tartar  (C of T)	
Dissolve	Mordant in Hot Water 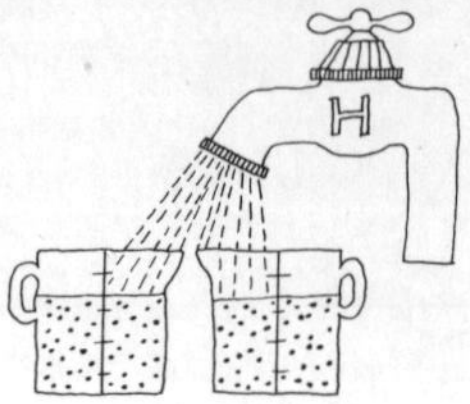	
Pour	Mordant Solution Into Pot of Hot Water 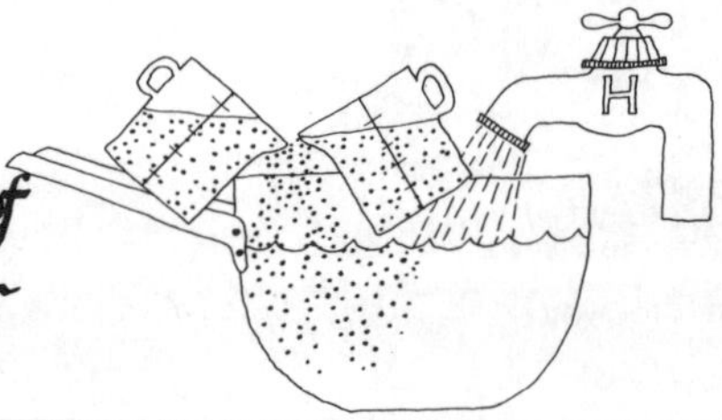	
Enter and Cover	Scoured Yarn 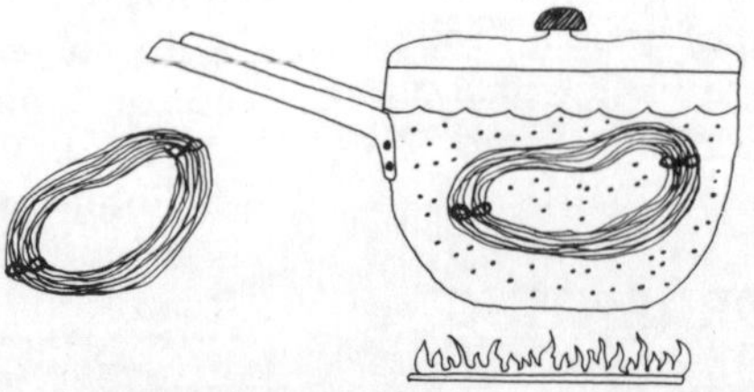	
Simmer 195° F	All Together	1½ hours
Cool	All Together	Overnight or longer
Remove	Yarn	
Proceed	To Dyeing or Store Wet or Dry	for future use

Figure 17 Pre-mordanting the textile (fiber, yarn, or fabric)

MORDANT
Potassium dichromate (½ ounce)

ASSISTANT
Cream of tartar (½ ounce)

WATER
Tap (4 gallons)

POT
Nonreacting (reserve for chrome mordanting) (large enough for water to cover and float textile)

METHOD
1. Dissolve chrome and cream of tartar in hot water.
2. Add to large pot of warm water.
3. Enter goods, cover pot.
4. Bring to simmer and simmer for 1 hour, covered. Turn goods occasionally. (Do not simmer silk.)
5. Cool to lukewarm and rinse.
6. Proceed directly to dyeing, or dry yarn and store in dark place.

WARNING: *Work in a well ventilated area. Some people are allergic to the steam.*

TIN PRE-MORDANTING RECIPE
METHOD
1. Substitute ⅔ ounce of tin for the chrome in the above recipe.
2. Substitute ⅓ ounce of cream of tartar for the cream of tartar in the above recipe.

NOTES: Do not store tin pre-mordanted yarn. Proceed immediately to dyeing. □ It is usually more convenient to add tin to the dye bath or as an afterbath. Tin brightens or "blooms" color.

TANNIN–ALUM–TANNIN MORDANTING RECIPE
(Used for vegetable fibers)
I: Tannin bath (may be used as the only mordanting procedure)
TEXTILE
Cotton, linen, sisal, raffia, jute (all preboiled in soap, water, and rinsed) (1 pound)

MORDANT
Tannin (3 ounces)

WATER
Tap (3 gallons)

POT
Nonreacting (large enough for water to cover and float textile)

METHOD
1. Dissolve tannin in warm water.
2. Enter vegetable fiber goods.
3. Heat to 150°F or 66°C for 1 hour.
4. Cool overnight.
5. Rinse lightly.

II: Alum bath (may be used as the only mordanting procedure)
TEXTILE
From above bath (1 pound)

MORDANT
Alum (4 ounces)

ASSISTANT
Washing soda (2 ounces)

WATER
Tap (3 gallons)

POT
Nonreacting (large enough for water to cover and float textile)

METHOD
1. Dissolve alum and washing soda in hot water.
2. Enter textile.
3. Boil for 1 hour.
4. Cool overnight.
5. Rinse lightly.

III: Tannin bath
METHOD
1. Repeat Step I.
2. Textile is ready for dyeing.

NOTES: Vegetable fibers may be mordanted in the usual ways—that is, with alum, chrome, or tin—or by the three-step tannin–alum–tannin method. □ Either Step I or II may also be used alone; however, the dye tends to be less fast.

AFTER-MORDANTING METHODS
It is sometimes useful to mordant after dyeing. Two methods are em-

ployed: (a) the mordant is added *into the dye bath* after the dyeing is completed, or (b) the mordanting is done *in a fresh water bath* after dyeing is completed.

After-mordanting can be done on yarn that was pre-mordanted, or it may be the only mordanting. Alum and chrome are suitable for pre- or after-mordanting. Tin is usually used during or after dyeing. Iron and copper are employed as afterbaths. Chrome after-mordanting may improve fastness to light. Copper after-mordanting may improve fastness to light and washing. All of this can be useful, except that the color is altered by after-mordanting. (Please refer to Table II in Appendix B: Chemicals Used in Dye Recipes: Percentage Amounts)

CHROME AFTER-MORDANTING RECIPE
(In Dye Bath, For 1 Pound of Textile)

Proceed as for direct dyeing, or follow a dye recipe.

METHOD

1. After the dyeing is completed, remove textile temporarily from dye bath.
2. Add 1/6 ounce chrome and 1/6 ounce cream of tartar (each dissolved in warm water).
3. Return textile to dye bath.
4. Simmer 10 minutes.
5. Remove textile from bath.
6. Rinse in hot water and dry.

CHROME AFTER-MORDANTING ALTERNATE RECIPE
(After Dye Bath, For 1 Pound of Textile)

Proceed as for direct dyeing, or follow a dye recipe.

METHOD

1. Remove textile from dye bath.
2. Prepare fresh dye bath of 1/6 ounce of chrome and 1/6 ounce of cream of tartar (per pound of textile) dissolved in water (3 to 5 gallons).
3. Enter dyed textile and simmer for 10 minutes, lid on.
4. Remove textile from bath.
5. Rinse in hot water and dry.

NOTE: This method improves fastness, but usually alters color of textile, dulling and browning it. Green colors suffer the least change.

ALUM AFTER-MORDANTING RECIPE
(In the Dye Bath, or as Afterbath, For 1 Pound of Textile)

METHOD

Same as for chrome after-mordanting recipe, but substitute 3 ounces of alum dissolved in hot water, and 1 ounce of cream of tartar.

NOTE: This method can be used following any dye procedure for increased fastness, but color is usually dulled.

CHROME-ALUM AFTER-MORDANTING RECIPE
(After Dye Bath, For 1 Pound of Textile)

METHOD

1. Follow regular dye recipe with afterbath of: 1/2 ounce of chrome-alum and 1/2 ounce of cream of tartar or 6 tablespoons of vinegar dissolved in 3 gallons of hot water. Simmer for 10 minutes, lid on.
2. Rinse and dry.

NOTE: This method increases fastness; it has the advantage of not changing color as much as chrome afterbath.

FERROUS SULFATE AFTER-MORDANTING RECIPE
(For 1 Pound of Textile)

METHOD

Same as for chrome after-mordanting recipe, but substitute ⅔ ounce of ferrous sulfate and 1 ounce of cream of tartar dissolved in hot water, or cook in iron pot.

NOTE: This method improves color fastness, but saddens (darkens) and changes the color. Yellows change to interesting greens.

CUPRIC SULFATE AFTER-MORDANTING RECIPE (For 1 Pound of Textile)

METHOD

Same as for chrome after-mordanting recipe, but substitute ⅕ ounce or 6 grams of cupric sulfate and ½ ounce of cream of tartar dissolved in 16 quarts of hot water.

NOTE: This method improves color fastness, but does modify the color. Greens are not affected as much as other colors.

CUPRIC SULFATE STOCK SOLUTION

This recipe is for preparing a stock solution of cupric sulfate. It can be stored in a dark, tightly-capped air-tight brown bottle for several months. One-half ounce in one quart of water makes an after-mordanting bath for one ounce of yarn.

METHOD

For use as afterbath on small amounts of textile.
1. Weigh out ⅙ ounce of cupric sulfate (or ¾ teaspoon).
2. Dissolve in 8 ounces of boiling water (liquid measure).
3. Store in air-tight, dark bottle. This is the stock solution.

Afterbath for 1 ounce of textile

1. Pour ½ ounce of stock solution (one tablespoon) into 1 quart of water.
2. Add ⅓ tablespoon of vinegar.
3. Add 1 ounce of textile.

4. Heat for 10 minutes (simmer), lid on.
5. Rinse and dry.

NOTE: Cupric sulfate is poisonous. Keep it away from food and eating utensils.

TIN (STANNOUS CHLORIDE) AFTER-MORDANTING RECIPE (In Bath or Afterbath, For 1 Pound of Textile)

METHOD

Same as for chrome after-mordanting recipe, but substitute a pinch of tin crystals (⅖ ounce or 11 grams) in the dye bath or in a separate afterbath.

NOTE: This chemical is an important adjunct to dye procedures. It not only improves fastness, but alters color considerably. Tin is a brightener and sometimes changes muted color to something much livelier. Yellows turn orange and browns may go red with tin. Eucalyptus leaves are strongly affected by tin. This chemical offers a very important variable in dye experiments and it is hard to understand how so valuable a dye chemical has gone unmentioned.

RINSES

After dyeing, the textile is always thoroughly rinsed in plain water. However, it is sometimes possible to change color dramatically by adding an acid or an alkaline substance to the last rinse. Not all dyes respond to a change of acidity. If a change is possible, it is sometimes observed that an acid may redden blues or purples, and a base (alkaline) makes blues a greener color. There are other possible changes: ammonia intensifies many yellows and reddens some orange colors, such as coreopsis and sorrel. Rinses are very useful in dye experiments. It is surprising

that this technique has gone unmentioned in popular works.

ACID RINSE
INGREDIENTS
Water
White vinegar, acetic acid, or
lemon juice
METHOD
1. Add just enough acid so that
rinse has a faint odor.
2. Litmus paper can be used to
check whether the bath is acidic,
basic, or neutral.
NOTE: Use nonreacting pot for the
rinse.

ALKALINE RINSE
INGREDIENTS
Water

Clear nondetergent ammonia
METHOD
Add just enough so that rinse has
faint ammonia odor ($1/2$ to $1 1/2$ teaspoons in 1 quart of water).

NOTES: After alkaline rinse, the
textile must be thoroughly rinsed
in plain water. ☐ Use nonreacting
pot for the rinse.

6

The city dweller and natural dyeing; foods as dye sources; dyeing macrame, crochet, and embroidery yarns

This chapter presents information concerning the immediate availability of dye material to city dwellers and the winter-bound. They need not be limited by the absence of plant material: dyestuff is as near as your cupboard or the corner grocery. Some excellent dyes are to be found in edibles. An interesting variation on onion skin dyeing is offered at the end of this chapter. We have spoken a great deal about plant collecting for dyes. It is a fascinating task. But what about the city-bound dyer who is nowhere near weeds and flowers? Or what about those who live in areas with severe winters? There is, of course, the possibility of planning ahead: perhaps you spent a summer month in Rhode Island and collected poke berries? Or a friend sent a bag full of eucalyptus leaves from California? Or you have stored away some exotic dyes that were ordered months before?

Let us assume you have had a sudden urge to plunge into natural dyeing. What cupboard contents might be useful as sources of dye? Spices, teas, herbs, vegetables, berries, and fruits all yield color. The spices turmeric and saffron have been admired since antiquity for their flavor and rich color. Both yield a lustrous orange-yellow. In India, turmeric is used to color rice, and in China, it is used to dye silk. Unfortunately, this beautiful color is fugitive, especially if washed. For this reason, its best use is for objects that are not washed. All fiber types take the dye, and the heavy cords used for macrame work are especially handsome. You can also dye a finished piece. Turmeric is available in 1-$\frac{1}{2}$ ounce tins at the grocery. It is inexpensive and easy to use (see Recipe 1).

Saffron is obtained from the pistils and stigma of the flower *Crocus sativus*. The spice is available in groceries, but it has become so precious that it is hardly worth considering as a dye. It makes more sense to grow crocus flowers. This way, two dyes would be available: yellow from the stigma, and blue or green from the petals (see Recipe 101).

Black tea is rich in tannin. This substance acts both as a mordant and a dye. We are all familiar with the staining properties of tea. It is such a strong dye that even used tea leaves or bags make an excellent dye source. The colors obtained range from beige to deep, rusty tans, according to the proportion of tea to textile. All natural fibers (and rayon) can be dyed. The dye is not only sunfast, but also washfast. As though these qualities were not enough, there is one more thing—tea is a substantive dyestuff and can be used following the direct method. As mentioned in Chapter II, boiling the dyestuff and the textile together in water is all that is required. In the case of tea, it is better to prepare the dye bath beforehand by boiling it for an hour. The tea leaves are then removed and the textile is entered and simmered until the desired color is achieved (see Recipe 3). Remember, the color looks darker when the textile is wet.

Some of the herb teas are dyes. Chamomile flowers dye wool, silk, and cotton a lovely gold color. Chamomile can be used as a hair tint for blondes and also as an ingredient of herbal douche. (See Appendix for hair-dye recipe.) It can be purchased as a tea or collected in early summer in fields and gardens. Lemon.verbena and mint tea also yield a pretty yellow.

Coffee grounds can be used for dyeing. Many a Boy Scout has freshened his khakis by steeping them in a strong infusion of coffee. If grounds are used, a four-to-one proportion will be necessary. Coffee tan is the color obtained, and all fibers can be used. It is not a direct dye on the plant fibers, so a tannin mordant will be necessary.

Two of our best sources of brown are food-related. These are pomegranate rinds and walnut husks, shells, or leaves. Tannin is an excellent source of brown dye. Pomegranates are so tannin-rich that they have been used for centuries for tanning leather and for dyeing. At holiday time in November and December, I save pomegranate rind and seeds. The leftovers from about six pomegranates can be used to dye about one-half pound of woolen goods. The rind and pulp can also be set aside in water and reserved for future need (see Recipes 258 and 259). Similarly, any part of the walnut tree, including the shells, can be used. Walnut husks stain the fingers and nails dark brown. Walnut parts, except nuts, can be collected in a crock or barrel and allowed to ferment until ready for use (see Recipe 266).

In Chapter III we mentioned berries as one of our best dye sources. Naturally, edible berries are included. Blackberries, blueberries, and huckleberries are infamous for the ineradicable stains they leave. I wish that all dye plants were as well-received by textiles.

In writing of berries, I feel a twinge of guilt. It seems improper to use a food directly for dye. Perhaps it is appropriate to point out that foods are not often used as dye sources in preindustrial cultures. We can guess the reason—only kings and nobles had more than enough food. (I can think of two exceptions: purple corn and black beans are used by the Hopi for dye. The purple corn, however, is not used for food because it stains the teeth and gums.) May I defend the use of edible berries for dye? In our economy, foods such as blackberries in season may be less expensive than synthetic dyes.

Concord grape skins are a good dye source. Enjoy the grape, then spit out the skin. Save them in a bottle and refrigerate until enough are collected. Wool and silk can be dyed blue or turquoise (see Recipes 236–238).

The purple cabbage is remarkable. It is said to be used as a dye in Russia. It is often mentioned as a dye source, yet no one offers a specific recipe! Two recipes will be found in this book (Recipes 231 and 232). We are certain of a lovely lavender and also a beautiful, though touchy blue that is fast to sunlight. If you try dyeing with cabbage, don't worry about the odor. It is fugitive. The whole head or just the outer leaves can be used. Supermarkets are a good place to collect cabbage trimmings. The proportion of cabbage to textile is best at about eight to one.

Perhaps the easiest edibles to use, and certainly the most pungent, are onion skins. The Romans found them useful for textile and food coloring. In European folk art, eggs are dyed in boiling water with onion skins. Beautiful shades of brown, rusty red, orange, ocher, yellow, and yellowish green can be obtained from this vegetable. The range of color depends upon the proportion of onion skin (brown or red) to textile and the chemical assistants. Onions in an iron pot yield the darkest color; onions and tin yield the brightest color; onions, tin, and ammonia yield the greenest color (see Recipes 14, 246, 247 and 248).

The only problem is collecting the quantity required. Unlike purple cabbage, onion skins are a more concentrated dye source. Therefore, as little as one-half pound will dye a pound of textile. At a ratio of one pound of skins to one pound of goods, a deep tone can be achieved. However, the average family is a long time collecting a pound of skins. For this reason, it is recommended that a contact be established with someone in the vegetable department of a grocery.

Ask a clerk to save the onion skins for you. Or better still, do you know a kindly and imaginative restaurant manager? (Unfortunately, the above advice has put me in competion with my own students here in Marin County. I can call by name at least one hundred natural dyers per school year who are depriving me of good onion skins!)

MACRAME, CROCHET, AND EMBROIDERY YARN DYEING

Any handcraft that uses yarn can benefit from natural dyeing. Hand skills deserve the best materials. Mass-produced yarns usually offer a limited range of color and texture. It is not that there are too few colors to choose from. What I refer to is the "dye lot" look. It is the flat, hard, "no nuance" appearance of synthetic color. There is also the too-perfect, smooth look of mass-produced textures.

Let us consider macrame yarns. Here is an old craft being used for new shapes and new purposes. But the yarns and colors that are available in packaged form cannot do full justice to the new ideas. Only natural, undyed yarns, such as jute, linen, and heavy cotton, seem pleasing.

Many knotters are unaware of yarn sources available to weavers. Most weaving shops have cordage items which are vastly interesting in knotted fabric. Jute is available in two-ply as well as five- to seven-ply rope. Natural linen is put up in skeins as well as cones and tubes. It is available in five-ply sacking twine and three-ply cordage. Sisal rope is glossy and creamy white— very pretty. Rug wool knots well. These fibers are pleasing in their natural state. They also can be dyed with natural color. It is still rather unusual to see natural dyed macrame. When one does see it, it sings!

Try any of the recipes suitable for the plant fibers: linen, cotton, jute, and sisal. Of the edibles, the following work on all fibers: turmeric, tea, coffee, onion skins, and walnut leaves.

Stitchery materials lend themselves very well to dyes from nature. The amount of yarn used is less than for weaving or even macrame. The yarns tend to be less bulky. Slight variations in color are an asset rather than a problem. Crochet yarn has tended to be the least interesting of all commercial yarns. Crochet craftsmen, on the other hand, have become more venturesome and are seeking interesting materials. The needle arts are now included in college textile arts programs. The result is invigorating.

Before dyeing, the yarn must be prepared according to the directions in Chapter IV, Basic Information. It must be wound into skeins, scoured, and thoroughly presoaked. If substantive dyes are used, such as turmeric or walnut leaves, mordanting will not be necessary. Piece dyeing, rather than yarn dyeing, is entirely feasible if an allover color is desired.

It is hoped that the suggestions made in this chapter are only the beginning for you. In the course of working with foods, keep your dyer's eye open. Observe sauces and stains for dye possibilities. I remember noticing a pretty blackberry pie stain on one of my daughter's white pillowcases. For two years this purple spot glared at me, underscoring the fact that I could not produce a *fast color* blackberry dye recipe! Suddenly it dawned on me—try a dye mixture that is similar to a pie mixture: add sugar and flour. The result is a fairly good berry dye recipe, and it has good

lightfastness too (see Recipe 230).

In general, onion skin dyeing is a good starting point for the city dweller. Skins are readily available, and effective on most fibers. By following the onion recipes in this book you can find an interesting color range: yellow, gold, orange, orangish-brown and some greens. Only blue is totally absent. With the addition of purple cabbage colors, a subtle, fairly broad palette is possible.

There follows a recipe using onion skins. Please refer to the recipe section for other recipes using foods and associated plants.

14/RED ONION SKINS (Allium sp.)

GOLD TO HENNA RED TO MAROON: ALUMED WOOL OR COTTON; FAIR TO GOOD LIGHTFASTNESS.

Amaryllis Family. The papery outer skin of the onion is used for dye.

TEXTILE

Scoured, presoaked, alum mordanted wool, cotton (see pages 37–39) (1 ounce)

INGREDIENTS

Red onion skins (3 ounces)

Iodized salt (1 tablespoon)

Vinegar, in 1 quart of water (2 tablespoons)

WATER

Tap (enough to cover textile)

POT

Nonreacting

METHOD

1. Cover skins and textile with water and soak overnight.
2. Add salt.
3. Simmer for 30 minutes.
4. Cool overnight in dye bath.
5. Remove textile from dye bath and dip in vinegar water.
6. Rinse thoroughly in fresh water.
7. Dry in shade.

NOTES: An ammonia rinse instead of vinegar darkens the color. □ For

½ pound of wool use 2 pounds of onion skins. Depth of color depends upon a large concentration of onion skins in proportion to a small amount of textile. □ For gold color, use 1-part textile by weight to ¾-part onion skin by weight. □ Yellow onion skins can be used instead of red.

7

Primitive dyeing methods: steeping, natural mordants, and vat dyeing

Some important, early dye methods applicable today are explained in this chapter. These include steeping and vat dyeing, neither of which requires fire. Natural mordants such as alum root, lichens, oak galls, dung, urine, smoke, and milk are considered. Six indigo blue and three magenta rose recipes are given at the end of the chapter.

A twentieth-century person practicing natural dyeing is an interesting, at-odds-with-the-time person. If we think about it we can find some remarkable things going on. For example, the way we take some basic needs for granted: cooking is one of the prime essentials of dyeing yet it is taken for granted. We know how absolutely important it is—that without heat there would usually be no permanent color. It is well-known that for a good dye

job it is necessary to simmer the textile for half an hour or more. Very important, but do we give it a passing thought? No. Why should we? Because of all the factors needed in a recipe, heat is the easiest for a modern dyer to obtain. And the utensils. And the water. Water is there with the flick of a finger. It is ready to gurgle out of the faucet, having run a long way through subterranean pipes from some mountain source. (It takes more effort to write "gurgle" than it does to turn on the faucet.)

Heat and water? As we move back in time to a preindustrial culture, we find that heat and water became vital concerns. The making of fire was a major task requiring a great deal of preplanning. Water was so important that settlements grew up wherever it was located. Utensils? Either a people produced baskets or clay utensils or traded for them, or depended upon vessels of shell or hollow tree parts. In Chapter III we indicated how a life style can affect needs: in a preindustrial culture such as the early Navajo's, one pot was enough for dyeing. It comes as no surprise to find that dye methods vary according to the degree of industrial development of a people.

Not that dyeing skill is less in so-called "primitive" cultures. (I use the word "primitive" to mean early, or nonindustrial.) It is, in fact, true that the more industrialized a country becomes, the less need there is for handcrafts. As a result, the training of craftsmen declines. Thus, when the dye industry was industrialized, the craftsman-dyer became obsolete. Now, if we look for skill in natural dyeing, it is more likely to be found in some remote, out-of-touch community. As time goes on it becomes less likely that such communities and information can be found. I am grateful to anthropologists for what information they have obtained. However, in attempting to work out recipes from the information they give, I have wondered just how much the informant may have withheld from the anthropologist. Dyers have trade secrets—why tell all to an outsider?

STEEPING

One of the earliest of dye procedures was soaking or steeping. Since some remarkable results can come from this method we are going to explain it. The essential ingredients are: the dye plant, the textile, a liquid, a container, and the passing of time. For the liquid, one could use stale urine or water. The length of time needed for dyeing to take place varies from a week to months, depending upon the plant and the weather.

The method is so simple that it strikes one as being miraculous. This is especially true if one has practiced dyeing by cooking. I still find it hard to believe that soaking red cactus fruit with white wool eventually results in wool dyed magenta. Or that soaking crocus flowers with white wool eventually yields turquoise-colored wool.

Perhaps it would be wise to explain a little of what happens. One of the purposes of cooking in the dye process is to liberate the dye from the plant cells. The heat breaks down the cell walls and dye can flow out into the liquid. In the steeping process there is no cooking. How then is the dye liberated into solution? Our miracle worker proves to be the process of fermentation. When we soak plants in water in a warm place, bacteria or yeast begin to grow, causing a breakdown of the plants. At the early stage, odors are not offensive as dyeing progresses. At later stages, rotting may set in. At this stage, odors can be bad, and dye color is usually destroyed. If urine is used instead of water, the whole process is odoriferous from beginning to end.

Who used this method? We have already mentioned that steeping was one of the earliest dye methods. It was probably in universal use before cooking methods were perfected. We can guess that such a dye method would be undertaken by a more or less sedentary people. People on the move probably could not afford to clutter their baggage with fermenting stuff in dye pots. We can guess that our dyers were not only relatively sedentary, but also well-versed in regulating a fermentation dye pot. I conclude this from the fact that the method is so seemingly loose, non-quantitative and dependent upon observation and sense of smell. All of which is to say that steeping as a dye method is seemingly easy, messy, tantalizing, disappointing, and rewarding. Why should we try it? For the same reason that primitive peoples continued its use *after* cooking methods were in use: we should learn the steeping method because it is the *only* way to achieve certain effects.

Magenta, for example. Dye books to the contrary, dandelion roots do not yield this color. At least, we do not get it on the West Coast. There are several dependable ways of achieving this color by natural methods. All require steeping, to my knowledge. Simmering destroys magenta dye. Cactus flowers, red cactus fruit and beets produce beautiful magentas by steeping (see recipes at the end of this chapter).

There are other reasons for using the soaking method. Sometimes it is used as the only way to extract dye preliminary to boiling methods. Rock lichens as a dye source are a case in point. The lichen *Parmelia sulcata* yields various shades of deep magenta and red. However, it must first be steeped in a strongly alkaline bath for several months. Either urine or water could be used. The dye liquor is ready when it is a deep red (see Recipe 28).

Steeping is also an excellent way to keep or preserve a dye bath. For example, walnut husks and shells can be soaked for months in water in a keg or jar. The ooze gets darker and darker. When the dyer needs a brown textile he pours the dark, steeped liquor into a pot, adds the textile, and proceeds in the usual manner by boiling.

NOTE: Only selected dyestuffs improve with steeping.

The above uses of steeping involve periods of time from one week to months. There is another form of steeping which I use routinely with cooking methods. With nearly all simmer methods of dyeing, allow the textile to cool overnight in the dye bath. In most cases, the color achieved is several shades darker because of the extra soaking.

It is interesting to experiment with dye plants by steeping. There are several ways to proceed. Try steeping a plant which has proved itself too tender for cooking. That is to say, if you lose a color by simmering, try again. Use fresh plant material and set it aside with yarn to ferment. Another approach would be to set aside cooked ooze which has already been used once for dyeing. Add fresh yarn or bits of fabric and set it aside to ferment. Examine your fermentation pots every several days. When the yarn seems dyed, remove it from the ooze and rinse. If the yarn retains

color, your test is promising. Dry the sample and test for fading in two places—interior, and in a bright window. (See Chapter VIII for light-testing information.)

What are the disadvantages of soaking–steeping–fermentation methods? The obvious difficulty is the clutter and space taken up by pots and jars waiting out their time. A dyer can only be happy with this method if he has a place for extra pots—an extra cabinet, or back porch, or dye shed. There is also the fact of unpleasant odor. Short periods of fermentation produce little or no odor. Naturally, plant material which is steeping for weeks begins to smell. Other organisms begin working and the process might become one of rotting or putrefaction. (Odor is affected by the type of organism in the dye bath and also by the nitrogen content of the dyestuff.) Some dyers are understandably fastidious. Some dyers' relatives are even more fastidious. Whether or not stale urine is used instead of water for steeping is primarily a matter of how much you or your family will tolerate!

There is another problem to be considered. Steeped reds and magentas are usually unstable in sunlight. They are beautiful, bright and clear, but they fade. However, these colors hold up quite well if protected from bright light. What should the attitude of a dyer or collector of folk art be? This is my view: many of our most beautiful textiles came from preindustrial cultures. Their colors are natural, and possibly achieved by steeping. Some of the colors fade. Don't worry. The quality and expression of folk art is unique. The *total* textile art quality is significant. What happens to an individual patch of color is less important. Similarly, with an individual craftsman's work. There is no use in agonizing over each color as though it were a be-all and an end-all. The way a color is used is more important than the color itself. Therefore, be bold. Try some steeped reds. Hang your work in the shady part of your parlor!

Steeping may have been the earliest dye method. Its most efficient use is seen in the indigo cold pot methods (see Recipes 22 and 23). Indigo dyeing is discussed later in this chapter.

EARLY MORDANTING TECHNIQUES

Steeping is a cold bath method of dyeing. Let us turn our attention to the hot bath. Direct heat came into use for food cooking and later it was used for dyeing. Direct heat makes dyeing easier and more efficient. Plant cells are broken down in hot water in a matter of minutes. Thus, dye can be released into the bath quickly. Heating or boiling also helps dye penetration into the textile. Heating also helps mordant chemicals penetrate textile fibers. Neither steeping nor direct dye techniques made *intentional* use of mordants. However, we know that most plant dyes require the addition of a mordant to fix color. A study of early dye procedures shows us that though unnamed for their special use, mordant-acting substances were used.

The use of mordants probably developed in the course of direct dyeing. Let us take the case of the club mosses (*Lycopodiaceae*). These little plants are a source of yellow dye. They are now also known to be a good source of alum. Such plants were used in early cultures as a source of yellow. They would eventually gain favor because of the permanence of color

associated with their use. Gradually, club mosses would be added to other dye recipes. The expectation would be that their good qualities would assist another dye plant. Thus, without knowing the chemical particulars, early peoples developed the use of mordant substances.

There are other plants in use which probably act as mordants. The Navajo make use of staghorn moss (*Letharia vulpina*), and a ground lichen (*Parmelia molluscula*) as dye assistants. Lichens and fungi may be found on trees, fences, and rocks. Staghorn moss, or "wolfmoss" may be found on trees in California and Canada.

It has been found that alum is present in about two hundred and fifty plants. Among these are most of the members of the Club Moss Family (*Lycopodiaceae*), nearly all *Symplocos* and lichens (*Primitive Dyeing Methods* by A. Bühler). It is no wonder many of these plants came to be indispensable. They are used wherever they grow by dyers all over the world. Club mosses occur in Humboldt County, California, in dampish places. They extend northwest to Alaska and eastward to the Atlantic Coast. (Wherever club mosses are plentiful they are used for Christmas decoration.)

The plants called alum root, genus *Heuchera*, were used as dye assistants by native American peoples. It is probable that they were used as dye assistants as well as medicine. There are a number of species of alum root, most of which contain usable quantities of alum. *Heuchera cylindrica var. glabella* grows in Oregon, Idaho, and Montana. Juice from the root was said to be used by Indians of the area. *Heuchera micrantha* is native to the Pacific states. Pomo and Yurok people of northern California are said to have used its long roots for dyeing.

· There are other species of this plant genus: *Heuchera americana* is a woodland plant of the eastern United States. Coral bells (*Heuchera sanguinea*) is the name of a domesticated member of the alum root genus above. Plants are available in garden nurseries. Roots from any of the above species would probably be suitable for use as mordants.

Another naturally occurring mordant is tannin. It is present in most woody, fibrous substances. Bark and juices of twigs and leaves are common sources. Oak galls are a fine source of tannin. When a wooden vessel is used for dyeing, tannin is obtained from the container. Thus a mordant is present in the dye bath without special

Natural Mordants

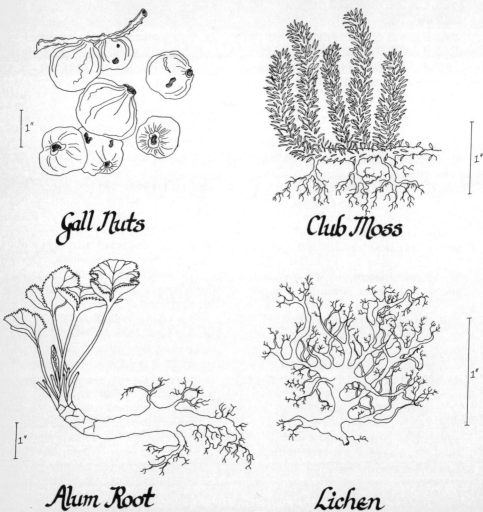

Gall Nuts

Club Moss

Alum Root

Lichen

Figure 18 Natural mordants

provision for it. It is likely that early dyers came to recognize the beneficial effect of dyeing in wooden vessels. A later refinement would be the addition of stems and leaves to a dye bath for wood effect (tannin mordant). Experienced dyers also came to know that tannin is not universally useful, since only cotton and linen benefit from this mordant.

Mineral iron (iron salts) was another mordant substance used in early times. It occurs in many clays. It is quite common to find iron-rich mud, and iron in creeks and springs. Colored fabrics were immersed in mineral springs. The effect is one of darkening a color, and making it fast to washing and light. It is said that in ancient times, sheep were dyed by coloring the fleece, and then dragging the ani-

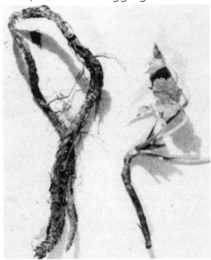

Figure 19 ALUM ROOT
(*Heuchera micrantha*)

mal through an iron-rich puddle (for a jaded king's amusement?).

The combination of tannic acid and iron salts was a universal way of achieving black. Mats woven of plant fibers were dipped in iron-rich spring water, or soaked in dark mud. The black color was a result

of the tannin in the fibers combining with the iron salts. The same effect can be had by soaking natural jute twine in a water-filled old iron pot.

EXPERIMENTING WITH NATURAL MORDANTS AND ASSISTANTS

Many craftsmen inquire about natural sources of dyeing ingredients. Some feel that all of the ingredients should be natural rather than artificial. I am not averse to the idea. It is especially worthwhile as a way of understanding how a craft developed. There is another reason for encouraging an ancient way: the simpler the approach, the more likely that art will come of it.

Following are a list of mordants and assistants used in earlier cultures. Suggestions are made for their use. It is advised that the following be undertaken *only after the dyer is experienced*. Without skillful handling, these natural mordants will give poor results.

CRUDE ALUM OR NATIVE ALUM, OR ALUNITE: Found in desert areas near sulfur springs. Use as is. One-fourth cup alum is needed for 1 pound of wool. Alum is added directly to the dye bath.

ALUM ROOT: Any member of the genus *Heuchera*. Two finger-lengths of the root were used for one dish pan full of dye. I estimate this to mean that two finger-lengths of alum root will mordant about one-half pound of yarn or basketry fiber. How should the root be used for mordanting? There are several possibilities:

1. One pot and mordant method: Precook the alum root. Soak overnight. Strain out roots. Add dye plant and textile and proceed as usual.

2. Pre-mordanting: Precook the alum root. Soak overnight. Add

scoured textile to bath and simmer for 1½ hours. Soak in bath for several days. Remove textile. Rinse, dry, and store, or proceed to dye bath. The textile is now pre-mordanted and ready for dyeing.

LICHEN OR MOSS (YIELD ALUM):

I have found no reference to amounts used for mordanting. Try one-half pound lichen to one pound of textile material. Proceed as for alum root. Try the one pot or pre-mordanting methods.

NOTE: Mordanted textile may be left a yellowish color from the mordant plant.

OAK GALLS. THESE YIELD TANNIN MORDANT FOR COTTON AND LINEN:

These are abnormal growths on certain oaks and must be crushed for use, a difficult job because of their resilience. Place them in a cloth bag and crush them with a heavy tool or rock. Boil in water for several hours. Strain out gall nuts. Use one pound of galls for one pound of cotton. This is the mordant bath. Enter scoured and pre-boiled linen or cotton in hot liquid and soak overnight. Dry and store yarn for future use.

NOTE: Oak galls leave the textile various shades of tan or brown. This means that only dark colors are suitable for overdyeing.

DUNGING: Liquid animal manure has been used as a mordant since time immemorial. The finest fabric printers in Europe were still using dung in 1874. (The best dung comes from dry-fodder-fed cows.) The Hopi mordanted cotton and wool in liquid sheep manure. Cotton is mordanted in cow dung in India. I use rabbit droppings soaked in water and strained off. Use dung as an after-mordant. Soak freshly-dyed yarn in liquid until color has barely changed. Rinse and dry.

URINE: It is likely that all preindustrial cultures have made varied use of this precious commodity. Allow urine to age for at least a week. Stale urine is usually used as an after-rinse. Enter dyed goods in the urine and steep for five minutes. Rinse. Dry. The Hopi pre-mordanted cotton in fermented urine.

SMOKE AND VAPOR: Dung and urine are used to produce smoke as a method of fixing color. According to Colton (*Hopi Dyes*), the Hopi have always used this method on dyed wool, basketry, and sometimes cotton. The technique consists of placing wet, dyed yarn on racks over dense smoke. The yarn is turned every few minutes and removed when dry. The smoke-drying can be done over an open fire or in a ventilated tin garbage can. An ideal situation would be over a campfire grill in the country. The Hopi burned fleece saturated with sheep dung and urine. Corn cobs were also burned.

In certain parts of Holland, urine vapors were employed to set color. Racks were placed over enclosed troughs partly filled with stale human urine. Freshly-dyed linen was placed on the racks and allowed to dry.

I have experimented with an approximation of the above. I used a five-gallon canner and fermented child's urine. (Child's urine is more concentrated. Use your own. It will work!) Freshly-dyed yarn was placed on a rack in the canner and the pot was covered. Turn the skeins often. Work outdoors.

MILK: Fatty substances have been used since early times by the dyer. The ancient Hindus steeped cotton in milk, sun-dried it, mordanted the fabric in alum, and then dyed it madder red. Fatty substances, such as rancid olive oil, milk, or castor oil, act as fixing agents for the subsequent alum mordant on cotton. Ugh! This one I have not tried. Being a believer in open-mindedness I have left myself a tantalizing *Out*.

VAT DYEING

We have spoken of vat dyes as a class of dyes that are insoluble in water. Mordant dyes are very different in this regard. They are soluble in water, especially with the application of heat. Cooking has no effect on the vat dye indigo. A very special process is involved in dyeing with indigo and other vat dyes. First, the insoluble dye must be acted upon chemically. The process is called reduction, and it results in a soluble, colorless substance called indigo white. At this stage, a textile is immersed in the vat and then aired. The exposure to air turns the textile blue. (The *indigotin* is oxidized.) The blue is once again insoluble, and fixed in the fibers of the textile.

The big question is, how do we achieve the chemical change that makes indigo soluble and ready to act as a dye? Does one add chemicals to the dye bath, and isn't doing this complex? No, there is a simple way, if we follow the primitive process of steeping. If indigo powder is steeped in stale urine for a week or so, it gradually goes into solution. Dyeing can then proceed by immersing the wetted textile for a shorter or longer time, and then hanging it out in the air. The shade of blue obtained varies according to the length of time spent in the blue vat. The textile is soaped and rinsed thoroughly and dried.

How does steeping assist the dye process? The stale urine provides alkalinity and nitrogen. Microbial action causes fermentation and the resulting reduction of the indigo. Since this process is carried out in specially constituted vats, all reduction dyeing is still termed vat dyeing. Nowadays, urine vat dyeing is probably only practiced in isolated instances. In 1940, however, it was still possible to obtain beautiful indigo cloth from West Africa; the surest way to determine urine-indigo-dyed goods was the unmistakable odor of the fabric.

Dyeing with indigo was one of the remarkable discoveries of early people. Actually, any form of dyeing was a cultural advance. The progress from direct dyeing to the use of mordants was in itself a technological achievement. As we have seen, the use of mordants added fastness and color range to textiles. Vat dyeing, however, is so complex that I am filled with wonder and respect for those primitive peoples who came upon its workings. May I say here that being "primitive" meant knowing a great deal more about immediate surroundings than modern man can conceive of.

I have asked myself many times: how was the indigo dyeing method discovered? First of all, how ancient is indigo dyeing? There is evidence to show that it has been in use in Asia as a dye and cosmetic for over 4,000 years. The plant is found not only in Asia but in Africa, the East Indies, the Philippines, and America. Spanish explorers have documented the use of an indigo-like dye by native Americans. In *Ancient and Medieval Dyes*, William Legett tells us that since early times, natives of all these countries seem to have had independent knowledge of the use of plants yielding indigo. Evidence of this knowledge comes from garments found in Egyptian tombs, Peruvian graves, and bits of primitive fabric from other finds.

There follow six recipes that describe early ways of achieving indigo blue, and three steeping recipes for magenta and red. The processes are workable and can be carried out today by craftsmen-dyers. There is even some practical application, especially for limited production and for artistic expression. If the reader is interested, I recommend Recipe 23, Blue Pot, for your first indigo attempt. It will take a relaxed attitude and patience. As you can guess, it is not possible to give minute by minute instructions when microbes are our assistants. I cannot describe the wonderment you will feel at your first successful "Blue Pot" dye job.

15/BEET ROOTS, STEEPED*
(Beta vulgaris)
MAGENTA TO DEEP RED: UNMORDANTED WOOL; POOR LIGHTFASTNESS.

Goosefoot Family. Beet red is a tantalizing example of magnicent, but fugitive, color. And yet it is so special that I write a recipe. This recipe is also an example of the fact that many red dyes are spoiled by heating but achieved by steeping. When preparing beets for eating, collect the unused parts and juice for your steeping vat. Canned beets are not cricket—their color is unreal! This is an ideal recipe for beet lovers.

TEXTILE
Scoured, presoaked unmordanted wool (1 ounce at a time)

INGREDIENT
Beet leftovers, simmered gently in small amount of salted water until tender. Use skin, root, juice, or whole beets if deeply colored. Overcooked beets are not used. Keep adding beets and trimmings when available to vat. Empty old vat and begin fresh every few months. (4 or 5 beets, or as available)

WATER
Tap (enough to cover textile)

POT
Large jar or pickle crock with lid (1-gallon)

METHOD
1. Cover beets and wool with water.
2. Put lid on and set steeping vat aside in a warm place.
3. Stir daily.
4. In 4 or 5 days take textile out and rinse. If color does not rinse out and it pleases you, it is done.
NOTE: For deeper color, soak longer. Add vinegar if scum forms.

16/PURPLE CACTUS FRUIT, STEEPED*
(Opuntia robusta)
MAGENTA TO ROSE: UNMORDANTED WOOL; POOR LIGHTFASTNESS.

Cactus Family. Yields a beautiful magenta color on wool, which lasts for a while in interior light. The Hopi and Navajo use this method for achieving magenta-rose colors.

TEXTILE
Scoured, presoaked wool (4 ounces)

INGREDIENT
Cactus fruit, ripe and mashed (8 ounces)

WATER
Distilled (1½ gallons)

POT
Large jar, crock or nonreacting pot with lid (3-gallon)

METHOD
1. Cover mashed cactus fruit and wool with water.
2. Set aside to steep in a warm place, lid on, for about a week.
3. Stir and keep mashing fruit into textile.
4. When color pleases you, remove textile from vat and rinse. If textile retains the color, it is dyed.
5. Dry in shade.

NOTES: Orange-colored cactus fruits yield an orange color by steeping. □ Ooze will spoil if allowed to steep too long. Color changes to tan.

17/RED FLOWERED ORCHID CACTUS, STEEPED*
(Epiphyllum sp.)

ORANGE TO ROSE: UNMORDANTED WOOL; POOR LIGHTFASTNESS.

Cactus Family. Here is another handsome, rosy color achieved on wool by steeping. The color will hold if the textile is protected from sunlight.

TEXTILE
Scoured, presoaked wool (1 ounce)

INGREDIENTS
Red flowers, picked as they fade but still colorful (20 flowers)
Vinegar (2 tablespoons)

WATER
Distilled (2 quarts)

POT
Glass or ceramic, with lid (4-quart)

METHOD
1. Put wool and water in crock.
2. Add 1 or 2 red flowers a day, as you pick them.
3. Set aside to steep in a warm place, lid on, for as long as ooze shows color (about 5 days).
4. Remove flowers from ooze when they become colorless.
5. Add vinegar to prevent early spoilage.
6. Rinse textile and dry in shade.

NOTE: This method of adding flowers day by day can be tried with other types of plants, especially those that mature over a long period.

18/INDIGO—WEST SUDANESE METHOD*
(Indigofera sp.)

BLUE: UNMORDANTED NATURAL FIBERS; LIGHTFAST AND WASHFAST.

Adapted from A. Bühler, *Indigo Dyeing Among Primitive Races.*

Fresh wood leaves may be used instead of indigo.

TEXTILE
All natural fibers, soaked and scoured (1 ounce)

INGREDIENTS
Indigofera leaves, fresh, ground up (about 4 pounds)
Wood ash lye (1 quart)

LIQUID
Urine, stale (keep in tightly capped jar for 5 or 6 weeks) (4 gallons)

POT
Earthenware, with lid, or large jar with tightly fitting lid (10-gallon)

METHOD
1. Grind up and pound indigo leaves.
2. Put in earthenware pot.
3. Add stale urine, lye water, and cover tightly.
4. Set aside to steep until fermentation is well-developed (several days).
5. Enter textile (keep covered by liquid) and cover tightly.
6. Set aside with lid on to steep overnight.
7. Lift textile out and expose to air. If it is a green which changes to blue, it is dyed.
8. If deeper color is desired, steep again.
9. Soap, rinse, and dry in shade.

NOTE: Burn wood on a fine-mesh screen placed over a pan. Pour hot water slowly over the ashes to obtain wood ash lye liquor.

19/INDIGO—AFRICAN METHOD*
(Indigofera tinctoria)

BLUE: UNMORDANTED NATURAL FIBERS; LIGHTFAST AND WASHFAST.

This is an African method using indigo, adapted from A. Bühler, *Indigo Dyeing Among Primitive Races.*

TEXTILE
All natural fibers, scoured and

presoaked (1 ounce)

INGREDIENTS
Indigo leaves, dried and pounded
(about 2 pounds)
Wood ash lye (see Recipe 18 for
method of making lye) (1 quart)

LIQUID
Urine, stale (set aside for 6 weeks
in tightly covered container)
(2 gallons)

POT
Earthenware, with lid (about
5-gallon)

METHOD
1. Grind up dried leaves and
pound.
2. Place in earthenware pot with
stale urine and lye water. Cover.
3. Steep several days in warm
place.
4. After fermentation is well-developed, enter textile (keep covered
by liquid).
5. Lift out to check color after 24
hours. If textile is a green which
turns blue in the air, it is dyed.
7. If deeper color is desired, steep
longer.
8. Soap, rinse, and dry in shade.

NOTES: Madagascar method of
preparing dye: ☐ Pound indigo
leaves and work into cakes. ☐ Dry
in sun. ☐ When ready to use, grind
up the cakes. ☐ Boil in water. ☐ Set
aside to ferment for several days.
☐ Enter textile and proceed as
above.

20/INDIGO—NORTH AFRICAN THREE-HOUR METHOD*
(Indigofera tinctoria)
BLUE: UNMORDANTED WOOL; LIGHTFAST
AND WASHFAST.

TEXTILE
Scoured, presoaked unmordanted
wool (3 pounds)

INGREDIENTS
Indigo crystals (½ pound)

Dates, pitted and ground up
(2 pounds)
Henna powder (12 ounces)
Lime (calcium oxide) (2 handfuls)

WATER
Any kind, warm (about 10 gallons)

POT
Iron, with lid (20-gallon)

METHOD
Step I
1. Mix a paste of indigo, dates, and
henna in a little warm water in the
dye pot.
2. Divide mixture in half, reserving
part of it for Step II.
3. Add the warm water.
4. Add lime powder, stirring all
together for 15 minutes.
5. Enter wool into dye bath and
cover.
6. Steep for 15 minutes.

Step II
1. Remove wool.
2. Stir in other half of paste from
Step I.
3. Beat or agitate the liquid for 5
minutes with a clean straw broom
or stick *submerged* in ooze.
4. Reenter wool and steep for 15
minutes, covered.
5. Repeat 7 times the beating of dye
mixture and the wool dipping.
If wool is a green which changes to
blue in the air, it is dyed.
6. Soap, rinse, and dry in shade.

21/INDIGO SAXON VAT*
(Indigofera tinctoria)
SAXON BLUE: UNMORDANTED FLEECE OR
FIBER; LIGHTFAST AND WASHFAST.

This method, adapted from J. Merritt
Mathews, *Application of Dyestuffs*,
represents indigo dyeing at its
earliest in Europe. Mathews tells us
that it was still being practiced in
Saxony in 1920. Substitute stale
urine for the potash if you want
to follow the old way. *Notice that
unscoured fleece is used.*

TEXTILE
Unscoured fleece or fiber

(2 ounces)

INGREDIENTS
Indigo powder or lump indigo ground to a powder ($\frac{1}{3}$ ounce)

Potash (potassium hydroxide pellets) ($\frac{1}{3}$ ounce)

DANGEROUS. Work only with small amounts. Handle with spatula. Keep away from skin.

WATER
Tap (enough to cover textile)

POT
Wooden or earthenware, with lid (about 6-quart)

METHOD
1. Dissolve potash in small amount of water. Add SLOWLY TO the water.
2. Stir in finely ground indigo.
3. Place unscoured fleece in vessel and pour indigo and potash solution over it.
4. Add sufficient water to cover wool.
5. Cover tightly.
6. Set aside to steep for a week or more in a warm place. Fermentation will set in and dissolve the indigo.
7. Check fleece for color by hanging it in the air for 5 to 10 minutes. If it is green which changes to blue, it is dyed.
8. For deeper color, it can be steeped longer.
9. Wash in soap and water. (Handle fleece gently.)
10. Dry in shade.

22/INDIGO, URINE VAT
(Indigofera tinctoria)
BLUE: ALUMED WOOL OR COTTON; LIGHT FAST AND WASHFAST.

This is a European and American method, adapted from J. J. Hummel, *The Dyeing of Textile Fabrics.* It was used by home craftsmen until manufactured dyes and goods became plentiful. It was suitable for limited and occasional production. It could still be a useful method for country craftsmen.

TEXTILE
Scoured, presoaked, alum mordanted wool or cotton (see pages 37–39) (1 to 2 pounds)

INGREDIENTS
Indigo powder (4 ounces)

Salt (12 ounces)

Madder root or dates, chopped up (4 ounces)

LIQUID
Urine, stale (at least 6 weeks old) (10 gallons)

POT
Wooden, earthenware or ceramic, with lid (20-gallon)

METHOD
1. Add salt to urine.
2. Heat to 120°F for 4 or 5 hours.
3. Stir often.
4. Add madder roots or dates and indigo and stir well.
5. Set aside to steep in a warm place, tightly covered. (Fermentation causes decomposition of urea, thus releasing ammonium carbonate which dissolves the "indigo white.")
6. Stir once a day.
7. When indigo is dissolved, enter textile for varying lengths of time, depending on shade of blue desired. If skeins are dyed, do several at a time, not all at once.
8. Hang up in air for blue color.
9. Resteep if darker blue is desired.
10. Soap, rinse and dry in shade.

23/INDIGO, BLUE POT*
(Indigofera tinctoria)
BLUE: WOOL OR COTTON; LIGHTFAST AND WASHFAST.

This is a modification of the Hopi method of small quantity indigo dyeing, and it is my favorite small quantity recipe.

TEXTILE
Presoaked wool or cotton (presoaking in urine works wonders!) four 4-ounce skeins, dyed one at a time (1 pound)

INGREDIENTS

Indigo powder (1 or 2 ounces)

Dates, pitted and chopped up (6 as needed)

LIQUID

Urine, stale (any kind will do but boy-child, collected in the morning, preferred) (3 quarts)

POT

Glass jar with lid (for dyeing larger amounts, use a larger jar) (2-gallon)

METHOD

Step I

1. Collect urine in a jar which can be kept tightly sealed.
2. Set aside in warm place to ferment.
3. When strong ammonia odor is given off, vat is ready; 7 to 14 days (lid lifted off for sniffs).

Step II

1. Stir in indigo and cover tightly.
2. Set in warm place for fermentation and stir once or twice daily. As fermentation progresses, indigo is being reduced to solubility; sediment decreases as this process progresses. This process takes several weeks, depending upon temperature.

Step III

1. Enter presoaked yarn, two 2-ounce skeins or one 4-ounce skein at a time.
2. Keep immersed for 24 hours.

Step IV

1. Lift out in 24 hours and hang in air for 10 minutes. If skein shows deep greenish color that turns blue in the air, you have achieved your goal.
2. Rinse thoroughly, soap, and rinse again.
3. Dry in shade.

Step V

1. Enter next skein(s) and repeat Steps III and above.
2. If color begins to lighten, discontinue dyeing temporarily and feed vat. This means, add 6 dates and

wait several days for fermentation to begin again. Enter 2 skeins of yarn and begin vat dye process again.

NOTES: Somewhere at midpoint, say, after you have dyed ½ pound of yarn, your indigo color may be less strong. The dyer has several choices:

1. Continue, and be content with paler and paler blues.
2. Redye. This means put your skeins back in for a second or third time. (Primitive peoples did this.)
3. Or, add one more ounce of indigo and proceed as you did the first time.

☐ When your dyeing is completed, the Blue Pot can be set aside tightly covered for future use. Months can go by. When you are ready to do some more indigo dyeing, reactivate the vat by adding dates. Eventually, however, you'll need a new batch of stale urine. ☐ *Please fear not.* Just try. It's easier than you think it is.

8

How to work out new recipes: a working method that leads to discovery

This chapter attempts to spell out a step-by-step procedure for experimenting. It will be of more use as the dyer gains skill and confidence. All the recipes in this book were worked out by the method set forth in this chapter.

One of the primary excitements of natural dyeing is the feeling of personal discovery. Every plant becomes a lure and a promise. Indeed, every different plant presents another possible dye source. What is the stuff of our dreams? Is it that we will find another source of blue as strong and as fade-proof as indigo? That we will unearth a red as useful as that from madder? Or that we will discover dyes that will "take" on cotton and linen?

Let us be realistic. Even working out another yellow can be useful—

your new yellow might dye cotton. It might be washfast. It might, with iron, yield a good green. Or, wonder of wonders, your yellow might turn red in an afterbath of tin! In addition to new sources, there is the possibility of experimenting with well-known recipes and plant materials. It is surprising how often an ingenious experimenter can make something new from something old.

METHOD AND IMPULSE IN EXPERIMENTING

How does one experiment? First of all, the craftsman–dyer must have a *methodical way of working.* Methodical usually means proceeding according to a definite system. The temptation is always present to let the system and records go to hell. There is a feeling that the next pinch of chemical will work magic. How do I know? Because I have felt the urge many times. Here is the situation: I am standing over my brew, puzzling. How to bring the color out? On impulse, I add a pinch or two of chemical. *Nothing happens.* Go ahead—add something else! Meanwhile, no records are being kept. Chances are, there will be no clear-cut results. No. Wait a minute. Look. A lovely mauve! How did this happen? What did I do? *I—don't know.* All right, let's start over. And this time, keep track of what is done!

THE DYER BECOMES FAMILIAR WITH TRADITIONAL RECIPES

Back to the old question: what is the best procedure for experimenting? First of all, it is wise to be familiar with some of the more straightforward recipes. By trying these, the dyer discovers the usual ways of dyeing with plants. She learns the methods that have been evolved by craftsmen. It is good to know that one bouquet of marigolds, dry or fresh, will dye approximately one pound of wool a deep *yellow* (Recipe 121). Remember that one large grocery bag full of red onion skins will dye one pound of wool or cotton a deep *orange-gold* (Recipe 14); that one large bag full of walnut leaves, dry or fresh, will dye one pound of wool *brown* (Recipe 265); and that skins from two pounds of Concord grapes are needed to dye one-half pound of wool *blue* (Recipes 237 and 238).

At this point, it is assumed that the dyer has read the preceding chapters and has used the above recipes. In so doing, you have practiced *direct, single bath and mordant*, and *pre-mordanting* methods (see Chapter V).

As a next step, it is suggested that the following recipes be noted: onion skins and tin (Recipe 247), Concord grape skins and ammonia afterbath (Recipe 236), marigolds in an iron pot (Recipe 121). One of these recipes demonstrates the effect of adding the metallic salt, tin, at the end of dyeing. In another recipe, the iron pot assists in the color change. In the concord grape skin recipe, the ammonia afterbath adds an alkalinity and thus changes blue to turquoise. These recipes demonstrate the innumerable possibilities of color change by afterbath treatment.

A PROCEDURE FOR EXPERIMENTING

Every recipe is made up of essential steps. Every recipe was once an experiment. We are now going to present a scheme for experimenting. Listed below in outline form are the essential parts or steps (components) of any recipe or experiment. These steps are: the plant, preparation, proportion, textile, kind of water, dye process,

chemicals added, temperature of bath, cooking time. In the outline, the components or essentials of a recipe are designated by Roman numerals. However, each step has variations or substitutions. Therefore, in our outline we will list under each step the possible variations or choices thus: under heading I, Plants, there would be nine possible choices for any experiment or recipe. Will we use the berries, or the flowers, or leaves, or stems, or roots, or bark, or all of it, or several combined? Will they be used fresh or dried? The reader–experimenter probably already knows that certain plant parts are more useful than others. The wonder of it all is that one cannot predict with certainty. An actual test must be made.

AN OUTLINE SCHEME FOR EXPERIMENTAL CHOICES

Here is the outline scheme for experimenting. The dyer can put his experiment together by making choices from each heading of the outline. What are the variables? Every recipe has the components from groups I–X. You choose the variables: I, 1; or I, 2; or I, 3; and so forth.

I. THE PLANT/(A) fresh or (B) dried
1. Fruit (berries and so forth)
2. Pods
3. Flower
4. Leaf
5. Stem
6. Root
7. Bark or skin
8. Juice
9. Entire plant

II. PREPARATION
1. Mash up
2. Cut or tear up
3. Chop up
4. Whole

III. PROPORTION OF PLANT TO TEXTILE, BY WEIGHT

1. *One* part plant to *one* part textile
2. *Two* parts plant to *one* part textile
3. *Three* parts plant to *one* part textile
4. *Four* parts plant to *one* part textile
5. *Eight* parts plant to *one* part textile, and so forth.

IV. TEXTILE/(A) plain or (B) pre-mordanted

1. Wool
2. Silk
3. Cotton
4. Linen
5. Jute
6. Rayon

V. WATER

1. Tap
2. Distilled
3. Rain
4. Spring
5. River

Figure 20 Collecting plant material for a dye experiment

6. Ocean

VI. DYE PROCESS
1. Direct and simmer
2. One-pot and mordant and simmer
3. Pre-mordant
4. After-mordant
5. Simmer
6. Pre-mordant and simmer and steep
7. Steep
8. Ferment
9. Vat dye

VII. CHEMICAL ADDED (MORDANTS)/(A) to dye bath or (B) to separate afterbath
1. Potassium alum or plant source of alum (alum)
2. Stannous chloride or use coffee tin (tin)
3. Cupric sulfate or use copper-lined dye pot (copper)
4. Ferrous sulfate or use iron dye pot (iron)
5. Potassium dichromate (chrome)
6. Potassium chromium sulfate (chrome-alum)
7. Aluminum or use aluminum pot

VIII. ACIDS, BASES, AND OTHER
ASSISTANTS/(A) added to dye bath or (B) to separate rinse or process
1. Vinegar or acetic acid
2. Lemon or citric acid
3. Oxalic acid
4. Tartaric acid (cream of tartar)
5. Tannic acid
6. Ammonia (base)
7. Vaporized ammonia (base)
8. Washing soda (base)
9. Soap
10. Lye (base)
11. Juniper ashes
12. Stale urine
13. Vaporized urine
14. Dung
15. Smoke

IX. TEMPERATURE OF DYE BATH
1. Cold
2. Hot
3. Simmer (180°–195°F or 83°–91°C)
4. Boil (212°F or 100°C)

X. LENGTH OF TIME OF COOKING
1. Fifteen minutes
2. Thirty minutes
3. One hour
4. Two hours
5. Three hours, and so forth.

Figure 21 Weighing plant material

Figure 22 Cutting up and entering plant material into dye pot

STEP-BY STEP WRITE-UP OF AN EXPERIMENT

Let us now make practical use of the scheme by plotting out an experiment. Here are the circumstances: we have collected one-half pound of flowers from New Zealand flax. Fine. We have the raw material. What happens next? Look over the scheme and jot down decisions. (I will also record the reasons for my decisions.)

I. THE PLANT: Use the flowers (I, 3), not the leaves and stems. The flowers look succulent; the leaves are huge and fibrous-looking, not promising.

II. PREPARATION: Cut up (II, 2), because this method is my usual practice.

III. PROPORTION OF PLANT TO TEXTILE BY WEIGHT: Let us divide out flowers and use only four ounces to begin with. If we use two ounces of yarn, the proportion will be two to one (III, 2). The flowers seem to have a strongly-colored juice so perhaps this proportion of two to one is sufficient.

IV. TEXTILE: Let's use three ½-ounce skeins of wool: unmordanted, alum-mordanted, and chrome-mordanted. Add ½ ounce jute, (IV, 1 and 5). Devise some system of marking each skein to avoid confusion. I tie one knot in an end of the unmordanted wool, two knots in the alum-mordanted wool, and three knots in the chrome-mordanted wool.

V. WATER: Distilled (V, 2), because it is not wise to use well water or city water for experiments. Chlorine, for example, would destroy color. The varying composition of some city water makes it unreliable for dye tests.

VI. DYE PROCESS: Steep overnight and simmer (VI, 3, 4, 6); that is, pre-mordanted, simmered, and steeped, because these represent *standard* procedure.

Figure 23 Lifting skeins from dye bath

VII. CHEMICALS ADDED: None. If the experiment proves a failure, I will try again and add some chemicals.

VIII. ACIDS, BASES, AND OTHER ASSISTANTS: After dyeing is completed I will try samples of the yarn in ammonia afterbath, (VIII, 6) and if the change obtained is desirable, I will afterbath all my samples. It is easy to test by afterbath, and therefore routine.

IX. TEMPERATURE OF DYE BATH: Try simmering (IX, 3) and if color appears, redo experiment and try lower temperature or steeping.

X. LENGTH OF TIME OF COOKING: Simmer thirty minutes, (X, 2) and if thirty minutes of simmering destroys color, I still have another four ounces of flax flowers to redo the experiment.

DECISION FOR AN EXPERIMENT

The dyer-experimenter has now read the discovery scheme and jotted down a proposal for himself. This is the way the above proposal to himself would appear, written in note form:

EXPERIMENT WITH NEW ZEALAND FLAX FLOWERS

4 ounces of cut up flowers.
2 ounces of yarn: ½ ounce of unmord. wool, ½ ounce of alum-mord. wool, ½ ounce of chrome-mord. wool, ½ ounce jute.

Distilled water to cover.
Simmer for 30 minutes.
Ammonia afterbath.

We recognize the above as a likely recipe and a list of needed materials. Once these are assembled, the experiment can begin: here I am, my ingredients are in the pot. I am at the simmer stage and it is dinner time! A pot of flax flowers is on the stove, and the guests are arriving . . .

"Hello, Ida. Mmmmmm . . . *that* is an interesting aroma. It makes us hungry. Let's try to guess what we are having for dinner!"

RESULT OF EXPERIMENT

Was the flax experiment successful? Did the plant yield a dye? What color was it? Was there a difference in color according to the mordant used? Did the ammonia after-rinse help any? Was it a fast color? Yes. No. First let us record the experimental results. Below is the information that was placed on tags and tied to each skein of the dyed yarn.

A verbal report of the experiment would go like this: New Zealand flax flowers dye a deep brown color on alumed, chromed and unmordanted wool. Is the experiment successful? Yes, the color is beautiful. Even the unmordanted wool was dyed. Does this mean I have discovered a substantive dye? Yes. Wow!

NEW ZEALAND FLAX FLOWERS: 4 ounces
Collected in Ida's garden, Mill Valley, 2/16/71

	SIMMER	LIGHT TEST	AFTER-RINSE AMMONIA
½ ounce of unmordanted wool	Brown	Good	Lightens color
½ ounce of alum pre-mordanted wool	Brown	Good	Lightens color
½ ounce of chrome pre-mordanted wool	Brown	Good	Lightens color
½ ounce of jute	Gold	Poor	

Distilled water to cover.
Simmer for 30 minutes in nonreacting pot.
Cool. Afterbath. Rinse. Dry in shade.

One question: do I care whether the color is more or less permanent? People are always asking, "Does it fade? Are your dyes as good as synthetic dyes?" Just for the fun of it, let's do a light test on samples of the dyed yarn. The results were indicated above: good fastness to light.

TESTING FOR COLORFASTNESS FASTNESS TO LIGHT: Samples of dyed yarn or fabric are partially covered with two pieces of cardboard. The cardboard edges are taped or clipped tightly together. The card is then placed in a sunny window, with a southern exposure. The yarn is checked at the end of

Figure 24 Page from a dye notebook showing pressed coreopsis, yarn sample, and recipe

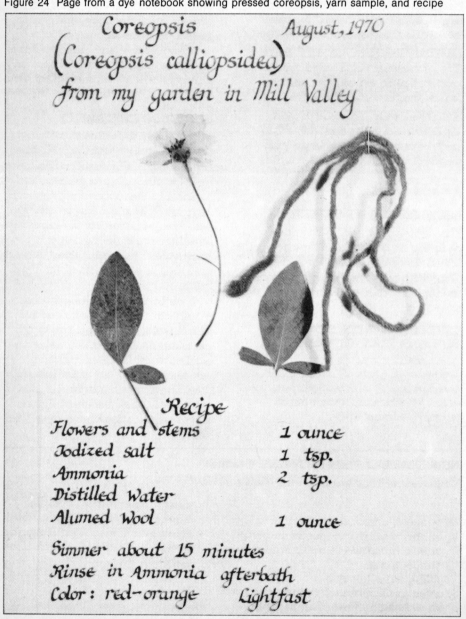

Coreopsis   August, 1970
(Coreopsis calliopsidea)
from my garden in Mill Valley

Recipe

Flowers and stems   1 ounce
Iodized salt   1 tsp.
Ammonia   2 tsp.
Distilled Water
Alumed Wool   1 ounce

Simmer about 15 minutes
Rinse in Ammonia afterbath
Color: red-orange   Lightfast

one week, and again in two weeks. Each time, the exposed part of the yarn or fabric is compared with the covered part. All recipes in this book have been tested and arbitrarily rated as follows:

No fading at the end of 2 weeks: good, or No. 1 rating. (Equivalent to fifty years in interior light—Mathews.)
No fading at the end of 1 week: acceptable, or No. 2 rating. (Equivalent to twenty-five years in interior lights—Mathews.)
Slight fading at the end of 1 week: fair, or No. 3 rating. (Remains a pleasing color.)
Fading after several days' exposure: poor, or No. 4 rating.

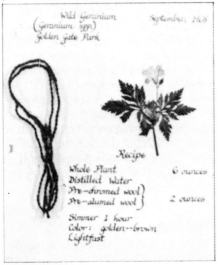

Figure 25
Page from a dye notebook showing pressed wild geranium, yarn sample, and recipe

FASTNESS TO WASHING: Samples of dyed yarn are plaited together with white yarn and subjected to ten minutes of handwashing with a mild soap. Rinse and dry. Following is an arbitrary system of rating:

No color in soap bath or on white yarn: fast, or No. 1 rating.
Tints soap bath, but not white yarn: acceptable, or No. 2 rating.

Tints the white yarn: poor, or No. 3 rating.
NOTE: It is much more difficult to achieve fastness to washing.

In conclusion, let it be said that colorfastness is a relative term. None of our colors are fast under all conditions. Some of our colors are not fast, but so beautiful that we make special use of them. A wall-hanging hung in filtered light will look the same for at least twenty-five years, even if it was made of materials rated *fair*.

KEEPING RECORDS

It is important that an experimenter keeps records of his dye experiences. This means that *notes have to be taken as you work*. It is astonishing how quickly one can forget weights, type of utensil used, whether or not the yarn was mordanted and pre-wetted, how old the dye material was, and so forth.

After the experiment is finished, it is essential to tag the dyed textile. At the same time, the experimental notes must be marked or illustrated with a sample of the dyed yarn or textile. The system used to accomplish this varies according to personal preference and experience. Many of my students keep a 9 × 12 loose-leaf notebook with dyed samples attached to each experiment or recipe.

As your confidence increases, other forms of record keeping are undertaken. Some dyers keep recipes on file cards; dyed samples are attached to each card and all are filed in a recipe box. If samples of plant material are included in a notebook, the recipe can become a beautiful thing.

9

Natural dyeing as design experience

This chapter presents natural dyeing as a direct design encounter. Special mention is made of experiencing the design elements: form, texture, color within texture, color relativeness, color relationships via differences and sharing, and designing with economy of means.
The preceding chapters set forth techniques of natural dyeing. Our focus has been on the skill or craft. Tangible matters were of concern to the reader, such as, where does one find dye plants? How is dye extracted from the plant? How is dye fixed on the cloth or yarn? Working in field and kitchen, the effort has centered upon capturing beautiful color. It is hoped that the reader has already set up his dye corner and begun his practice.

However, there is something beyond the practical to be derived from our craft. Natural dyeing also offers a subtle but basic kind of design training. Even without an art teacher, the dyer is directly encountering some important principles of design. Our very method of seeking new recipes and new

colors is also a method of studying texture-color as one might in an unusually vital design class. In fact, I am willing to go out on a limb and say that there is no better introduction to textile design than through the study of natural dyeing (and spinning).

What design experiences are inherent in natural dye practice? Let us briefly consider several basic experiences.

FORM

Color, texture, and form are the building stones of any artistic project. Every creation has these elements. However, these are only words on paper, and without concrete application. On the other hand, any dye experience makes intimate use of form, texture and color. Take the word "form." Plant prospecting involves form experience. Looking for plants involves intense seeing experiences. The eye learns to scan a landscape or a group of plants as though one's life depended upon it. Looking for a plant is almost like drawing: the eye follows contour quickly as it searches. Soon, new shapes are recognized: one sees endless variation of line and curve.

TEXTURE

Take the word "texture." What artist could have created the endless surface variations that exist in nature? Our dye work helps us appreciate texture variation visually, and *manually*. It is the latter, the constant touching, stroking, and squeezing of plant and textile material that becomes a vital part of texture appreciation. The natural dyer is in constant manual communication with his plants and textiles. He learns to associate the *look* of a plant or yarn texture with the *feel* of it to the touch. This is the reality of texture: the look–feel combination. The relationship between the appearance of texture and its tactile quality is of vital concern to the textile artist.

Texture awareness has become a basic part of art instruction since the Bauhaus school led the way. This school also introduced ways of teaching and studying texture, color, and form. *Experience* was the key word. The basic attitude involved experience by *doing*. Not the old way of teaching design by precept drawing, and painting alone; but by touching, tearing, interlacing, and building with the raw materials and tools of the art medium.

COLOR IN TEXTURE

Looking back on our dye experience, what can we conclude about color? The most basic statement would be that *color is part of substance*. It does not exist separately or abstractly. It is inextricably part of the material from which it was extracted. A natural dyer knows the truth of this statement. We know where the dye color is to be found —in flowers, in stems, in berries, in twigs, in clay. Always within a substance.

The second most basic conclusion about color is that *color is part of the substance into which it is introduced*. That is, once a fiber is dyed, the color exists *within* the fiber (or fabric, or paper, or plastic) not separately. The natural dyer knows the truth of this principle also. We know the importance of different fibers and textures in their ways of combining with, or repelling dye.

The design principle that derives from these conclusions is that *color is part of surface or texture, and is affected by it*. The designer must always be aware of this fact. For example, the orange in orange-colored jute has a different quality than a similar orange in silk or cotton. A certain red in percale cloth is very much different than the same red in taffeta. A blue plastic plate looks (and feels) very different from a similar blue in ceramic. A green lawn has a totally different look (and feel) than the same green in a shag carpet. Have you ever tried to match blue linen place mats with blue ceramic table ware? Blue linen can never appear the same as blue ceramic. It is so because dyed linen and fired glaze are two very different media, with differing surfaces and textures.

To repeat: color exists within the medium substance and is a unity with substance. The resulting design element is best thought of as *color–texture* rather than just color. A designer who works with color-texture awareness, rather than color, achieves much richer, more meaningful results. For example, in terms of yarn, don't think "blue." Think "blue wool," or "blue jute," or "blue cotton." Try the following exercise: *visualize* as you read the following words: blue candle, blue grass, blue sky, blue velvet, blue eyes, blue paper, blue lilies. Color does not exist separately or abstractly. Color wheels are more useful as pretty pictures than for practical design purposes because the designer must be aware of his materials, his medium. He must work with color as part of his medium, be it clay, fiber, metal, or whatever.

The natural dyer is one of the few colorists who experiences these truths as he works. We are forever viewing color in texture (the plant) and trying to isolate the color from the texture (the dye). If we are successful and a dye is extracted, we immediately face the reality of trying to get the color *into another* texture, the yarn or fabric. On the other hand, the craftsman who works with ready-made pigments and dyes, and already-dyed yarns and fabrics is much less likely to appreciate the strong color-texture bond. Such craftsmen work with color as though it were dominant and *independent of medium*. This attitude may work for the painter, but it proves to be a severe handicap for the textile artist.

(Note: No attempt will be made here to discuss the three qualities of color that are usually well-known: *hue*, which means color name; *value* or tone, which means the lightness or darkness of a color; and *intensity*, which means how much pure color. Nor will color-system theories be discussed. The author is emphasizing color facts or phenomena that may be less well-known to the craftsman and student.)

COLOR RELATIVITY

We have brought out the fact that texture or surface quality affects color. Let us now briefly consider how color is affected *by color*. It is perhaps startling to find that any color depends upon other colors for its being. Take redness, for example. Our visual experience of the uniqueness of red is based on the fact that we have seen colors which are *not* red, like blue or green. These are very different from red. If everything around us were red, there would probably not be a word for red, or for any other color. Color is a relative matter. We see it, and have a name for it, because there are other colors which differ from it.

COLOR RELATIONSHIPS— DIFFERENCES

The designer can make use of the above color fact by juxtaposing any two different hues. A tapestry or pillow that is half red and half blue makes a sharp, pleasurable impact of redness and blueness. The relationship of these two colors is one of *difference*.

COLOR RELATIONSHIPS— SIMILARITY AND DIFFERENCE

Colors are not only related by being different from one another, but can also be related by being similar to each other. Our previous example demonstrated the uniqueness of red by color difference. Red. Blue. The specialness of red can be experienced and exploited in another manner. Two colors can be juxtaposed that are different from one another, but share redness. Examples of shared redness are orange and pink. True, the impact of red is perhaps more direct in the case of our red-blue composition. However, the fact of shared color can be subtler, and at least helps us understand why red, pink, and orange can be exciting used side by side.

Color sharing is an everyday occurrence in nature. It is frequently seen in natural dyeing. Colors derived from the same plant have a relatedness which has to be seen to be appreciated. Visualize the maroon-colored leaves of the Japanese plum. When simmered, they yield a reddish-violet dye bath. Wool dyed in this bath turns plum color. (This is one of the few instances of color name and color source and common knowledge converging on one word: plum!)

The plum-colored yarn can be reddened by using a vinegar rinse. It can be changed to green-colored yarn by using an ammonia rinse. A stannous chloride (tin) afterbath yields purple-colored yarn. We can have plum color, green and purple yarn, all from the leaves of the Japanese plum. Yarns dyed in these three ways are different, but similar. The effect of sharing comes across to the eye even when juxtaposing the green and plum-colored yarn. There exists an *undertone* of plumness. There is also an exact sameness of tonality ("tone" meaning the lightness or darkness of a color). Where, except in natural dyed yarn, can one experience green and purple as closely related?

TEXTILE DESIGNERS' PALETTE—LESS IS MORE

The words "designers' palette" usually bring to mind the range or extended variety of color. I would like to discuss the opposite concept: the principle of *limited palette*. Not that the natural dyer has limited resources. He can produce color and tone variations more varied than mass-production is interested in. Even so, it is sometimes helpful to design from a self-limited range of color. Various artists have worked with this idea in mind.

The idea of a limited palette or limiting the means is a matter of aesthetics. It is a design outlook or point of view, and as such, is not subject to scientific proof. Throughout the ages, good design has often displayed the quality of economy of means. I suggest this as a conscious way of working that is especially useful in our time of too many ready-made colors, yarn types, textures, fabrics, and so forth.

The concept of limited color palette is especially useful to the textile craftsman who produces his own textile (by weaving, twining, knotting, crocheting, or knitting). This craftsman is a "builder." He must consider not only the appearance but also the strength of his materials. He works with yarn, the interlacement of weave or knot, the texture and color of the fabric after

it is woven, and finally, *the form or shape* that the fabric assumes. The form might be flat and rectangular as a rug, or multisurfaced as a sculpture. It can be understood from this that although color is an important design element, it is not the only element which must be considered.

Natural dyes offer an unlimited subtle gradation of color. A designer would be tempted by the profusion. It can be confusing to create from a full color range. A practical way might be to use the dye palette derived from one or several plants.

I propose that the craftsman begin by limiting his color ideas to one or two plants at a time. Instead of arbitrarily working from a palette that includes all of the colors, pretend a limitation. For example, weave a tapestry or crochet a scarf or tie-and-dye a pillow cover in materials dyed with onion skin. What might the palette be? Yellows, orange, almost maroon, dull green. Almost too many colors? Or, tie-and-dye a silk undershirt or pillow cover in a dye bath of Japanese plum leaves. What would the palette be? Plum color, lavender, purple, and green. These ideas are offered only as a taking off point. The dyer–craftsman can go on exploring and expanding his color experience. Only delight and peace can come of it.

10

About the dye recipes

There are 268 recipe formulas in this book. All of them are the direct result of experimentation. The method of discovery used is described in Chapter VIII, How to Work Out New Recipes. It is hoped that the reader will use these as a stepping stone to a life-time practice of natural dyeing. The recipes are divided into plant groups from which the dyes were obtained:

Lichens
Wild flowers and weeds
Garden flowers
Wild shrubs
Garden shrubs
Trees
Food and food-related plants

RECIPE PRESENTATION

Several innovations in dye recipe writing will be noted. One of these is the tabular form of presentation. The recipe appears in a table with each item clearly visible. Thus the reader can scan a recipe and within seconds pick out the important items:

Name of plant
Dye result, light test information
Type of fiber and mordant used
Ingredients
Type of water
Type of pot
Dye methods
Notes

Remember, an asterisk (*) after the plant name will indicate that an *unmordanted* textile (fabric, yarn, or fiber) is used. Such a recipe is easier than one which requires a mordanted textile.

RECIPE PROPORTIONS

Another innovation in this book is the use of small amounts of fiber and dye plant. Most of my dye recipes are written for one ounce of yarn and about four to six ounces of plant material. In recent years recipe writers have favored a proportion of one pound of wool which automatically calls for huge amounts of plant material (unless exotic dyes are used).

Years of teaching convince me that a dyer seldom dyes one pound of wool at a time. It is more usual to dye much smaller or much larger amounts. One pound of wool requires four to five gallons of water and two to four pounds of plant material! This amount is unwieldy for the inexperienced dyer. It places emphasis on production rather than on gaining experience and designing. Technique and experience are far more important for good dye results than are big dye lots. *It is better to have practiced a number of dyeings than it is to produce several large batches.* An example of the importance of practice is the following: working with the same formulas experienced dyers tend to achieve more color *variety* and *deeper* color than do beginners. Why? Because they have practiced dyeing for a longer time.

Small dye batches are also congruent with the facts of life (the life of natural dyeing). It is not easy to find three pounds of canterbury bells or hollyhock, or one pound of goldenrod. If we were buying all of our dyestuff any requirement is practical as long as we can afford it. Exotic dyes were once inexpensive. They are also potent and therefore require much smaller amounts.

SMALL DYE LOTS ADD VARIETY AND RICHNESS

The experienced dyer has varying needs. She may require a variety of color in small amounts or a few colors in large amounts. Here again a one-pound-based dye formula is an abstraction. Many weavers are working with multicolored wall hangings, tapestries, sculpture. It might be of interest to note the weight of some handwoven objects in my studio: stole, 10 ounces; purse, 1½ ounces; evening skirt, 7 ounces; pillow (17 × 21 inches), 8 ounces; tapestry (16 × 25 inches), 13 ounces; pillow cover (31 × 46 inches), 2 pounds. Remember, the weight of a fabric includes both warp and weft. Each of these can be and usually is a different color.

Handmade textiles are *enriched by subtle variation* rather than spoiled. Slight changes within a color are beautiful to behold. Dye lot be damned! Here is anti-art propaganda: "Be sure to buy enough yarn of the same dye lot to avoid unsightly *dye lot* streaks." Or: "Our white bread is smooth, even-textured, fresh, *always the same* and dependable." All of which is my way of saying that small dye batches can be an aesthetic blessing and loaf after loaf of bread can be depended upon to *look the same.*

All other considerations aside, I am convinced that *small dye batches yield deeper color and better lightfastness.* One of the reasons for greater color depth is possibly the *overconcentration* of plant material in my recipes. The other reason for color depth is probably the *combining of plant material and textile in the same pot* and processing them together. This too is a consequence of working with small batches. Large batches of yarn and dye plant cannot be processed conveniently in one pot unless the pot is very large. The above remarks do not apply if exotic dyes are used. (If I had to dye wool material to be made into pantaloons for an army *red,* I would whip out my forty-gallon caldron and my pounds of madder root. Yes, I would!)

FOLLOWING THE RECIPE

Let the recipe guide you and give you ideas for further experiment. Do not become enslaved by it.

(NOTE: The reader is reminded that it is not always necessary to cook plant and textile together. Strong dye plants may be precooked and strained out before dyeing begins.) A little bit more or less of textile or plant material is of no consequence. Particularly plant material can be increased or decreased. Naturally, if the ratio of textile to plant increases, the dye becomes paler and changes.

The critical items in a recipe are:

1. Using the correct fiber for the dye. If the fiber listed is wool, then it is important to use wool—*100 percent wool.*
2. Using the *correct mordant* and following the correct mordanting technique.
3. Using the *correct chemical* ingredient in the *amount* indicated.
4. Following the *heating directions* with reasonable care.
5. Following the method indicated until experienced, then improvising on these and other themes.
6. Mastering the basic techniques

of presoaking, scouring and mordanting. I have long suspected that herein lie the answers to many dye problems.

7. Try a recipe at several different growing seasons.

8. Collect plants from various growing conditions.

9. VERY IMPORTANT: Each dye recipe will list the correct mordant if it is needed. However, it does *not* give mordanting directions. Chapter V gives mordant recipes and techniques. *Always refer to Chapter V for mordant information!*

METHODS OF DECREASING AND INCREASING RECIPE AMOUNTS

The experienced dyer likes to modify a recipe to suit his needs: There may not be enough plant material; a larger quantity of dyed textile is needed; the dye pot may be too small. For these reasons and others, recipe amounts may have to be decreased, increased, or varied. The reader is referred to the appendices where the following choices for adjusting a recipe are explained:

Decreasing the amounts—see Appendix A.
Increasing the amounts—see Appendix A and Table I.
Percentage calculation—see Appendix B and Table II and III.

There is also a way of modifying a recipe which I call *rule-of-thumb*. Experienced craftsmen sometimes appear to be guessing or approximating amounts of *dyestuff* instead of measuring and weighing. Can one achieve results in this manner? I think so—providing you are working with a well-known, stable dye plant and are a dyer of some experience. Please note this: experienced dyers *do not* guess at the amounts of textile and chemicals

used in a recipe. *We measure.* For rule of thumb methods see Appendix C.

COLOR EXPECTATIONS

The word "color" has been on my mind constantly while writing this book. The reader has also been thinking color, or having color expectations, especially when studying the recipe section. I must therefore tell you that it was frustrating to have to choose color words or names for each recipe. One reason for this is that our language lacks specific words for the wonderful, subtle *color in texture* range that my eyes behold.

Take a range of phrases describing green. There is bottle green, turquoise green, olive green, avocado green, grass green, leaf green, apple green, and pea green. Or, malachite green, earth green, and chrome green, to name a few mineral colors. Or green with envy. Or green in artists' oil paints, in acrylics, in house paint. Or green color terms used by decorators, textile designers, and advertising writers. Would any of these serve our purpose? Not quite. I have nonetheless decided to use color names in common use, particularly those used to describe everyday objects, such as foods, glass, or wood.

The prospective dyer must also be reminded of the unpredictable dye variations due to nature's rhythms. There is always dye-lot difference. By this is meant the inevitable differences seen from batch to batch—even in factory artificial dyeing. Remember that plants vary from day to day and season to season. There are variations due to soil chemistry and to moisture conditions. Experiments show that moisture variations affect the dye content of plants. This is a relatively unknown fact, probably because natural dyes are of little economic importance. But grapes have money value. So, listen to this: grape growers dread unseasonal rain, because rain lowers the sugar content. Grapes harvested after a rain bring in less money. Crocus harvested after a rain brings in less dye!

Am I saying that we can expect only the unexpected? Not quite. There are stable dye plants and these yield fairly dependable results from batch to batch. There are good dye plants that yield handsome, somewhat varied results. There are sensitive dye plants that please us from time to time, but unpredictably. There are also varying people conditions, aren't there?

All of which is to say that natural dyeing is similar to food preparation in many ways:

We use plants.

Plant conditions vary.

We try the recipes until we find favorites.

There will be failures and successes.

We innovate.

Small portions are easier to manage.

Small portions yield better results.

Each person develops his special touch.

Natural dyeing is not a science: it is an art.

11

Lichen recipes

24 / BROWN ROCK LICHEN, OYSTER LICHEN*
(Umbilicaria sp.)

MAGENTA-VIOLET: UNMORDANTED WOOL; ACCEPTABLE LIGHTFASTNESS; AROMATIC.

These magentas are beautiful to behold. However, they are subject to fading in sunlight. Use for textiles that are kept indoors, or for textiles which can be dyed over.

TEXTILE
Scoured, presoaked wool (1 ounce)

INGREDIENTS
Lichens, broken up (about ¼ cup)
Ammonia, clear (in 2 cups of hot water) (½ cup)

WATER
Distilled (enough to cover textile)

POTS
Step I
Glass jar with lid

Step II
Nonreacting

METHOD
Step I
1. Cover lichens with solution of ammonia and water and close tightly.
2. Set aside in warm corner to steep for several months. (Ooze gradually turns deep purple—and becomes concentrated.)

Step II
1. Measure out some concentrate

into dye pot (vary amount according to strength of dye).
2. Add sufficient water to float wool.
3. Enter wool and simmer for 40 minutes (add more concentrate for deeper color).
4. Cool overnight in dye bath.
5. Rinse and dry in shade.

25 / LICHEN ON OAK TREES*
(Parmelia perlata)

DEEP ORANGE-RUSSET: UNMORDANTED WOOL; GOOD LIGHTFASTNESS AND GOOD WASHFASTNESS; AROMATIC.

TEXTILE
Scoured, presoaked wool (1 ounce)

INGREDIENT
Lichen, free of bark and torn up (2 ounces)

WATER
Distilled (enough to cover textile)

POT
Nonreacting

METHOD
1. Cover textile and lichens with water.
2. Simmer for 1 hour.
3. Cool overnight in dye bath.
4. Rinse and dry in shade.

NOTES: 15 minutes of simmering yields yellow. ☐ 30 minutes of simmering yields dark yellow. ☐ 60 minutes of simmering yields deep orange.

26 / LICHEN ON OAK TREES, STEEPED*
(Parmelia perlata)

BRIGHT PINK-MAGENTA: UNMORDANTED WOOL; GOOD LIGHTFASTNESS.

This recipe makes use of the same lichen species as in the previous recipe. However, with a change in technique (and time elapsed) a beautiful bright-pink is obtained.

TEXTILE
Scoured, presoaked unmordanted wool (1 ounce)

INGREDIENTS
Lichens, free of bark and torn up

(2 ounces)

Ammonia, clear (in 2 cups of water) (½ cup)

WATER
Distilled (enough to cover textile)

POT
Large tin with lid (honey tin)

METHOD
1. Cover lichens with ammonia and water and close tightly.
2. Set aside in a warm corner to steep for a month or so. When ooze changes from orange to cranberry the time has come.
3. Enter wet textile.
4. Steep until textile turns a bright pink that does not rinse out.
5. Rinse thoroughly.
6. Dry in shade.

NOTE: Season of collecting seems to make a difference. Lichens for this recipe have usually been collected during the winter season.

27 / OLD MAN'S BEARD LICHEN*
(Usnea barbata)
ORANGE: UNMORDANTED WOOL; GOOD LIGHTFASTNESS AND WASHFASTNESS; AROMATIC.

TEXTILE
Scoured, presoaked wool (1 ounce)

INGREDIENT
Lichens, free of bark and torn up (3 ounces)

WATER
Distilled (enough to cover textile)

POT
Nonreacting

METHOD
1. Cover lichens with water and soak several days.
2. Enter wool.
3. Simmer for 1 hour.
4. Set dye bath with wool aside to steep 2 days.
5. Rinse and dry in shade.

NOTE: The dye yield of this lichen is subject to seasonal variation.

28 / LICHEN ON ROCKS*
(Parmelia sulcata)
MAGENTA: UNMORDANTED WOOL; FAIR LIGHTFASTNESS; AROMATIC.

TEXTILE
Scoured, presoaked wool (1 ounce)

INGREDIENTS
Lichens, ground to a paste in a little water (about ¼ cup)

Ammonia, clear (in 2 cups of hot water) (½ cup)

WATER
Distilled (enough to cover textile)

POTS
Step I
Glass jar with lid

Step II
Nonreacting

METHOD
Step I
1. Cover lichens with solution of ammonia and water and close tightly.
2. Set aside in warm corner to steep for about 2 months. When dark-red color shows, the dye concentrate is ready to use.

Step II
1. Measure out some concentrate into dye pot. Vary amount according to strength of concentrate.
2. Add sufficient water to cover wool.
3. Enter wool and simmer 40 minutes. Add more concentrate for deeper color.
4. Cool overnight in dye bath.
5. Rinse and dry in shade.

12

Wild flower and weed recipes

Figure 26 BRASS-BUTTONS
(*Cotula coronopifolia*)

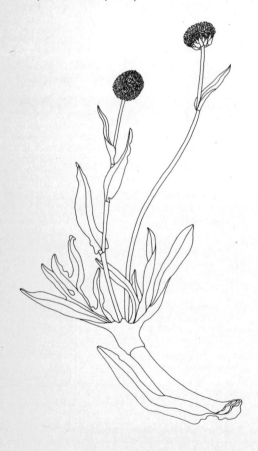

29/BRASS-BUTTONS
(Cotula coronopifolia)

DEEP BRASSY GOLD: CHROMED WOOL;
GOOD LIGHTFASTNESS.

Perennial, low-growing member of
Sunflower Family. Somewhat succulent and strong scented. Originated in South Africa.

TEXTILE
Scoured, presoaked, alum- or
chrome-mordanted wool (see pages
37–39) (2 ounces)

INGREDIENT
Whole plant, torn up (4 ounces)

WATER
Tap (enough to cover textile)

POT
Tin can or coffee tin

METHOD
1. Cover plants and textile with
water.
2. Simmer for about 30 minutes.
3. Cool overnight in ooze.
4. Rinse thoroughly.
5. Dry in shade.

NOTE: For 1 pound of wool use 1
pound of plant material.

30/FETID CHAMOMILE,
STINKWEED, MAYWEED
(Anthemis cotula)

DEEP GOLD: ALUMED WOOL; GOOD LIGHT-
FASTNESS.
TAN-GOLD: CHROMED WOOL; GOOD
LIGHTFASTNESS.

Annual. Relative of garden chamomile. Introduced from Europe during Spanish exploration. Common
in gardens, fields, and waste
places. Intense odor has been described as "naughty." I find it
pleasingly pungent and an excellent dye subject.

TEXTILE
Scoured, presoaked, alum- or
chrome-mordanted wool (see pages
37–39) (1 ounce)

INGREDIENTS
Whole plant, torn up (4 ounces)
Alum, dissolved in 1 cup of hot
water (2 teaspoons)

Figure 27 FETID CHAMOMILE (*Anthemis cotula*)

WATER
Tap (enough to cover textile)

POT
Nonreacting

METHOD
1. Cover plants with water and steep overnight.
2. Stir in alum dissolved in hot water..
3. Enter wool and simmer 45 minutes.
4. Cool overnight in ooze.
5. Rinse thoroughly.
6. Dry in shade.

NOTES: An ammonia after-rinse (½ teaspoon in 1 quart of water) will brighten the colors. Rinse thoroughly in plain water. □ Use nonreacting pot for any after-rinse.

31 / COREOPSIS
(Coreopsis auriculata and Coreopsis calliopsidea)
ORANGE TO RED-ORANGE: ALUMED OR CHROMED WOOL; GOOD LIGHTFASTNESS.

Coreopsis auriculata is a wild plant found in eastern North America,

sometimes cultivated in gardens. Six or so inches tall. *Coreopsis calliopsidea* is also low-growing. It is a California plant found in the San Francisco Bay region. Both species yield similar dye results.

TEXTILE
Scoured, presoaked, alum- or chrome-mordanted wool (see pages 37–39) (1 ounce)

INGREDIENTS
Flowers and stems (1 to 2 ounces)
Iodized salt (1 teaspoon)
Ammonia, clear (in quart of water) (2 teaspoons)

WATER
Distilled (enough to cover textile)

POT
Nonreacting

METHOD
Step I (orange)
1. Cover plants and textile with water.
2. Simmer until full color appears (15 minutes or so).
3. Cool overnight in ooze.

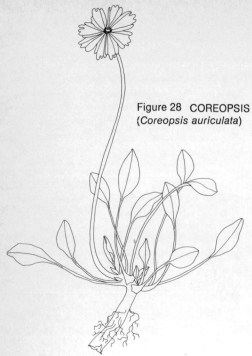

Figure 28 COREOPSIS
(*Coreopsis auriculata*)

4. Rinse thoroughly.
5. Dry in shade.

Step II (red-orange)
1. Omit rinse stage.
2. Remove textile from ooze.
3. Dip in ammonia afterbath (fresh water and ammonia).
4. Rinse in fresh water.
5. Dry in shade.

32/GIANT COREOPSIS
(Coreopsis gigantea)

LIGHT ORANGE: ALUMED WOOL; GOOD LIGHTFASTNESS.
DEEP ORANGE: CHROMED WOOL; GOOD LIGHTFASTNESS.

Somewhat shrubby, two to four feet tall, California native found on coast on rocky sea cliffs and the Channel Islands. Easily grown from seed (if you can find them!). Shaggy, bizarre-looking weedy plant. An exciting dye discovery.

TEXTILE
Scoured, presoaked, alum- or chrome-mordanted wool (see pages 37–39) (2 ounces)

INGREDIENTS
Old flower heads, seed pods, and stems (fresh material, if you ever do your dyeing on the Channel Islands) (2 ounces)

WATER
Distilled (enough to cover textile)

POT
Nonreacting

METHOD
1. Cover plant and textile with water.
2. Simmer for 30 minutes.
3. Cool overnight in ooze.
4. Rinse thoroughly.
5. Dry in shade.

NOTE: As amount of coreopsis is increased, the proportion changes: for 1 pound of textile use about ½ to ¾ pound of plant.

33/CUDWEED IN IRON POT
(Gnaphalium spp.)

YELLOW (STEP I): ALUMED WOOL; GOOD-LIGHTFASTNESSS. GREEN (STEP II): ALUMED WOOL; GOOD LIGHTFASTNESS.

Sunflower Family. Woolly, low-growing aromatic plant. Introduced from Europe. Other species found in California and elsewhere in North America. Pillows can be stuffed with dry flowers and enjoyed for their fragrance. Colds are said to improve by inhaling the fragrance.

TEXTILE
Scoured, presoaked, alum-mordanted wool (see pages 37–39) (1 ounce)

INGREDIENT
Whole plant, torn up (5 ounces)

WATER
Tap

POTS
Step I
Nonreacting

Step II
Iron

METHOD
Step I
1. Cover plant and textile with water.

2. Simmer for 1 hour (the textile is yellow at this stage).

Step II

1. Transfer ooze and textile to iron pot.
2. Simmer for 15 minutes or until textile is green.
3. Remove textile from pot when it is cool.
4. Rinse thoroughly.
5. Dry in shade.

34/DOCK ROOT, WILD RHUBARB, STEEPED*
(Rumex spp.)

PALE TO DEEP GOLD: UNMORDANTED WOOL OR COTTON; GOOD LIGHTFASTNESS.

Perennial. Member of Buckwheat Family. Many species found throughout North America. Young leaves of certain species were used as greens. Canaigre or wild rhubarb is native to the west. The long yellow roots are very rich in tannin and a mustard-colored dye. "Padre's gold" was the name of this color which was used in early California mission days. Said to have a number of medicinal properties including astringent action. Certain skin disorders of the eczema type seem to benefit from the application of dock root juice or a strong infusion.

TEXTILE

Scoured, presoaked, unmordanted cotton or wool (1 ounce)

INGREDIENT

Dock roots, ground up or pounded (1 ounce to 1 cup)

WATER

Tap (enough to cover textile)

POT

Nonreacting

METHOD

1. Boil dock root in water for 1 hour.
2. Cool.
3. Add textile and set aside to ferment. A week may be sufficient.
4. When color does not rinse out of textile, the dyeing is completed.

5. Rinse thoroughly.
6. Dry in shade.

NOTES: A vinegar rinse yields a warm tan. ☐ An ammonia rinse yields a greenish gold.

35/DOCK ROOT
(Rumex spp.)

DARK TAN TO OLD GOLD: ALUMED WOOL OR COTTON; GOOD LIGHTFASTNESS.

Roots vary in dye content according to season and type of soil in which they grow.

TEXTILE

Scoured, presoaked, alum-mordanted wool or cotton (see pages 37–39) (1 ounce)

Figure 29 DOCK (*Rumex* sp.)

INGREDIENT

Dock roots, washed and chopped up or pounded (Roots should look yellow inside and not be woody.) (3 ounces or more)

WATER

Tap (enough to cover textile)

POT

Nonreacting

METHOD

1. Cover roots with water and boil for 1 hour.

2. Add textile and simmer for 1 more hour.
3. Cool overnight in ooze.
4. Rinse thoroughly.
5. Dry in shade.

NOTE: For 1 pound of textile, use ½ pound of roots.

36/DOCK ROOT IN IRON POT OR WITH NAILS*
(Rumex spp.)

DARK GREEN TO BROWN: UNMORDANTED WOOL; GOOD LIGHTFASTNESS.
DARK GRAY: UNMORDANTED COTTON; GOOD LIGHTFASTNESS.

TEXTILE
Scoured, presoaked, unmordanted cotton or wool (1 ounce)

INGREDIENT
Dockroot (washed, chopped, or ground) (4 ounces)

WATER
Tap (enough to cover textile)

POT
Iron

METHOD
1. Boil dock roots in iron pot for 1 hour (or longer depending on need).
2. Enter textile and simmer for 1 hour.
3. Cool overnight in ooze.
4. Rinse thoroughly.
5. Dry in shade.

NOTE: A nonreacting pot can be used instead of the iron pot if nails are introduced into the dye bath.

37/DOCK BLOSSOMS
(Rumex spp.)

ROSE BEIGE TO TERRA-COTTA: ALUMED WOOL OR COTTON; GOOD LIGHTFASTNESS.

TEXTILE
Scoured, presoaked, alum-mordanted wool or cotton (see pages 37–39) (1 ounce)

INGREDIENT
Dock blossoms, torn up (2 ounces)

WATER
Tap (enough to cover textile)

POT
Nonreacting

METHOD
1. Cover textile and blossoms with water.
2. Boil for 1 hour.
3. Cool overnight in ooze.
4. Rinse thoroughly.
5. Dry in shade.

38/DODDER AND BITS OF PICKLEWEED
(Cuscuta sp. and Salicornia sp.)

YELLOW: ALUMED WOOL; GOOD LIGHT-FASTNESS.
OCHER: CHROMED WOOL; GOOD LIGHT-FASTNESS.

TEXTILE
Scoured, presoaked alum- or chrome-mordanted wool (4 ounces)

Figure 30 DODDER AND BITS OF PICKLEWEED (Cuscuta sp.)

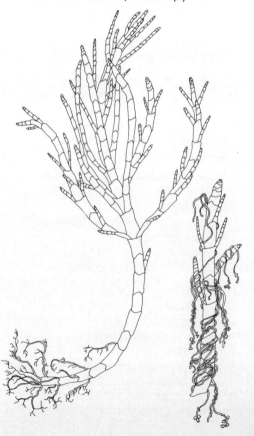

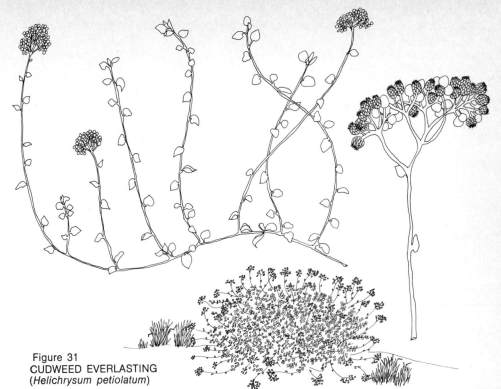

Figure 31
CUDWEED EVERLASTING
(*Helichrysum petiolatum*)

INGREDIENT
Dodder (bits of pickleweed which adhere to dodder) (1 pound)

WATER
Tap (enough to cover textile)

POT
Nonreacting

METHOD
1. Cover plants with water.
2. Simmer for 1 hour.
3. Cool.
4. Enter textile.
5. Simmer for 30 minutes.
6. Cool overnight in ooze.
7. Rinse thoroughly.
8. Dry in shade.

NOTE: An ammonia rinse brightens the colors.

39/CUDWEED EVER-LASTING
(Helichrysum petiolatum)
LIGHT GOLDEN YELLOW: ALUMED WOOL; GOOD LIGHTFASTNESS; AROMATIC.
BROWN: CHROMED WOOL; GOOD LIGHT-FASTNESS; AROMATIC.

Shrubby plant, 2 to 4 feet, from South Africa, sometimes grown in gardens. White woolly leaves and creamy-white strawlike flowers in clusters. Dried flowers are beautiful. Related to the annual cudweed. Yields a lasting fragrance on wool and fast colors ranging from yellow through green to sienna brown.

TEXTILE
Scoured, presoaked, alum- or chrome-mordanted wool (2 ounces)

INGREDIENTS
Flowers and leaves (4 ounces)

WATER
Distilled (enough to cover textile)

POT
Nonreacting

METHOD
1. Combine plant material, textile, and water.
2. Simmer for 20 minutes.
3. Cool overnight in ooze.
4. Rinse thoroughly.
5. Dry in shade.

NOTE: A pinch of tin added to dye bath brightens the colors.

40 / CUDWEED EVER-LASTING AND CUPRIC SULFATE
(Helichrysum petiolatum)

KHAKI GREEN: ALUMED WOOL; GOOD LIGHTFASTNESS.
LIGHT BROWN; CHROMED WOOL; GOOD LIGHTFASTNESS.

TEXTILE
Scoured, presoaked, alum- or chrome-mordanted wool (2 ounces)

INGREDIENTS
Flowers and leaves (4 ounces)
Cupric sulfate stock solution (mixed into 2 quarts of hot water) (See page 43 for cupric sulfate solution directions.) (1 ounce or 2 table-spoons)

WATER
Distilled (enough to cover textile)

POT
Nonreacting or copper

METHOD
1. Combine plants, textile, and water.
2. Simmer for 20 minutes.
3. Cool overnight in ooze.
4. Enter textile in copper afterbath.
5. Heat for 10 minutes.
6. Rinse thoroughly in fresh water.
7. Dry in shade.

41 / PEARLY EVERLASTING
(Anaphalis margaritacea)

YELLOW-GOLD: ALUMED WOOL; GOOD LIGHTFASTNESS.
ORANGE-GOLD: CHROMED WOOL; GOOD LIGHTFASTNESS.

Figure 32 Here and above right:
PEARLY EVERLASTING
(*Anaphalis margaritacea*)

Perennial. Member of Sunflower Family. Found throughout woods and hillsides of North America. Name of genus refers to natural drying of flower without wilting and to its ageless look. Looks fresh when old. A bouquet in the parlor marks one as a weed-loving, anti-establishment type. Indians used the plant as an antiseptic.

TEXTILE
Scoured, presoaked, alum- or chrome-mordanted wool (1 ounce)

INGREDIENTS
Flowers, stems, and leaves (torn up) (4 ounces)

WATER
Tap (enough to cover textile)

POT
Nonreacting

METHOD
1. Cover plant material and textile

with water.
2. Simmer for 30 minutes.
3. Cool overnight in ooze.
4. Rinse thoroughly.
5. Dry in shade.

42/PEARLY EVERLASTING AND CUPRIC SULFATE (Anaphalis margaritacea)

LIGHT OLIVE GREEN: ALUMED WOOL; GOOD LIGHTFASTNESS.
LIGHT BROWN; CHROMED WOOL; GOOD LIGHTFASTNESS.

TEXTILE
Scoured, presoaked alum- or chrome-mordanted wool (1 ounce)

INGREDIENTS
Flowers, stems, leaves, torn up (4 ounces)

Cupric sulfate stock solution (in 1 quart of water) (See page 41 for cupric sulfate stock solution directions.) (½ ounce c: 1 tablespoon)

WATER
Tap (enough to cover textile)

POT
Nonreacting

METHOD
1. Cover plant material and textile with water.
2. Simmer for 30 minutes.
3. Cool.
4. Transfer textile to cupric sulfate solution.
5. Heat gently for 10 minutes.
6. Rinse thoroughly.
7. Dry in shade.

43/FENNEL (Foeniculum vulgare)

MUSTARD YELLOW: ALUMED WOOL; FAIR LIGHTFASTNESS; AROMATIC.
GOLDEN BROWN: CHROMED WOOL; GOOD LIGHTFASTNESS; AROMATIC.

Perennial member of the Carrot Family. Originated in Europe. Common in Central and Southern California. Rampant in the San Francisco Bay area. I firmly believe that this pest could take over in the Bay Area. I mean "take over" in science-fiction style: the fennel gets taller and denser; the roots, thicker and longer. Gradually, patches of growth ruin gardens, crowd the highways, and choke off neighborhoods! (*Almost* true. Ask a gardener when she feels frustrated.) The seed tastes like anise. Can be used for seasoning.

TEXTILE
Scoured, presoaked, alum- or chrome-mordanted wool (1 ounce)

INGREDIENTS
Flowers and leaves (4 ounces)

WATER
Tap (enough to cover textile)

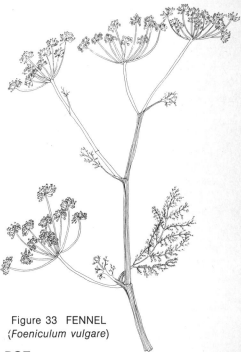

Figure 33 FENNEL
(*Foeniculum vulgare*)

POT
Nonreacting

METHOD
1. Combine plants, textile, and water.
2. Simmer for 30 minutes.
3. Cool overnight in ooze.
4. Rinse thoroughly.
5. Dry in shade.

NOTE: A cupric sulfate afterbath on the alumed, dyed yarn will make it lightfast. (See page 41 for cupric sulfate afterbath directions.)

44/FILAREE, CLOCKS, ONE POT AND MORDANT*
(Erodium spp.)

BROWN-GREEN: UNMORDANTED WOOL; GOOD LIGHTFASTNESS.
GREEN-GRAY: UNMORDANTED COTTON OR LINEN; GOOD LIGHTFASTNESS.
MOSS GREEN: UNMORDANTED JUTE; GOOD LIGHTFASTNESS.

European annuals of the Geranium Family. Widely naturalized in California. Food for sheep and cattle. Excellent fare for race horses and rabbits. Rich in protein.

TEXTILE
Presoaked, scoured, unmordanted wool, cotton, jute, or linen (1 ounce)

INGREDIENTS
Filaree plants, cut up (5 ounces)
Alum (in 1 cup of hot water) (2 teaspoons)
Cream of tartar (in 1 cup of hot water) (1 teaspoon)

WATER
Tap

POTS
Step I
Nonreacting
Step II
Iron

METHOD
Step I
1. Cover plants with water in non-reacting pot.
2. Simmer for 45 minutes.
3. Add alum, cream of tartar, and textile.
4. Simmer for another 30 minutes.

Step II
1. Pour ooze and textile into iron pot.
2. Simmer for 15 minutes.
3. Cool.
4. Remove textile if using wool.
(If vegetable fibers are used, allow to steep in ooze for 2 days.)
5. Rinse thoroughly.
6. Dry in shade.

45/GODETIA, FAREWELL TO SPRING AND CUPRIC SULFATE
(Clarkia sp.)

DARK GOLD: ALUMED COTTON; GOOD LIGHTFASTNESS.

Native California wild flower. Evening Primrose Family.

TEXTILE
Scoured, presoaked, alum-mordanted cotton (1 ounce)

INGREDIENTS
Flowers (4 ounces)
Cupric sulfate stock solution (in 1 quart of water) ($\frac{1}{2}$ ounce or 1 tablespoon)

WATER
Distilled (enough to cover textile)

POT
Nonreacting

METHOD
1. Cover flowers and textile with water.
2. Simmer for 20 minutes.
3. Steep in ooze 2 days.
4. Prepare copper afterbath.
5. Enter dyed cotton.
6. Heat for 10 minutes.
7. Cool.
8. Rinse thoroughly.
9. Dry in shade.

46/GODETIA, FAREWELL TO SPRING IN IRON POT
(Clarkia sp.)

GREENISH GRAY: ALUMED COTTON; GOOD LIGHTFASTNESS.

TEXTILE
Scoured, presoaked, alum-mordanted cotton (1 ounce)

INGREDIENT
Flowers (4 ounces)

WATER
Distilled (enough to cover textile)

POTS
Step I
Nonreacting
Step II
Iron

METHOD

Step I

1. Pre-simmer flowers only in non-reacting pot for 10 minutes.
2. Cool.

Step II

1. Enter ooze and textile in iron pot.
2. Heat for 10 minutes.
3. Remove textile.
4. Cool.
5. Rinse thoroughly.
6. Dry in shade.

47 / GOLDENROD IN IRON POT
(Solidago spp.)

MUSTARD (STEP I): ALUMED WOOL; GOOD LIGHTFASTNESS.
TAN-ORANGE (STEP I): CHROMED WOOL; GOOD LIGHTFASTNESS.
BROWN-OLIVE (STEP II): CHROMED WOOL; GOOD LIGHTFASTNESS.

Native North American perennials. Members of Sunflower Family. The name *Solidago* is from the Greek "to heal" because these plants were believed to have healing properties. A solution of the boiled stems and leaves is said to be an antiseptic. The leaves and stems may be dried and pulverized to make an antiseptic powder. The dried flowers and leaves may be used to make a tea. The goldenrod is more appreciated for its beauty in Europe than in the United States. An excellent dye subject. Try dyeing the hair of dolls (if natural hair or fibers) with it.

TEXTILE

Scoured, presoaked, alum- or chrome-mordanted wool (1 ounce)

INGREDIENT

Whole plant, cut up (3 ounces)

WATER

Distilled (enough to cover textile)

POTS

Step I
Nonreacting

Step II
Iron

METHOD

Step I

1. Cover plant material and textile with water.
2. Simmer for 1 hour.

Step II

1. Transfer contents into iron pot.
2. Simmer for 40 minutes.
3. Cool for 2 hours.
4. Rinse thoroughly.
5. Dry in shade.

48 / GOOSEFOOT IN UN-LINED COPPER POT OR WITH CUPRIC SULFATE
(Chenopodium sp.)

DARK GREEN: ALUMED WOOL; GOOD LIGHTFASTNESS.
GREEN-GOLD: CHROMED WOOL; GOOD LIGHTFASTNESS.

Annual weed, member of Goosefoot Family. Leaves can be cooked for greens. Excellent spinach substitute. One species furnishes oil of chenopodium which is used for intestinal worms.

TEXTILE

Scoured, presoaked alum- or chrome-mordanted wool (1 ounce)

INGREDIENTS

Plants, cut up (8 ounces)

Cupric sulfate stock solution (in 1 quart of water) if copper pot is not available (½ ounce or 1 tablespoon)

WATER

Tap

POT

Unlined copper pot

METHOD

1. Cover plants with water.
2. Simmer for 1 hour.
3. Remove plants.
4. Cool.
5. Enter textile.
6. Simmer for 30 minutes.
7. Cool overnight in ooze.
8. Rinse thoroughly.
9. Dry in shade.

NOTES: If copper pot is not available, heat dyed yarn in cupric sulfate afterbath for 10 minutes. Rinse thoroughly and dry in shade. □ For 1 pound of wool use about 3 pounds of plants.

49/GUM PLANT, GUM WEED, GRINDELIA
(Grindelia sp.)

YELLOW AND GOLD (STEP I): ALUMED WOOL; GOOD LIGHTFASTNESS; AROMATIC. OLIVE GREEN (STEP II): ALUMED WOOL; GOOD LIGHTFASTNESS; AROMATIC.

Coarse, resinous, somewhat woody perennial. Member of the Sunflower Family. Young buds exude a milky resin. Brew of the dried leaves and stems used to relieve symptoms of asthma and bronchitis. Brew used externally to re-

Figure 34 GUM PLANT
(Grindelia sp.)

lieve skin irritations, including poison oak. Cough medicine made from sticky buds. For toothache, hold a small quantity in the mouth. Do not swallow. Native Americans and pioneers used the plant in similar ways. Excellent dye plant.

TEXTILE
Scoured, presoaked, alum-mordanted wool (1 ounce)

INGREDIENTS
Flowering heads and pods (5 ounces)
Ammonia, clear (in 1 quart of water)—for yellow and gold only (1 teaspoon)

WATER
Tap (enough to cover textile)

POTS
Step I
Nonreacting
Step II
Iron

METHOD
Step I
1. Combine plant parts and water in nonreacting pot.
2. Simmer for 30 minutes.
3. Cool.
4. Enter wool.
5. Simmer for 30 minutes/*For yellow*: Rinse wool in ammonia and water; wash and dry/*For green*: Proceed to Step II.

Step II
1. Transfer ooze and textile to iron pot.
2. Simmer for 40 minutes.
3. Cool for 1 hour in iron pot.
4. Rinse thoroughly.
5. Dry in shade.

50/HEDGE-NETTLE, BETONY
(Stachys sp.)

CHARTREUSE GREEN: ALUMED WOOL; GOOD LIGHTFASTNESS.

This weed was the most despised in my garden until I tested it for dye. Perennial garden pest of the Mint Family. An infusion of the leaves in water is said to be useful as a wash for sores.

TEXTILE
Scoured, presoaked, alum-mordanted wool (2 ounces)

INGREDIENTS
Hedge-nettle plants, fresh (about 7 ounces)

Salt (1 teaspoon)

Cupric sulfate (in 1 quart of water) (pinch or 1/16 teaspoon)

WATER
Tap (enough to cover textile)

POT
Nonreacting

METHOD
1. Combine plants, textile, and water.

·2. Simmer for 25 minutes.
3. Cool overnight in ooze.
4. Remove textile.
5. Enter textile in cupric sulfate afterbath.
6. Heat for 10 minutes.
7. Cool.
8. Rinse thoroughly.
9. Dry in shade.

51 / HERB ROBERT, WILD GERANIUM, RED ROBIN (Geranium robertianum)
LIGHT GOLDEN BROWN TO RICH BROWN; ALUMED WOOL; GOOD LIGHTFASTNESS.

The fruits of all geraniums resemble a crane's beak. The Greek word for crane is *geranos*, hence the name *Geranium*.

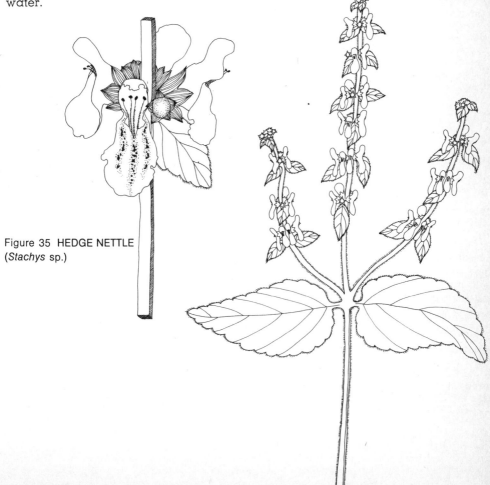

Figure 35 HEDGE NETTLE
(*Stachys* sp.)

TEXTILE

Scoured, presoaked, alum-mordanted wool (1 ounce)

INGREDIENT

Geranium weeds, cut up (about 5 ounces)

WATER

Tap (enough to cover textile)

POT

Nonreacting

METHOD

1. Cover plants and textile with water.
2. Simmer for 1 hour.
3. Cool overnight in ooze.
4. Rinse thoroughly.
5. Dry in shade.

NOTE: Using an iron pot in the above recipe results in darker color.

52/KLAMATH WEED AND AMMONIA
(Hypericum perforatum)

MUSTARD GOLD: ALUMED WOOL; GOOD LIGHTFASTNESS.
RAW SIENNA: CHROMED WOOL; GOOD LIGHTFASTNESS.

Saint-John's-Wort Family. Naturalized from Europe. Found along roadsides and dry pastures. See Saint-John's-Wort Recipe in Chapter XIII.

TEXTILE

Scoured, presoaked, alum- or chrome-mordanted wool (1 ounce)

INGREDIENTS

Flowers and leaves (3 ounces)

Ammonia, clear (in 1 quart of water) (1 teaspoon)

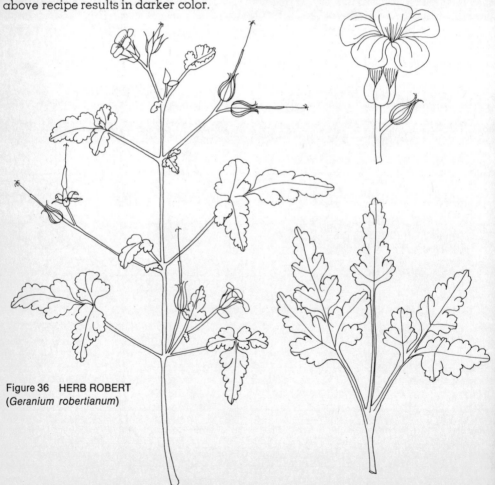

Figure 36   HERB ROBERT
(*Geranium robertianum*)

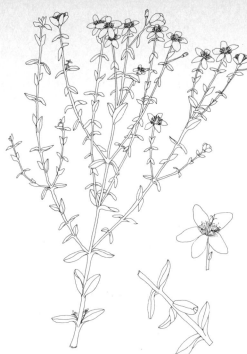

Figure 37 KLAMATH WEED
(*Hypericum perforatum*)

WATER
Tap (enough to cover textile)

POT
Nonreacting

METHOD
1. Cover textile and plant with water and soak overnight.
2. Simmer for 30 minutes.
3. Cool overnight in ooze.
4. Dip in ammonia rinse until color brightens.
5. Rinse thoroughly.
6. Dry in shade.

53/KLAMATH WEED AND CUPRIC SULFATE (Hypericum perforatum)
DARK YELLOW-GREEN: ALUMED WOOL; GOOD LIGHTFASTNESS.
LIGHT BROWN: CHROMED WOOL; GOOD LIGHTFASTNESS.

TEXTILE
Scoured, presoaked, alum- or chrome-mordanted wool (1 ounce)

INGREDIENTS
Flowers and leaves (3 ounces)

Cupric sulfate stock solution (in 1 quart of water) (1 tablespoon)

WATER
Distilled (enough to cover textile)

POT
Nonreacting

METHOD
1. Cover textile and plant material with water.
2. Soak overnight.
3. Simmer for 30 minutes.
4. Cool overnight.
5. Transfer textile to cupric sulfate solution.
6. Heat gently for 10 minutes.
7. Cool.
8. Rinse thoroughly.
9. Dry in shade.

54/KNOTWEED, DOOR-WEED, MAT-GRASS (Polygonum aviculare)
CREAMY YELLOW: ALUMED WOOL; GOOD LIGHTFASTNESS.
BRIGHTER YELLOW: ALUMED WOOL WITH AMMONIA; GOOD LIGHTFASTNESS.
BRASSY YELLOW: CHROMED WOOL; GOOD LIGHTFASTNESS.

Weedy annual member of Buckwheat Family, native to Eurasia. Found mainly in hard-trampled ground, such as paths and yards. The only nice thing to be said about this nuisance is that it makes a useful dye. Remember also that dock and rhubarb are relatives. (That makes me feel more kindly disposed toward knotweed.)

TEXTILE
Scoured, presoaked, alum- or chrome-mordanted wool (1 ounce)

INGREDIENTS
Knotweed, cut up (about 8 ounces)
Ammonia, clear (1 teaspoon)

WATER
Tap (enough to cover textile)

POT
Nonreacting

METHOD
1. Combine plants, textile, and water.

2. Simmer for 30 minutes.
3. Cool overnight in ooze.
4. *If desired*: Add ammonia to plain water and dip dyed textile.
5. Rinse thoroughly.
6. Dry in shade.

NOTE: For 1 pound of wool use about 8 quarts (dry measure) or about 3 pounds of weeds.

55/KNOTWEED IN UNLINED COPPER POT
(Polygonum aviculare)

MOSS GREEN: ALUMED WOOL; GOOD LIGHTFASTNESS.
BRASSY MOSS GREEN: CHROMED WOOL; GOOD LIGHTFASTNESS.

TEXTILE
Scoured, presoaked, alum- or chrome-mordanted wool (1 ounce)

INGREDIENTS
Knotweed, cut up (about 8 ounces)
Cupric sulfate stock solution (if copper pot is not available) (½ ounce or 1 tablespoon)

WATER
Tap (enough to cover textile)

POT
Unlined copper pot (or use cupric sulfate afterbath instead)

METHOD
1. Combine plants, water, and textile.
2. Simmer for 1 hour.
3. Cool overnight in ooze.
4. Rinse thoroughly.
5. Dry in shade.

56/PURPLE LUPINE
(Lupinus spp.)

BRIGHT YELLOW-GREEN (STEP I): CHROMED WOOL; FAIR LIGHTFASTNESS.
DULLED GREEN (STEP II): CHROMED WOOL WITH CUPRIC SULFATE; GOOD LIGHT-FASTNESS.

Annual, perennial, and shrubby species in North America. Until thirty years ago, lupines were used mainly for fodder and soil improvement. Being members of the Pea Family, the plants have the capacity of fixing nitrogen in the soil and

Figure 38 LUPINE (*Lupinus* sp.)

thus enriching it. Purple lupine furnishes a lively green dye. Though only fairly fast (after one week in the sun the green is somewhat paler), it is still a worthwhile dye plant.

TEXTILE
Scoured, presoaked, chrome-mordanted wool (1 ounce)

INGREDIENTS
Purple lupine blossoms (6 ounces)
Cupric sulfate stock solution (in 1 quart of water) (½ ounce or 1 tablespoon)

WATER
Distilled (enough to cover textile)

POT
Nonreacting

METHOD
Step I
1. Combine flowers, textile, and water.
2. Simmer for 30 minutes.
3. Cool overnight in ooze.
4. Rinse thoroughly.

5. *For bright yellow-green*: Dry in shade.
For dull green: Proceed to Step II.

Step II
Prepare copper afterbath of cupric sulfate in water.
2. Enter dyed textile in afterbath.
3. Heat for 10 minutes.
4. Cool.
5. Rinse thoroughly.
6. Dry in shade.

57/TREE MALLOW, STEEPED
(Malva sp.)
MEDIUM BLUE: ALUMED WOOL; GOOD LIGHTFASTNESS.

Mallow Family. Here is a so-called "weed" that produces a rare color: blue: I must admit this coarse-looking plant hardly belongs in a garden. We found it growing near the beach. Like its cultivated relatives, hollyhock, abutilon, rose of sharon and okra, it produces a mucilaginous ooze. The greens are also endowed with sugar, vitamin C, carotene, and coloring matter. No doubt, the deer would relish this plant. I have a specimen now growing, guarded by a fence.

TEXTILE
Scoured, presoaked, alum-mordanted wool (1 ounce)

INGREDIENTS
Mallow flowers (6 ounces)
Iodized salt (dissolved in 1 cup of hot water) (2 teaspoons)

WATER
Distilled (enough to cover textile)
POT
Nonreacting
METHOD
1. Combine flowers, textile, salt solution, and water. Set aside for 24 hours.
2. Remove textile from ooze.
3. Rinse thoroughly.
4. Dry in shade.

NOTE: *Save ooze. It can be reused for lighter colors.*

58/TREE MALLOW AND TIN CRYSTALS
(Malva sp.)
DEEP BLUE: ALUMED WOOL; GOOD LIGHT-FASTNESS.

TEXTILE
Scoured, presoaked, alum-mordanted wool (1 ounce)

INGREDIENTS
Mallow flowers (6 ounces)
Iodized salt (dissolved in 1 cup of hot water) (2 teaspoons)
Tin crystals (dissolved in 1 cup of hot water immediately before using) (pinch, 1/16 teaspoon)

WATER
Distilled (enough to cover textile)
POT
Nonreacting or tin
METHOD
1. Combine flowers, textile, salt solution and water.
2. Simmer for 50 minutes.
3. Remove textile from ooze.
4. Stir in tin solution.
5. Reenter textile into dye bath.
6. Simmer for 10 more minutes.
7. Cool overnight in ooze.
8. Rinse thoroughly.
9. Dry in shade.

59/MALVA WEED, CHEESES IN IRON POT
(Malva sp.)
CREAM COLOR (STEP I): ALUMED WOOL; GOOD LIGHTFASTNESS.
BRIGHT YELLOW (STEP II): ALUMED WOOL WITH AMMONIA; GOOD LIGHTFASTNESS.
KHAKI GREEN (STEP III): ALUMED WOOL IN IRON POT; GOOD LIGHTFASTNESS.

Annual or biennial member of Mallow Family. Wayside weed. Thought to be a potent medicinal herb. Has high mineral content (17 percent) and according to one report, has highest vitamin A content of any herb. Spanish peoples used it for centuries in salads and soup.

TEXTILE
Scoured, presoaked, alum-mordanted wool (1 ounce)

Figure 39   MALVA WEED (*Malva* sp.)

INGREDIENTS
Malva plants and seeds (6 ounces)

Ammonia, clear (in 1 quart of water) (1 teaspoon) for bright yellow

WATER
Tap (enough to cover textile)

POTS
Step I
Nonreacting

Step II
Iron

METHOD
Step I
1. Combine plant, textile, and water in nonreacting pot.
2. Simmer for 30 minutes. Textile is cream color at this stage.

Step II
1. Ammonia rinse yields a bright yellow.
2. *For khaki green:* Skip Step II and go to Step III.

Step III
1. Pour ooze and textile into iron pot.
2. Add water to cover if necessary.
3. Simmer for 30 minutes.
4. Cool in ooze for a few hours.

5. Rinse thoroughly.
6. Dry in shade.

60/MEADOW RUE
(Thalictrum polycarpum)
BRIGHT YELLOW: ALUMED WOOL, GOOD LIGHTFASTNESS AND GOOD WASHFASTNESS; AROMATIC.

Perennial. Member of Ranunculus Family.

TEXTILE
Scoured, presoaked, alum-mordanted wool (1 ounce)

INGREDIENTS
Meadow rue plants, torn up (6 ounces)

Ammonia, clear (in 1 quart of water) (1 teaspoon)

WATER
Tap (enough to cover textile)

POT
Nonreacting

METHOD
1. Combine plants, textile, and water.
2. Simmer for 30 minutes.
3. Cool overnight in ooze.
4. Dip textile in ammonia rinse.

5. Rinse thoroughly.
6. Dry in shade.

NOTE: Try this plant with cupric sulfate, or in an iron pot. We ran out of plants.

61 / SHOWY MILKWEED AND CUPRIC SULFATE OR UNLINED COPPER POT (Asclepias speciosa)

MOSS GREEN: ALUMED WOOL; GOOD LIGHTFASTNESS.
BRASS GREEN: CHROMED WOOL; GOOD LIGHTFASTNESS.

Native perennial. Member of Milkweed Family. Found in dry meadows and pastures throughout the West. Other species growing in Eastern United States. Milkweed is named in honor of the Greek god of medicine Asclepius. This was so because of the many medicinal uses attributed to some of the members of this plant family. The milky juice is said to cure warts. The inner layer just under the bark contains fibers which were used for rope and fish nets by native Americans. If you are interested in the fibers, wait for the milkweed plant to dry at the end of its season. The Indians

Figure 40 SHOWY MILKWEED (Aesclepias speciosa)

collected the old, dry plants, not the green ones. It works. Try it. The seed hairs found in the pods can be mixed with fleece and spun into a thread.

TEXTILE
Scoured, presoaked, alum- or chrome-mordanted wool (1 ounce)

INGREDIENTS
Milkweed leaves and flowers (7 ounces)
Cupric sulfate stock solution (in 1 quart of water) (½ ounce or 1 tablespoon)

WATER
Tap (enough to cover textile)

POT
Nonreacting

METHOD
1. Combine plants, textile, and water.
2. Simmer for 30 minutes.
3. Cool overnight in ooze.
4. Remove textile.
5. Enter textile in cupric sulfate afterbath.
6. Heat slowly for 10 minutes.
7. Rinse thoroughly.
8. Dry in shade.

62 / MORNING-GLORY, BINDWEED (Convolvulus arvensis)

DULL GREEN: ALUMED WOOL IN COPPER POT; GOOD LIGHTFASTNESS.
KHAKI GREEN TO YELLOW: ALUMED WOOL IN PLAIN POT; GOOD LIGHTFASTNESS.

Perennial. Member of Morning Glory Family. Sprawling, climbing garden pest. It is a pleasure to find some use for this nuisance.

TEXTILE
Scoured, presoaked, alum-mordanted wool (1 ounce)

INGREDIENT
Whole plants, torn up (5 ounces)

WATER
Tap (enough to cover textile)

POT
Copper or nonreacting

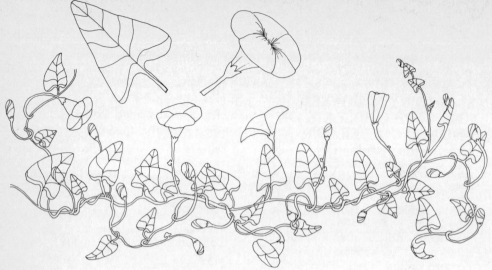

Figure 41 MORNING GLORY (*Convolvulus arvensis*)

METHOD

1. Cover plants and textile with water.
2. *For dull green:* Use copper pot. *For khaki green and yellow:* Use nonreacting pot. Simmer for 1 hour.
3. Cool overnight in ooze.
4. Rinse thoroughly.
5. Dry in shade.

63/CALIFORNIA MUG-WORT IN IRON POT (**Artemisia** sp.)

GOLD (STEP I): CHROMED WOOL; GOOD LIGHTFASTNESS; AROMATIC.
CHARTREUSE AND VARIOUS GREENS (STEP II): ALUMED WOOL; GOOD LIGHTFASTNESS; AROMATIC.

Sunflower Family. Native to California. Perennial herb. Grows in Eastern United States. Aromatic, bitter. Can be used as a condiment like tansy. Used in China for moxybustion (heating acupuncture needles).

TEXTILE

Scoured, presoaked, alum- or chrome-mordanted wool (1 ounce)

INGREDIENT

Whole plants, torn up (4 ounces)

WATER

Tap (enough to cover textile)

POTS

Step I
Nonreacting

Step II
Iron

METHOD

Step I
1. Cover plant and textile with water.
2. Simmer for 30 minutes.
3. *For yellow:* Cool overnight in ooze, rinse, and dry.
For chartreuse: Proceed to Step II.

Step II
1. Transfer textile and ooze to iron pot.
2. Simmer an additional hour.
3. Cool overnight in ooze.
4. Rinse thoroughly.
5. Dry in shade.

NOTE: Steeping for several days after 1 hour simmer yields various greens.

64/MULE EARS (**Wyethia angustifolia**)

GOLD TO BRASS: ALUMED WOOL; GOOD LIGHTFASTNESS.

Perennial. Member of Sunflower Family. The large seeds can be ground and used as pinole, a favorite Indian food. Young leaves can be used for salad.

TEXTILE

Scoured, presoaked, alum-mordanted wool (1 ounce)

INGREDIENTS

Flowers, leaves and stems (8 ounces)

WATER

Tap (enough to cover textile)

POT

Nonreacting

METHOD

1. Combine plant, textile, and water.
2. Simmer for 30 minutes.
3. Cool overnight in ooze.
4. Rinse thoroughly.
5. Dry in shade.

NOTE: Flowers alone (without leaves or stems) yield lemon yellow.

65/MULLEIN AND AMMONIA
(Verbascum thapsus)

BRIGHT YELLOW: ALUMED WOOL; GOOD LIGHTFASTNESS.
CHARTREUSE: CHROMED WOOL; GOOD LIGHTFASTNESS.

Common field and roadside biennial, naturalized in the United States. Introduced from Eurasia. Member of the Figwort Family.
Woolly, gray foliage and stalks or spikes up to six feet tall, with tiny yellow flowers. Penstemon, calceolaria, and foxglove, to name a few, are also in the same family. Many qualities—medicinal, practical, and spiritual—are attributed to this plant. Of the practical, I can attest to: the spikes dipped in suet, oil, or paraffin do burn well. Witches are said to have used the leaves as wicks and candles. The whole flower spike was once used as a torch in funeral processions. The leaves are woolly enough to serve as a child's "security feeler." I knew several children who actu-

ally used the plant in this way!
As a dye, the plant yields excellent yellows and greens. As a hair dye, I am still at the experimental stage. Roman ladies used the flowers to make a yellow hair dye. Their concoction included flowers steeped in urine. I am exceedingly fond of this plant. My intuition urges me to experiment with it some more.

Figure 42 MULLEIN (*Verbascum thapsus*)

TEXTILE

Scoured, presoaked, alum- or chrome-mordanted wool (1 ounce)

INGREDIENTS

Mullein leaves, torn up (6 ounces)
Ammonia, clear (in quart of water) (1 teaspoon)

WATER

Tap (enough to cover textile)

POT

Nonreacting

METHOD

1. Combine leaves, water and textile.
2. Simmer for 30 minutes.
3. Cool overnight in ooze.
4. An ammonia rinse deepens the yellow.
5. Rinse thoroughly.
6. Dry in shade.

NOTE: The chartreuse color is very similar to the color obtained from nightshade and cupric sulfate, see Recipe 68.

66/MULLEIN, TORCHES, CANDLEWICK, BIG TAPER, OUR LADY'S FLANNEL AND CUPRIC SULFATE
(Verbascum thapsus)

MOSS GREEN: ALUMED WOOL; GOOD LIGHTFASTNESS.
DARK YELLOW-GREEN: CHROMED WOOL; GOOD LIGHTFASTNESS.

TEXTILE

Scoured, presoaked, alum- or chrome-mordanted wool (1 ounce)

INGREDIENTS

Leaves and flowers, torn up (6 ounces)

Cupric sulfate stock solution (in 1 quart of water) (½ ounce or 1 tablespoon)

WATER

Tap (enough to cover textile)

POT

Nonreacting

METHOD

1. Combine leaves, water, and textile.
2. Simmer for 30 minutes.
3. Cool overnight in ooze.
4. Prepare cupric sulfate afterbath.
5. Enter textile in solution and heat for 10 minutes.
6. Rinse thoroughly.
7. Dry in shade.

NOTES: An unlined copper pot can be used instead of the cupric sulfate afterbath. □ An iron pot may be used instead of the copper pot or the cupric sulfate bath.

67/NIGHTSHADE
(Solanum sp.)

BRIGHT YELLOW (STEP I): ALUMED WOOL; GOOD LIGHTFASTNESS.
DULL GOLD (STEP I): CHROMED WOOL; GOOD LIGHTFASTNESS.
VARIOUS KHAKI GREENS (STEP II): ALUMED OR CHROMED WOOL; GOOD LIGHTFASTNESS.

Annual, growing in shady places in fields and waste places. Member of the Potato Family, which includes the tomato, potato, eggplant, green pepper, and the very poisonous jimson weed. Nightshade berries contain solanine, a poison. Green potato skins, sprouts, and vines contain solanine and are also poisonous. The black berry of this species promises to be an excellent dye subject.

TEXTILE

Scoured, presoaked, alum- or chrome-mordanted wool (1 ounce)

INGREDIENTS

Nightshade plants and green berries (8 ounces)

WATER

Tap (enough to cover textile)

POTS

Step I
Nonreacting

Step II
Iron

METHOD

Step I
1. Combine plants, textile, and water in nonreacting pot.
2. Simmer for 30 minutes.
3. *For bright yellow or gold*: Cool in ooze overnight, rinse, and dry.
For various khaki greens: Proceed to Step II.

Step II
1. Pour ooze and textile into iron pot.
2. Simmer for 30 minutes.
3. Cool in iron pot for about 1 hour.
4. Rinse thoroughly.
5. Dry in shade.

NOTE: For ½ pound of textile use about 2 to 3 pounds plants.

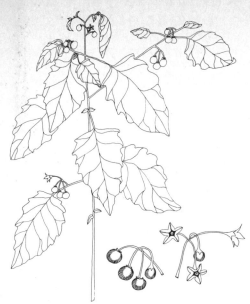

Figure 43 NIGHTSHADE (*Solanum* sp.)

68/NIGHTSHADE AND CUPRIC SULFATE (Solanum sp.)

CHARTREUSE: ALUMED WOOL; GOOD LIGHTFASTNESS.
DEEPER CHARTREUSE: CHROMED WOOL; GOOD LIGHTFASTNESS.

TEXTILE

Scoured, presoaked, alum- or chrome-mordanted wool (1 ounce)

INGREDIENTS

Nightshade plants, and green berries (8 ounces)

Cupric sulfate stock solution (in 1 quart of water) (½ ounce or 1 tablespoon)

WATER

Tap (enough to cover textile)

POT

Nonreacting

METHOD

1. Combine plants, textile, and water.
2. Simmer for 30 minutes.
3. Cool overnight in ooze.
4. Prepare cupric sulfate solution.
5. Enter dyed textile.
6. Heat for 10 minutes.
7. Rinse thoroughly in tap water.
8. Dry in shade.

NOTE: Black nightshade berries with tin yield a pretty blue dye. Experiment and see if you can make a useful dye recipe.

69/OWL'S CLOVER* (Orthocarpus spp.)

LEMON YELLOW: UNMORDANTED WOOL; GOOD LIGHTFASTNESS. MUSTARD COLOR: ALUMED COTTON OR WOOL; GOOD LIGHTFASTNESS.
OCHER COLOR: CHROMED COTTON, GOOD LIGHTFASTNESS.

California annual spring wild flower. Member of Figwort Family.

TEXTILE

Scoured, presoaked, unmordanted wool or alum- or chrome-mordanted wool (Choose color you want and proceed accordingly.) (1 ounce)

INGREDIENT

Owl's clover plants, torn up (6 ounces)

WATER

Tap (enough to cover textile)

POT

Nonreacting

METHOD

1. Combine plants, water and textile.
2. Boil for 20 minutes.

Figure 44 OWL'S CLOVER (*Orthocarpus* sp.)

3. Cool overnight in ooze.
4. Rinse thoroughly.
5. Dry in shade.

NOTE: For 1 pound of wool use 1½ to 2 pounds of plant.

70/OWL'S CLOVER IN IRON POT
(Orthocarpus sp.)

YELLOWISH GRAY: ALUMED COTTON; GOOD LIGHTFASTNESS.
BRASS GREENS TO KHAKI GREENS: ALUMED WOOL; GOOD LIGHTFASTNESS.

TEXTILE
Scoured, presoaked, alum-mordanted cotton or wool (1 ounce)

INGREDIENT
Owl's clover plants (6 ounces)

WATER
Tap (enough to cover textile)

POTS
Step I
Nonreacting

Step II
Iron

METHOD
Step I
1. Combine plants and water in nonreacting pot.
2. Simmer for 30 minutes.
3. Cool.

Step II
1. Pour ooze into iron pot and add water if necessary.
2. Enter textile.
3. Simmer for 30 minutes in iron pot.
4. Cool in ooze for about 1 hour.
5. Rinse thoroughly.
6. Dry in shade.

NOTE: For 1 pound of textile, use 1½ to 2 pounds of plant.

71/PICKLEWEED, GLASS-WORT, SAMPHIRE IN IRON POT
(Salicornia sp.)

GRAY-GREEN: ALUMED WOOL; GOOD LIGHTFASTNESS.

Goosefoot Family. Grows along coastal beaches, marshes, and lakes. Pleasant salty-sour taste in shoots and tops. Eaten raw, like pickles, or used as seasoning in cooking. Rich soda content made glasswort useful in soap making. The ashes, mixed with animal fat, were used to make soap.

TEXTILE
Scoured, presoaked, alum-mordanted wool (1 ounce)

INGREDIENT
Pickleweed (6 ounces)

WATER
Tap (enough to cover textile)

POT
Iron

METHOD
1. Cover plants with water.
2. Simmer in iron pot for 1 hour.
3. Cool.
4. Enter textile and simmer for 1 hour.
5. Cool overnight in ooze.
6. Rinse thoroughly.
7. Dry in shade.

72/PIGWEED
(Amaranthus sp.)

MOSS GREEN: ALUMED WOOL; GOOD LIGHTFASTNESS.
PALE YELLOW: STEEPED ALUMED WOOL; GOOD LIGHTFASTNESS.
BRASS: CHROMED WOOL; GOOD LIGHTFASTNESS.'

Figure 45 Here and above right: PIGWEED (*Amaranthus* sp.)

Annual weed of the Amaranth Family. Many native to North America. The garden flower, cockscomb, is a relative. Seeds of a red species are used by the Hopi to color corn-bread pink. Greens from young plants make a tasty vegetable.

TEXTILE
Scoured, presoaked, alum- or chrome-mordanted wool (1 ounce)

INGREDIENT
Pigweed plants, cut up (about 8 ounces)

WATER
Tap (enough to cover textile)

POT
Nonreacting

METHOD
1. Combine plants and water.
2. Boil for 1 hour.
3. Cool.
4. Enter textile.

·5. Simmer for 40 minutes.
6. Cool overnight in ooze.
7. Rinse thoroughly.
8. Dry in shade.

NOTES: A pale yellow can be obtained by *steeping* alumed wool for 5 days instead of simmering. If the pale-yellow textile is dipped in an ammonia after-rinse, a bright yellow results. □ For 1 pound of wool use 8 quarts (dry measure) of pigweed, or about 3 pounds. □ If bath is not exhausted it can be used for a steeping recipe.

73/PIGWEED IN IRON POT
(Amaranthus sp.)
FOREST GREEN: ALUMED WOOL; GOOD LIGHTFASTNESS.
KHAKI GREEN: CHROMED WOOL; GOOD LIGHTFASTNESS.

TEXTILE
Scoured, presoaked, alum- or chrome-mordanted wool (1 ounce)

INGREDIENTS
Whole plant (About 8 ounces)
Vinegar (4 teaspoons)

WATER
Tap (enough to cover textile)

POTS
Step I
Nonreacting

Step II
Iron

METHOD
Step I
1. Combine plants and water in nonreacting pot.
2. Gently boil for 1 hour.
3. Cool.
4. Enter textile.
5. Simmer for 30 minutes. Add water if needed.

Step II
1. Pour liquid ooze and textile into iron pot.
2. Add vinegar.
3. Simmer for 45 minutes.
4. Cool for about 1 hour.
5. Rinse thoroughly.
6. Dry in shade.

NOTES: For 1 pound of wool use about 3 pounds of weeds. ☐ Because the weeds are bulky, it is advisable to precook them. Cool and remove plants from dye pot. The remaining liquid is the dye bath.

74/PLANTAIN
(Plantago lanceolata)

DULL GOLD: ALUMED WOOL; GOOD LIGHT-FASTNESS.
DARK CAMEL: CHROMED WOOL; GOOD LIGHTFASTNESS.

Perennial. Member of Plantain Family. Introduced from Europe, widely distributed in fields and cities of North America. The seeds can be ground into meal and eaten or soaked in cold water and taken as a laxative. The leaves can be cooked and eaten as a vegetable. The liquid from steeped leaves is said to make a good hair rinse. Half a handful of crushed leaves, steeped in a cup of hot water,

Figure 46 PLANTAIN (*Plantago lanceolata*)

makes a tea. After three cupfuls, the drinker can begin dyeing.

TEXTILE
Scoured, presoaked, alum- or chrome-mordanted wool (1 ounce)

INGREDIENT
Whole plant, torn up (6 ounces)

WATER
Tap (enough to cover textile)

POT
Nonreacting

METHOD
1. Cover plants and textile with water.
2. Simmer for 1 hour.
3. Cool overnight in ooze.
4. Rinse thoroughly.
5. Dry in shade.

NOTE: Save ooze. It can be set aside for several days and re-used. Add a little water. (See following recipe.)

75/PLANTAIN, OLD OOZE
(Plantago lanceolata)

BROWN: ALUMED WOOL; GOOD LIGHTFASTNESS.

Fermentation improves this dye bath.

TEXTILE
Scoured, presoaked, alum-mordanted wool (1 ounce)

INGREDIENT
Old ooze from previous recipe, or cook new plant material and set aside for at least 2 days (about 2 quarts of old ooze or 6 ounces of new plant)

WATER
Tap (enough to cover textile)

POT
Nonreacting

METHOD
1. Enter plant and textile in ooze.
2. Simmer for 1 hour.
3. Cool overnight in ooze.
4. Rinse thoroughly.
5. Dry in shade.

76 / RABBIT BRUSH
(Chrysothamnus sp.)

LEMON YELLOW: ALUMED WOOL; GOOD LIGHTFASTNESS.
GOLD-COPPER: CHROMED WOOL; GOOD LIGHTFASTNESS.

Shrub growing in desert areas of Arizona and parts of California. Sunflower Family. The Hopi make extensive use of this plant. They call it siva'pi: used for wind-breaks, arrows, wicker plaques. The yellow flowers are used to make a yellow dye. Green is obtained from the bark. The Navajo got a bright yellow from one species of this genus. They use three pounds of blossoms and twigs to one pound of wool, in a one pot and mordant method. I have found that a pre-mordanted textile will require less plant material. If stannous chloride is used, a deep-orange dye results. It is likely that the plant may be dried and used for dye as needed.

TEXTILE
Scoured, presoaked, alum- or chrome mordanted wool (1 ounce)

INGREDIENT
Rabbit brush flower heads (1 ounce)

WATER
Tap (enough to cover textile)

POT
Nonreacting

METHOD
1. Cover plants with water.
2. Simmer for 1 hour.
3. Cool.
4. Enter textile.
5. Simmer for 45 minutes.
6. Cool overnight in ooze.
7. Rinse thoroughly.
8. Dry in shade.

NOTE: For one pound of wool use 1 to 2 pounds of plant material.

77 / RABBIT BRUSH AND TIN CRYSTALS
(Chrysothamnus sp.)

Figure 47
RABBIT BRUSH
(*Chrysothamnus* sp.)

YELLOW-ORANGE: ALUMED WOOL; GOOD LIGHTFASTNESS.
PUMPKIN ORANGE: CHROMED WOOL; GOOD LIGHTFASTNESS.

TEXTILE
Scoured, presoaked, alum- or chrome-mordanted wool (1 ounce)

INGREDIENTS
Flower heads (1 ounce)
Tin crystals (dissolved in 1 cup of hot water immediately before using) (pinch or 1/16 teaspoon)

WATER
Tap (enough to cover textile)

POT
Nonreacting

METHOD

1. Cover plants and textile with water.
2. Simmer for 1 hour.
3. Cool.
4. Remove textile.
5. Stir in tin solution.
6. Reenter textile and simmer for 45 minutes.
7. Cool overnight in ooze.
8. Rinse thoroughly.
9. Dry in shade.

78/RAGWORT, TANSY-RAGWORT, STINKING WILLIE
(Senecio jacobaea)

BRIGHT YELLOW: ALUMED WOOL; GOOD LIGHTFASTNESS.
BRASSY GOLD: CHROMED WOOL; GOOD LIGHTFASTNESS.

Sunflower Family. Perennial or biennial. Introduced from Europe, naturalized in Northern California.

TEXTILE
Scoured, presoaked, alum- or chrome-mordanted wool (1 ounce)

INGREDIENTS
Flower tops (7 ounces)
Ammonia, clear (in 1 quart of water) (1 teaspoon)

WATER
Tap (enough to cover textile)

POT
Nonreacting

METHOD
1. Combine flowers, textile, and water.
2. Simmer for 40 minutes.
3. Cool overnight in ooze.
4. Remove textile.
5. Dip textile in ammonia rinse.
6. Wash thoroughly and rinse.
7. Dry in shade.

NOTE: The ammonia rinse intensifies the colors.

79/RAGWORT AND CUPRIC SULFATE
(Senecio jacobaea)

CHARTREUSE: ALUMED WOOL; GOOD LIGHTFASTNESS.

Figure 48 RAGWORT
(*Senecio jacobea*)

MUSTARD BROWN: CHROMED WOOL; GOOD LIGHTFASTNESS.

TEXTILE
Scoured, presoaked, alum- or chrome-mordanted wool (1 ounce)

INGREDIENTS
Flower heads (7 ounces)
Cupric sulfate stock solution (in 1 quart of water) (½ ounce or 1 tablespoon)

WATER
Distilled (enough to cover textile)

POT
Nonreacting or unlined copper

METHOD
1. Combine flower heads, textile, and water.
2. Simmer for 30 minutes.
3. Cool overnight in ooze.
4. Remove textile.
5. Enter textile in cupric sulfate afterbath.
6. Heat for 10 minutes.
7. Rinse thoroughly.
8. Dry in shade.

NOTE: Omit cupric sulfate if an unlined copper pot is used.

80/RAGWORT AND TIN CRYSTALS
(Senecio jacobaea)

ORANGE: ALUMED WOOL; GOOD LIGHT-FASTNESS.
LIGHT BURNT ORANGE: CHROMED WOOL; GOOD LIGHTFASTNESS.
PALE YELLOW: ALUMED COTTON; GOOD LIGHTFASTNESS.

TEXTILE
Scoured, presoaked, alum- or chrome-mordanted wool or alum-mordanted cotton (1 ounce)

INGREDIENTS
Flower tops (7 ounces)

Tin crystals (dissolved in 1 cup of hot water immediately before using) (pinch or 1/16 teaspoon)

WATER
Distilled (enough to cover textile)

POT
Nonreacting

METHOD
1. Combine flowers, textile, and water.
2. Simmer for 20 minutes.
3. Remove textile.
4. Add tin solution.
5. Re-enter textile.
6. Simmer for 40 minutes.
7. Cool overnight in ooze.
8. Rinse thoroughly.
9. Dry in shade.

81/SAGEBRUSH
(Artemisia tridentata)

VARIOUS TAN-GOLDS: ALUMED OR CHROMED WOOL; GOOD LIGHTFASTNESS.
BRILLIANT YELLOW: ALUMED FLEECE; GOOD LIGHTFASTNESS.
YELLOW: UNMORDANTED RAFFIA OR REED; GOOD LIGHTFASTNESS.

Silver gray, aromatic shrub. Member of the Sunflower Family. Grows in arid areas of the West. The Hopi name is wi:'kwapi, it being used for digestive ailments. The seeds can be eaten raw or dried and pounded to make pinole. Medicinally used as hair tonic for dandruff and falling hair: steep one teaspoon of leaves to one cup of boiling water. Use hot or cold. As a dye subject, sage yields vibrant yellows and greens. Fleece takes dye especially well.

TEXTILE
Scoured, presoaked, alum- or chrome-mordanted wool, or un-mordanted raffia or reed (2 ounces)

INGREDIENTS
Leaves, buds, and stems (6 ounces)

WATER
Tap (enough to cover textile)

POT
Nonreacting

METHOD
1. Combine plants and water.
2. Simmer for 30 minutes.
3. Cool.
4. Enter textile.
5. Simmer for 30 minutes.
6. Cool overnight in ooze.
7. Rinse thoroughly.
8. Dry in shade.

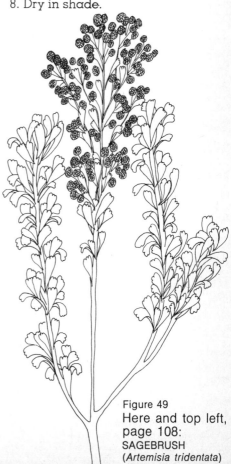

Figure 49
Here and top left, page 108:
SAGEBRUSH
(Artemisia tridentata)

82/SAGEBRUSH IN IRON POT (Artemisia tridentata)

VARIATIONS OF DARK GREEN; CHROMED WOOL; GOOD LIGHTFASTNESS.
SAGE GREEN; ALUMED WOOL; GOOD LIGHT-FASTNESS.
BROWN: UNMORDANTED RAFFIA; GOOD LIGHTFASTNESS.

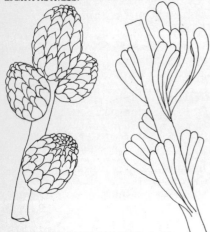

SAGEBRUSH (*Artemisia tridentata*)

TEXTILE
Scoured, presoaked, alum-or chrome-mordanted wool, or un-mordanted raffia (2 ounces)

INGREDIENTS
Leaves, buds, and stems (6 ounces)

WATER
Tap (enough to cover textile)

POT
Step I
Nonreacting
Step II
Iron

METHOD
Step I
1. Simmer plants in water in non-reacting pot for 30 minutes. Cool.
2. Enter textile and simmer for 30 minutes.
Step II
1. Pour textile and ooze into iron pot.
2. Simmer for 30 minutes.
3. Cool.
4. Rinse thoroughly.
5. Dry in shade.

83/SELF-HEAL, HEAL-ALL (Prunella vulgaris)

BRIGHT OLIVE GREEN: ALUMED WOOL; GOOD LIGHTFASTNESS.

Perennial wild flower of the Mint Family. Originated in Europe. Occurs as a weed in California. Makes a tasty drink if soaked in cold water. The leaves can be dried and stored for future use. The name "Heal-All" indicates the esteem in which the plant was held in earlier times.

TEXTILE
Scoured, presoaked, alum-mordanted wool (1 ounce)

INGREDIENTS
Flowers and stems (4 ounces)

WATER
Distilled (enough to cover textile)

POT
Nonreacting

METHOD
1. Combine plant material, water, and wool.
2. Simmer for 30 minutes.
3. Cool overnight in ooze.
4. Rinse thoroughly.
5. Dry in shade.

84/SOUR-GRASS, YELLOW OXALIS, WOOD SORREL (Oxalis corniculata)

MAIZE YELLOW (STEP I): ALUMED JUTE, COTTON, OR WOOL; GOOD LIGHTFASTNESS.
NEON ORANGE (STEP II): ALUMED JUTE, COTTON, OR WOOL; GOOD LIGHTFASTNESS.

Perennial. Member of Wood Sorrel Family. Introduced from Europe to North America. Common in California in shady places, mainly lawns. In eastern North America is seen along roadsides, cultivated fields, and waste places. Leaves may be used in a salad with other greens. Plants contain oxalic acid, so be cautious.

TEXTILE
Scoured, presoaked, alum-mordanted jute, cotton, or wool (1 ounce)

INGREDIENTS
Oxalis flowers (1 cup or 1 ounce)
Ammonia, clear (in 1 quart of water) (1 teaspoon)

WATER
Tap (enough to cover textile)

POT
Tin can

METHOD
Step I
1. Combine flowers, water, and textile in tin can.
2. Simmer for 30 minutes.
3. Cool overnight in ooze.
4. *For orange:* Proceed to Step II.
Step II
1. Prepare ammonia rinse by combining ammonia and water.
2. Dip cooled, dyed textile in ammonia solution until orange appears.
3. Rinse thoroughly.
4. Dry in shade.

85/SOUR GRASS, WOOD SORREL, AND TIN CRYSTALS
(Oxalis corniculata)
DEEP ORANGE-RED TO BROWN: CHROMED WOOL; FAIR TO GOOD LIGHTFASTNESS.

TEXTILE
Scoured, presoaked, chrome-mordanted wool (1 ounce)

INGREDIENTS
Sorrel flowers and stems (2 ounces or 2 cups)

Tin crystals (dissolved in 1 cup of hot water immediately before using) (pinch or 1/16 teaspoon)

Ammonia, clear (in 1 quart of water) (1 teaspoon)

WATER
Distilled (enough to cover textile)

POT
Nonreacting

METHOD
1. Combine plant, water, and textile.
2. Heat.
3. Remove textile and stir in tin solution.

4. Reenter textile and simmer for 30 minutes.
5. Cool overnight in ooze.
6. Prepare ammonia rinse.
7. Dip dyed textile until color changes.
8. Rinse thoroughly.
9. Dry in shade.

86/TARWEED
(Hemizonia luzulaefolia)
GOLDEN YELLOW: ALUMED WOOL; GOOD LIGHTFASTNESS; AROMATIC.
LIGHT YELLOW: ALUMED COTTON AND JUTE; GOOD LIGHTFASTNESS; AROMATIC.

This pungent sticky, nondescript weed yields an excellent dye and spicy fragrance. Cook outdoors and keep particles *out* of eyes! Native of California. Member of Sunflower Family. Excellent dye plant.

TEXTILE
Scoured, presoaked, alum-mordanted wool, cotton, or jute (1 ounce)

INGREDIENTS
Whole plant, torn up (about 4 ounces)

Ammonia, clear (in 1 quart of water) (1 teaspoon)

Figure 50   TARWEED
(*Hemizonia luzulaefolia*)

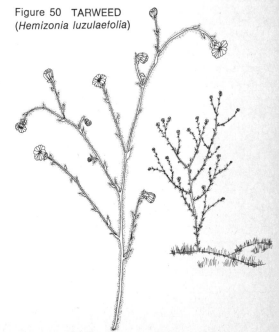

WATER
Tap (enough to cover textile)

POT
Nonreacting or brass (improves cotton color)

METHOD
1. Combine flowers, water, and textile.
2. Simmer for 45 minutes.
3. Steep in ooze for 2 days.
4. Dip in rinse of ammonia and water.
5. Rinse thoroughly in fresh water.
6. Dry in shade.

NOTE: For 1 pound of textile use about 2½ to 3 pounds of weeds.

87 / TARWEED IN IRON POT
(Hemizonia luzulaefolia)
DARK BRASSY GREEN: ALUMED WOOL OR COTTON; GOOD LIGHTFASTNESS; AROMATIC.

TEXTILE
Scoured, presoaked, alum-mordanted wool or cotton (1 ounce)

INGREDIENT
Hemizonia plants (about 4 ounces)

WATER
Tap (enough to cover textile)

POT
Iron

METHOD
1. Combine plants, textile, and water.
2. Simmer for 45 minutes.
3. Cool overnight in ooze.
4. Rinse thoroughly.
5. Dry in shade.

88 / VETCH, HAIRY VETCH, WINTER VETCH
(Vicia benghalensis)
VARIATIONS OF DEEP TURQUOISE GREEN: ALUMED AND CHROMED WOOL; GOOD LIGHTFASTNESS.

Annual. Member of the Pea Family. Grown as a cover crop and for green manure. Escaped from cultivation and seen as weed in various localities. A surprisingly handsome dye is extracted from this delicate, trailing plant.

TEXTILE
Scoured, presoaked, alum- or chrome-mordanted wool (1 ounce)

INGREDIENTS
Magenta flowers (or purple) (6 ounces)
Tin crystals (dissolved in 1 cup of hot water immediately before using) (pinch, $\frac{1}{16}$ teaspoon)

WATER
Tap (enough to cover textile)

POT
Nonreacting

METHOD
1. Combine plant and water. Heat slowly (under simmer).
2. Add tin solution to bath and stir thoroughly.
3. Add textile to bath and simmer for 30 minutes.
4. Cool overnight in ooze.
5. Rinse thoroughly.
6. Dry in shade.

89 / VETCH AND CUPRIC SULFATE
(Vicia benghalensis)
VARIATIONS OF BRIGHT YELLOW-GREEN: ALUMED AND CHROMED WOOL; GOOD LIGHTFASTNESS.

TEXTILE
Scoured, presoaked, alum- or chrome-mordanted wool (1 ounce)

INGREDIENTS
Magenta flowers (or purple) (6 ounces)
Cupric sulfate (dissolved in 1 cup of hot water immediately before using) ($\frac{1}{8}$ teaspoon)

WATER
Tap (enough to cover textile)

POT
Nonreacting

METHOD
1. Combine plant, water, and heat slowly (under simmer).
2. Add cupric sulfate dissolved in water and stir thoroughly.
3. Cool.
4. Add textile and simmer for 30

Figure 51 Vetch (*Vicia bengalensis*)

minutes.

5. Cool overnight in ooze.
6. Rinse thoroughly.
7. Dry in shade.

90/YARROW
(Achillea millefolium
and spp.)

YELLOW TO MAIZE (STEP I): ALUMED OR
CHROMED WOOL; GOOD LIGHTFASTNESS.
DARK GREEN (STEP II): ALUMED WOOL;
GOOD LIGHTFASTNESS.

Perennial. Native to North America
and Europe. Member of the Sunflower Family. Found in pastures
and meadows. Sharp, pleasantly
pungent odor. Named after the
Greek god Achilles, who was said
to have used the plant first on his
own wounds and later on the
wounds of his soldiers. Many healing properties are attributed to this
plant. The photograph above
shows a garden relative—*Achillea
filipendulina*.

TEXTILE
Scoured, presoaked, alum- or
chrome-mordanted wool (1 ounce)

INGREDIENTS
Yarrow flowers (about 4 ounces)
Tin crystals (dissolved in 1 cup of
hot water immediately before using
for maize color) (pinch or 1/16 teaspoon)

POTS
Step I
Nonreacting

Step II
Iron

METHOD
Step I
1. Combine flowers, water and textile in nonreacting pot. (Add tin for
yellow to maize only.)
2. Simmer for 20 minutes.
For yellow to maize: Cool overnight in ooze, rinse, and dry.

For dark green: Proceed to Step II.

Step II

1. Pour dye bath and textile into iron pot.
2. Add water to cover if necessary.
3. Simmer for 20 minutes more.
4. Cool overnight in ooze.

Figure 52 YARROW (*Achillea filipendulina*)

5. Rinse thoroughly.
6. Dry in shade.

NOTE: Yarrow leaves used alone yield a darker color.

91/YARROW IN COPPER POT
(Achillea millefolium)

CHARTREUSE TO TAN-GREENS: ALUMED WOOL; GOOD LIGHTFASTNESS.

TEXTILE
Scoured, presoaked, alum-mordanted wool (1 ounce)

INGREDIENTS
Yarrow flowers, or whole plant (4 ounces)

Cupric sulfate stock solution if copper pot is not available (1 tablespoon)

WATER
Tap (enough to cover textile)

POT
Copper, *not tinned*

METHOD
1. Combine flowers, water, and textile in copper pot. Add cupric sulfate if copper pot is not available.
2. Simmer for 40 minutes.
3. Cool overnight in ooze.
4. Rinse thoroughly.
5. Dry in shade.

NOTE: Yarrow leaves may be used instead of flowers or whole plants, but the color is duller.

13

Garden flower recipes

92/BLUE ANEMONE (Anemone sp.)

TEAL BLUE: ALUMED WOOL; FAIR TO GOOD LIGHTFASTNESS.
LIGHT GREEN: CHROMED WOOL; FAIR TO GOOD LIGHTFASTNESS.

Corm. Member of the Buttercup Family. Variable dye plant.

TEXTILE
Scoured, presoaked, alum- or chrome-mordanted wool (1 ounce)

INGREDIENT
Flowers (4 ounces)

WATER
Distilled (enough to cover textile)

POT
Nonreacting

METHOD
1. Cover flowers and textile with water.
2. Heat gently for 15 minutes.
3. Cool in ooze overnight.
4. Rinse thoroughly.
5. Dry in shade.

NOTE: An ammonia afterbath yields a darker color.

93/PURPLE CANTERBURY BELLS (Campanula medium)

MEDIUM GREEN: CHROMED OR ALUMED WOOL; FAIR LIGHTFASTNESS.
PALE BLUE: ALUMED COTTON; FAIR LIGHTFASTNESS.

Old-fashioned favorite garden flower. Belongs to the Bellflower Family. Native to southern Europe. Biennial and hardy. The whole family is especially noteworthy for furnishing many of the blue garden flowers. The deer and I are fond of the flower.

TEXTILE
Scoured, presoaked, alum-mordanted wool or cotton, or chrome-mordanted wool (2 ounces)

INGREDIENTS
Flowers (6 ounces)
Alum (dissolved in 1 cup of hot water) (1 teaspoon)
Tin crystals (dissolved in 1 cup of hot water immediately before using) (pinch or 1/16 teaspoon)

Figure 53 PURPLE CANTERBURY BELLS (*Campanula medium*)

WATER
Distilled (enough to cover textile)

POT
Nonreacting

METHOD
1. Heat flowers, water, and textile for 10 minutes.
2. Remove textile.
3. Add dissolved alum and dissolved tin. Cool.

4. Reenter textile.
5. Bring to simmer and keep hot for 15 minutes.
6. Cool textile in ooze.
7. Repeat heating and cooling 3 times.
8. Cool overnight in ooze.
9. Rinse thoroughly.
10. Dry in shade.

94/CHRYSANTHE-MUM LEAVES
(Chrysanthemum spp.)

GOLD-YELLOW: ALUMED WOOL; GOOD LIGHTFASTNESS.
GREEN: NATURAL GRAY ALUMED WOOL; GOOD LIGHTFASTNESS.

Strongly scented perennial. Grown in temperate climates all over the world. Cultivated and admired in China and Japan for thousands of years. Unknown in Europe until about 1812. Usually fall-blooming. The deer who live in my meadow are particularly fond of this flower. I am also. The outcome? Heartbreak.

TEXTILE
Scoured, presoaked, alum-mordanted wool (1 ounce)

INGREDIENTS
Leaves and stems (6 ounces)

WATER
Distilled (enough to cover textile)

POT
Nonreacting

METHOD
1. Cover plant material and textile with water.
2. Boil for 1 hour.
3. Cool overnight in ooze.
4. Rinse thoroughly.
5. Dry in shade.

95/MAROON CHRYSANTHEMUM
(Chrysanthemum spp.)

VARIATIONS OF GRAY-TURQUOISE: ALUMED WOOL OR COTTON; GOOD LIGHTFASTNESS.
Perennial garden flower. Sunflower Family.

TEXTILE
Scoured, presoaked, alum-mordanted wool (1 ounce)

INGREDIENT
Wine-color or purple flowers (5 ounces)

WATER
Distilled (enough to cover textile)

POT
Nonreacting

METHOD
1. Combine flowers, textile, and water.
2. Simmer for 25 minutes.
3. Cool overnight in ooze.
4. Rinse thoroughly.
5. Dry in shade.

96/DARK-BLUE FLORIST'S CINERARIA
(Senecio hybridus, or Senecio cruentus)

VARIATIONS OF TURQUOISE: ALUMED WOOL; GOOD LIGHTFASTNESS.
VARIATIONS OF GREEN; CHROMED WOOL; GOOD LIGHTFASTNESS.

Annual. Brilliantly colored blue, purple, and magenta and easy to grow in a mild, cool climate. At least this once, the flower is related to the dye color. A purplish color is yielded by purple flowers and greenish-bluish colors are yielded by dark-blue cineraria.

TEXTILE
Scoured, presoaked alum- or chrome-mordanted wool (1 ounce)

INGREDIENT
Petals (about 2 ounces)

WATER
Distilled (enough to cover textile)

POT
Nonreacting

METHOD
1. Cover petals with water.
2. Steep overnight.
3. Enter textile.
4. Simmer for 20 minutes.
5. Cool overnight in ooze.
6. Rinse thoroughly.

7. Dry in shade.

97 / DARK-BLUE FLORIST'S CINERARIA AND TIN CRYSTALS*
(Senecio hybridus, or Senecio cruentus)

MEDIUM BLUE; UNMORDANTED WOOL; GOOD LIGHTFASTNESS.
DARK BLUE: ALUMED OR CHROMED WOOL; GOOD LIGHTFASTNESS.

TEXTILE
Scoured, presoaked, unmordanted or alum-mordanted wool (1 ounce)

INGREDIENTS
Petals (about 2 ounces)
Tin crystals (dissolved in 1 cup of hot water immediately before using) (pinch or 1/16 teaspoon)

WATER
Distilled (enough to cover textile)

POT
Nonreacting

METHOD
1. Cover petals with water.
2. Steep overnight.
3. Heat slowly for 10 minutes. Do not simmer.
4. Stir in tin solution. Cool.
5. Enter textile.
6. Simmer for 20 minutes.
7. Cool overnight in ooze.
8. Rinse thoroughly.
9. Dry in shade..

98 / PURPLE FLORIST'S CINERARIA AND TIN CRYSTALS*
(Senecio hybridus, or Senecio cruentus)

WINE RED: ALUMED WOOL; GOOD LIGHT-FASTNESS.
PURPLE: UNMORDANTED JUTE OR LINEN; GOOD LIGHTFASTNESS.
LAVENDER: UNMORDANTED JUTE OR LINEN; GOOD LIGHTFASTNESS.

TEXTILE
Scoured, presoaked alum-mordanted wool or unmordanted jute or linen (1 ounce)

INGREDIENTS
Petals (2 ounces)

Tin crystals (dissolved in 1 cup of hot water immediately before using) (pinch or 1/16 teaspoon)
Cupric sulfate stock solution (in 1 quart water) (1/2 ounce or 1 table-spoon)

WATER
Distilled (enough to cover textile)

POT
Nonreacting

METHOD
1. Combine petals, water, and textile.
2. Steep overnight.
3. Remove textile from dye bath.
4. Stir in tin solution.
5. Reenter textile.
6. Simmer for 15 minutes. If wool is used it can be entered just before heating.
7. Cool overnight in ooze.
8. Prepare cupric sulfate rinse and dip textile.
9. Rinse thoroughly.
10. Dry in shade.

NOTE: It is my experience that dye potency is affected by the amount of water the plant has received—how recently watered or rained upon.

99 / COREOPSIS
(Coreopsis spp.)

NEON ORANGE TO ORANGE RED: ALUMED OR CHROMED WOOL; GOOD LIGHTFASTNESS.

Native to America, tropical Africa, and the Hawaiian Islands. Old-fashioned perennial related to the sunflower. Commonly called tick-seed. Reseeds easily. Excellent dye plant. If there were no other source of red dye, the coreopsis and am-monia orange-red recipe would substitute very well. It yields a glowingly brilliant color.

TEXTILE
Scoured, presoaked, alum- or chrome-mordanted wool (6 ounces)

INGREDIENTS
Flowers (8 ounces)

Iodized salt (dissolved in 1 cup of hot water) (1 teaspoon)

Ammonia, clear (in 1 quart of water) (1 teaspoon)

WATER

Distilled (enough to cover textile)

POT

Nonreacting

METHOD

1. Combine flowers, water, salt solution, and textile.
2. Simmer for 20 minutes.
3. *For neon orange:* Cool overnight in ooze. Remove textile.
4. *For red-orange:* Dip textile in ammonia solution, rinse thoroughly, and dry in shade.

100/COREOPSIS SEED HEADS*
(Coreopsis spp.)

GOLDEN BROWN: ALUMED WOOL; GOOD LIGHTFASTNESS.
BRIGHT OLIVE GREEN: CHROMED WOOL; GOOD LIGHTFASTNESS.
GOLD: UNMORDANTED WOOL; GOOD LIGHT-FASTNESS.

TEXTILE

Scoured, presoaked, alum- or chrome-mordanted wool or unmordanted wool, according to color desired (2 ounces)

INGREDIENTS

Seed heads, fresh (4 ounces)

Alum (dissolved in 1 cup of hot water) (1 tablespoon)

Cream of tartar (dissolved in 1 cup of hot water) (1 teaspoon)

WATER

Tap (enough to cover textile)

POT

Nonreacting

METHOD

1. Cover seed heads with water.
2. Heat for 10 minutes.
3. Stir in alum and cream of tartar solutions. Cool.
4. Enter textile.
5. Simmer for 45 minutes.
6. Cool overnight in ooze.
7. Rinse thoroughly.

8. Dry in shade.

101/PURPLE CROCUS
(Crocus vernus)

MEDIUM BLUE TO TURQUOISE: ALUMED WOOL; GOOD LIGHTFASTNESS.
APPLE GREEN: CHROMED WOOL; GOOD LIGHTFASTNESS.

Popular low-growing tulip-like flower from the Iris Family. Grows from bulb-like stem called a corm. Originated in Europe. The name comes from Latin meaning saffron.

TEXTILE

Scoured, presoaked, chrome-mordanted wool (1 ounce)

INGREDIENT

Purple crocus flowers (2 ounces)

WATER

Tap (enough to cover textile)

POT

Nonreacting

METHOD

1. Cover wool and flowers with water.
2. Simmer for 30 minutes.
3. Cool overnight in ooze.
4. Dry in shade.

NOTES: Flowers picked after rain or heavy fog do not give the same results. Variable dye plant. Australian experiments with eucalyptus indicate that dye content is affected and colors changed by varying moisture conditions. ☐ Stigma parts will yield a yellow dye.

102/PURPLE CROCUS AND HYACINTH
(Crocus vernus and Hyacinthus sp.)

MEDIUM BLUE: ALUMED WOOL; GOOD LIGHTFASTNESS.

TEXTILE

Scoured, presoaked, alum-mordanted wool (1 ounce)

INGREDIENTS

Crocus petals, dry (½ ounce)

Hyacinth flowers, dry (½ ounce)

WATER

Tap (enough to cover textile)

POT

Nonreacting

METHOD

1. Soak crocus petals overnight.
2. Add wool to soaked petals.
3. Simmer for 30 minutes.
4. Add hyacinth flowers to dye bath.
5. Simmer for 30 minutes longer.
6. Cool overnight in ooze.
7. Rinse thoroughly.
8. Dry in shade.

NOTE: Variable dye plant.

103/YELLOW DAFFODILS
(Narcissus pseudo-narcissus)

BRIGHT YELLOW: ALUMED WOOL; GOOD LIGHTFASTNESS.
DEEP GOLD: CHROMED WOOL; GOOD LIGHTFASTNESS.

Grown from bulbs. Amaryllis Family. Originated in Europe where its ancestor is the wild narcissus. Daffodils are long-trumpeted narcissus. Jonquils are short-trumpeted narcissus. The word narcissus derives from the Greek *Narkao* (to be numb), referring to the narcotic properties of the bulb. It is poisonous and emetic. No wonder daffodils thrive and multiply, unmolested by gophers.

TEXTILE

Scoured, presoaked, alum- or chrome-mordanted wool (1 ounce)

INGREDIENTS

Yellow flowers (4 ounces)
Ammonia, clear (in 1 quart of water) (1 teaspoon)

WATER

Distilled (enough to cover textile)

POT

Nonreacting

METHOD

1. Cover flowers and textile with water.
2. Simmer for 30 minutes.
3. Cool overnight in ooze.
4. Remove textile.
5. Dip in ammonia afterbath.
6. Rinse thoroughly.
7. Dry in shade.

DAHLIA
(Dahlia pinnata)

Perennial, strong-growing favorite. Grown from tubers. Descendant of Mexican single-flowered variety. The first three plants known in Europe were sent to Madrid in 1797. The flower was named after the Swedish botanist Dahl. Seeds were sent from Mexico to the Berlin botanical garden in 1804. Two years later, fifty-five varieties had been developed! Interest in the flower increased to the point of being called a craze. There were 2,000 varieties developed in Germany alone, including all the variations we know today: small to sixteen-inch monsters; single-flowered to double; and many color variations. In England in 1840, a prize of £1000 was offered for a blue-colored dahlia. (There isn't one to this day.) In France, a dahlia mania developed. A well-tended and planned dahlia bed was bought for 70,000 francs. A single, rare plant was traded for one rare diamond! The dahlia has been offered as an example that man improves nature rather than destroys it. (See *Flowers Through the Ages* by Gabriele Tergit.)

For dyers, the dahlia is an excellent subject. It is abundant both in the size of flowers and the flowering rate. One medium-sized flower can easily weigh two ounces. You are doing the gardener a favor to pluck off the overripe heads. So, whether the flower grows in your garden or a neighbor's, there need be no problem of quantity. The dye color is lovely—it is possible to achieve brilliant orange to vibrant orange-red. (See dahlia and ammonia recipes.)

Producing a lightfast dahlia color has been tricky. There is no difficulty with chrome-mordanted wool. The problem was to produce lightfastness in alum-mordanted wool. My method of experimenting was to combine dahlia and some other plant. The latter was chosen from plants known to produce lightfast colors. In addition, these plants had to yield colors which combined well, or enhanced the dahlia color. Several recipes have been worked out using dahlia and pearly everlasting, dahlia and walnut leaves, and so forth. This proved to be a good procedure. I have discussed it at length, hoping the reader will be intrigued and invent some recipes along these lines.

104/YELLOW-RED DAHLIAS AND AMMONIA (Dahlia pinnata)

BRILLIANT BURNT ORANGE: CHROMED WOOL; GOOD LIGHTFASTNESS.

Flowers can be used fresh or dry. Even the fresh seed heads yield a dye. Best color is obtained from deep-yellow to bronze flowers.

TEXTILE
Scoured, presoaked, chrome-mordanted wool (1 ounce)

INGREDIENTS
Dahlia flowers, fresh or dry (2 ounces, or about 1 quart) (dry measure)
Ammonia, clear (in 1 quart of water) (1 teaspoon)

WATER
Distilled (enough to cover textile)

POT
Nonreacting

METHOD
1. Cover flowers and textile with water.
2. Simmer for 20 minutes.
3. Cool overnight in ooze.
4. Remove textile.
5. Dip textile in ammonia afterbath.
6. Rinse thoroughly.
7. Dry in shade.

NOTES: For 1 pound of wool use about 1½ pounds dahlias. □ If dahlias are available, try an overconcentration; for instance, 4 or 5 pounds of dahlias to 1 pound of wool. An almost-red can be achieved.

105/OLD DAHLIA— COREOPSIS BOUQUET (Dahlia sp. and Coreopsis sp.)

INTENSE YELLOW-ORANGE: ALUMED WOOL; GOOD LIGHTFASTNESS.
ORANGE: CHROMED WOOL; GOOD LIGHTFASTNESS.

Coreopsis improves the lightfastness, and the color also, if fresh.

TEXTILE
Scoured, presoaked, alum- or chrome-mordanted wool (1 ounce)

INGREDIENTS
Old yellow dahlias (about 4 ounces)
Coreopsis seed heads, or left-over ooze from coreopsis recipe (about 1 ounce or 2 quarts ooze)
Ammonia (in 1 quart of water) (1 teaspoon)

WATER
Distilled (enough to cover textile)

POT
Nonreacting

METHOD
1. Cover plants and textile with water.
2. Simmer for 45 minutes.
3. *For yellow-orange:* Cool overnight in ooze. Remove textile.
4. *For orange:* Dip textile in ammonia afterbath, rinse thoroughly, and dry in shade.

NOTE: If fresh dahlia and coreopsis flowers are used instead of seed heads, the wool dyes a blazing burnt orange.

106/YELLOW DAHLIAS AND ONION SKINS IN IRON POT (Dahlia pinnata)

MAIZE YELLOW (STEP I): ALUMED WOOL; GOOD LIGHTFASTNESS.
GOLDEN BROWN (STEP II): ALUMED WOOL; GOOD LIGHTFASTNESS.

PURPLE CACTUS FRUIT, steeped (*Opuntia robusta*) and ORANGE CACTUS FRUIT /16

Nature's Colors: Dyes from Plants

(References are to Recipe number.)

FENNEL (*Foeniculum vulgare*) /43,44

Steeping experiments; ooze is shown in glass containers for visibility

LUPINE (*Lupinus* sp.), outdoors /56

GUM PLANT (*Grindelia* sp.) /49

LUPINE (*Lupinus* sp.)

TARWEED (*Hemizonia luzulaefolia*) /86, 87

SOUR GRASS (*Oxalis corniculata*) /84

CINERARIA (*Senicio hybridus*) /96, 97

COREOPSIS (*Coreopsis* sp.) /99, 100

RED HOLLYHOCK (*Althaea rosea*) /114,115

INDIA HAWTHORN (*Raphiolepsis indica*) /178,179

EUCALYPTUS SILVER DOLLAR (*Eucalyptus polyanthemus*) /199, 200, 201

OREGON GRAPE (*Mahonia* sp.) /145,146

ACACIA (*Acacia* sp.) /189

PITTOSPORUM (*Pittosporum crassifolium*) /223, 224

EUCALYPTUS ASHY STRINGYBARK (*Eucalyptus cinerea*) /207

PURPLE CABBAGE (*Brassica oleracea var. capitata*) /232

PRIVET BERRIES (*Ligustrum* sp.) /226

BLACK MULBERRY TREE, berries (*Morus nigra*) /239

ONIONS (*Allium* sp.) /14, 246, 247, 248

Skeins of yarn dyed with onion skins /14, 246, 247, 248

PLUM LEAVES (*Prunus* sp.) /254, 255

WALNUT LEAVES (*Juglens* sp.) /265, 266

RED-FLOWERED SUCCULENT, steeped (*Epiphyllum* sp.) /17

Skeins of yarn: wool, cotton, jute, and linen dyed with plants of the countryside

Bluish series, skeins of yarn: wool, cotton, jute, and linen dyed with plants of the countryside

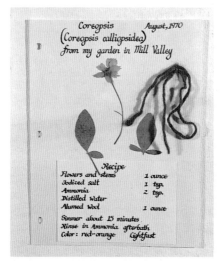

Page from dye notebook showing pressed coreopsis, yarn sample, and recipe

Reddish series, skeins of yarn: wool, cotton , jute, and linen dyed with plants of the countryside

Yellowish series, skeins of yarn: wool, cotton, jute, and linen dyed with plants of the countryside

Knitted and sewn dolls by Jessie Wold and crocheted lion by Judy Spaier: yarns dyed with plants of the countryside; orange doll is iron buff dyed (blue doll costume is an indigo dyed heirloom lent by Lotte Schiller, Mill Valley, Calif.)

Carved wood dolls: wood stained with blackberry, bindweed, broom, soot, sour grass, and tulip (*Dominican College, California*)

Knitted doll by Mary K. Mihal and carved figure by Marc Kapellas: wool yarn dyed with canary wood, eucalyptus, hawthorn, silk oak, and tea; wood stained with blackberry and iris

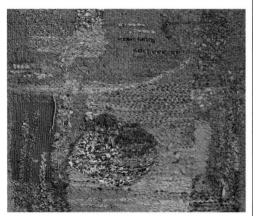

"The Meaning of Blue" tapestry by Ida Grae: wool, cotton, linen, and rags dyed with plants of the countryside and indigo

Stole and pillow by Ida Grae: wool dyed with indigo and purple cabbage

Pillow, stole, and rug by Ida Grae: wool dyed with eucalyptus, mulberry, sage, and tea

"The King" tapestry by Ida Grae: wool, cotton, and rags dyed with coralline, mulberry, privet, sage, and sour grass

"Mask," macramé wall hanging by Jessie Wold: jute rope dyed with madder, mulberry, osage, and sour grass

Pillow by Ida Grae: wool dyed with tree dahlia flowers

Embroidered and woven tapestry by Jessie Wold: natural linen and wool dyed with gum plant, sour grass, tarweed, and tea

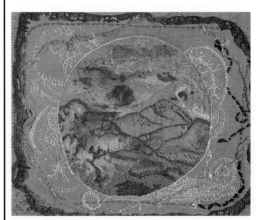

"Microcosm," embroidered landscape by Dot Rosenfield: wool, cotton, linen dyed with acacia, coralline, grape, iris, milkweed, plantain, scabiosa, and ragwort

Dahlias on alumed wool do not yield a lightfast dye. For this reason, onion skins have been added in this recipe. The iron pot also helps fastness.

TEXTILE
Scoured, presoaked, alum-mordanted wool (1 ounce)

INGREDIENTS
Flowers (about 2 ounces)

Onion skins (1 ounce)

Tin crystals (dissolved in 1 cup of hot water immediately before using) (pinch or 1/16 teaspoon)

WATER
Tap (enough to cover textile)

POTS
Step I

Nonreacting

Step II

Iron

METHOD
Step I

1. Cover onion skins with water.

2. Simmer for 20 minutes.
3. Add flowers and tin solution. Cool.
4. Enter textile.
5. Simmer for 30 minutes.
6. *For maize yellow*: Cool overnight in ooze, rinse thoroughly, and dry in shade.
7. *For golden brown*: Proceed to Step II.

Step II

1. Pour ooze and textile from non-reacting pot into iron pot.
2. Simmer for 30 minutes.
3. Cool in ooze for about 1 hour.
4. Rinse thoroughly.
5. Dry in shade.

107/DAHLIA SEED HEADS (Dahlia pinnata)
BRIGHT ORANGE: CHROMED WOOL; GOOD LIGHTFASTNESS.

TEXTILE
Scoured, presoaked, chrome-mordanted wool (1 ounce)

INGREDIENTS
Flower centers, old or fresh (1 cup)

Figure 54 Collecting dahlias for an experiment

Ammonia, clear (in 1 quart of water) (1 teaspoon)

WATER
Distilled (enough to cover textile)

POT
Nonreacting

METHOD
1. Combine seed heads, textile, and water.
2. Simmer for 30 minutes.
3. Cool overnight in ooze.
4. Remove textile.
5. Dip textile in ammonia afterbath.
6. Rinse thoroughly.
7. Dry in shade.

108/YELLOW DAHLIAS AND ENGLISH WALNUT LEAVES
(Dahlia pinnata and Juglans regia)

BURNT ORANGE: ALUMED WOOL; GOOD LIGHTFASTNESS.

Walnut leaves are used to make a more lightfast product.

TEXTILE
Scoured, presoaked, alum-mordanted wool (1 ounce)

INGREDIENTS
Dahlias (2 ounces)
Walnut leaves (1 ounce)
Ammonia, clear (in 1 quart of water) (1 teaspoon)

WATER
Tap (enough to cover textile)

POT
Nonreacting

METHOD
1. Combine dahlia petals, walnut leaves, textile, and water.
2. Simmer for 45 minutes.
3. Cool overnight in ooze.
4. Remove textile.
5. Dip textile in ammonia afterbath.
6. Rinse thoroughly.
7. Dry in shade.

NOTE: Dahlias alone on alumed wool do not make a lightfast dye.

109/PURPLE OR ORANGE AFRICAN DAISY
(Arctotis sp.)

VARIOUS GREENS: ALUMED WOOL; GOOD LIGHTFASTNESS.
OLIVE GREEN: CHROMED WOOL; GOOD LIGHTFASTNESS.

Perennial. South African native. Sunflower Family. Attractive gray-green foliage. Blooms from late fall to early spring.

TEXTILE
Scoured, presoaked, chrome-mordanted wool (1 ounce)

INGREDIENTS
Flowers (3 ounces)
Cupric sulfate (dissolved in 1 cup of hot water) (1/8 teaspoon)

WATER
Tap (enough to cover textile)

POT
Nonreacting

METHOD
1. Cover flowers and textile with water.
2. Simmer for 45 minutes.
3. Cool overnight in ooze.
4. Remove textile and plant material from dye pot.

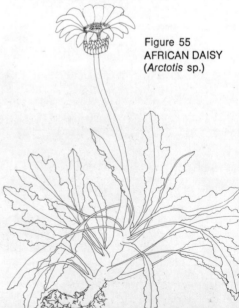

Figure 55
AFRICAN DAISY
(Arctotis sp.)

5. Stir cupric sulfate solution into dye pot.
6. Enter dyed textile and heat for 10 minutes.
7. Rinse thoroughly.
8. Dry in shade.

110/BROWNISH GLORIOSA DAISY, BLACK-EYED SUSAN (Rudbeckia sp.)

BRIGHT OLIVE GREEN TO DARK GREEN: CHROMED WOOL; GOOD LIGHTFASTNESS.

Perennial. Member of the Sunflower Family. Started from seed or seedlings.

TEXTILE
Scoured, presoaked, chrome-mordanted wool (1 ounce)

INGREDIENT
Flowers (6 ounces)

WATER
Tap (enough to cover textile)

POT
Nonreacting

METHOD
1. Cover flowers and textile with water.
2. Simmer for 30 minutes.
3. Cool overnight in ooze.
4. Rinse thoroughly.
5. Dry in shade.

NOTE: Gloriosa daisy and rudbeckia (see recipe for rudbeckia) yield similar green colors with chrome mordant.

111/PURPLE FOXGLOVE (Digitalis purpurea)

CHARTREUSE: ALUMED WOOL; GOOD LIGHT-FASTNESS.

Introduced from Europe as a garden plant. Tall, old-fashioned garden flower. Biennial, reseeds easily. Has escaped into the countryside in Oregon, Washington, and Eastern United States. The powerful drug digitalis is made from the dried leaves. Do *not* self-medicate. Dangerous.

TEXTILE
Scoured, presoaked, alum-mordanted wool (1 ounce)

INGREDIENT
Flowers (5 ounces)

WATER
Distilled (enough to cover textile)

POT
Nonreacting

METHOD
1. Cover flowers and textile with water.
2. Simmer gently for 30 minutes.
3. Cool overnight in ooze.
4. Rinse thoroughly.
5. Dry in shade.

112/RED GERANIUM, FISH GERANIUM* (Pelargonium hortorum)

DARK BROWN: UNMORDANTED WOOL; GOOD LIGHTFASTNESS.
GREENISH BROWN: ALUMED WOOL; GOOD LIGHTFASTNESS.

Brought from Cape of Good Hope to Leyden in 1690. Became fashionable in Europe in the early 1800s. Have become the mainstay of public squares and window boxes in all countries. In California they seem to thrive even on neglect. The leaves are rich in tannin and therefore yield an excellent brown dye. The weedy relatives, cranesbill (*Geranium maculatum*, and *Geranium dissectum*), are equally potent dye sources.

TEXTILE
Scoured, presoaked, unmordanted or alum-mordanted wool (1 ounce)

INGREDIENTS
Dry flowers (4 ounces)
Tin crystals (dissolved in 1 cup of hot water immediately before using) (pinch or 1/16 teaspoon)
Cream of tartar (dissolved in 1 cup of hot water immediately before using) (1/2 teaspoon)

WATER
Distilled (enough to cover textile)

POTS
Step I
Nonreacting

Step II
Iron

METHOD
Step I
1. Cover flowers and textile with water.
2. Bring to simmer.
3. Remove textile.
4. Add dissolved tin crystals and cream of tartar.
5. Reenter textile.
6. Simmer for 1 hour.

Step II
1. Transfer contents to iron pot.
2. Cool overnight in ooze.
3. Simmer for 30 minutes.
4. Cool.
5. Rinse thoroughly.
6. Dry in shade.

113/RED GERANIUM LEAVES
(Pelargonium hortorum)
DARK PURPLE TO GRAY: ALUMED COTTON; GOOD LIGHTFASTNESS.

TEXTILE
Scoured, presoaked, alum-mordanted cotton (1 ounce)

INGREDIENT
Geranium leaves, fresh (8 ounces)

WATER
Distilled (enough to cover textile)

POT
Iron

METHOD
1. Cover leaves with water.
2. Simmer for 1 hour.
3. Enter cotton.
4. Simmer for 1 hour.
5. Cool in pot overnight.
6. Rinse thoroughly.
7. Dry in shade.

RED HOLLYHOCK
(Althaea rosea)

Perennial. Belongs to the Mallow Family (Malvaceae). Originated in China. Known for a long time in Europe. Charlemagne's garden list in A.D. 812 contained five flowers: sunflower, hollyhock, poppy, lovage, and Christ's eye. It was an old established flower in England, being known before 1500. The name is Anglo-Saxon in origin: holyoak, holihec. By 1850 most English gardens included hollyhock.

In the United States, the hollyhock is an old-fashioned garden subject. Cotton, abutilon, hibiscus, marshmallow, okra, rose of sharon, and malva weed are all members of the Mallow Family. *Please note* the number of dye-yielding plants in the mallows. It is interesting to note that the dye bath of all of these is mucilaginous, like okra soup, and softening to the skin. This characteristic of the mallows was known when the family name was applied: "malva" means emollient, or soothing or softening (to the skin). Mallows provide excellent forage for animals, including the deer in my garden.

114/RED HOLLYHOCK IN IRON POT
(Althaea rosea)
BROWN: ALUMED WOOL; GOOD LIGHTFASTNESS.

I find it easier to grow this flower from young plants rather than from seed.

TEXTILE
Scoured, presoaked, alum-mordanted wool (1 ounce)

INGREDIENTS
Petals, fresh (2 ounces)
Tin crystals (dissolved in 1 cup of hot water immediately before using) (pinch or 1/16 teaspoon)
Cream of tartar (dissolved in 1 cup of hot water) (1 teaspoon)

WATER
Distilled (enough to cover textile)

POTS
Step I
Nonreacting

Figure 56   HOLLYHOCK (*Althaea rosea*)

Step II
Iron

METHOD
Step I
1. Combine petals, tin and cream of tartar solutions, and textile.
2. Simmer in nonreacting pot for 20 minutes.

Step II
1. Pour ooze and textile into iron pot.
2. Simmer for 15 minutes.
3. Cool overnight in ooze.
4. Rinse thoroughly.
5. Dry in shade.

NOTE: If color is dark, do not cool overnight in iron pot.

115 / RED HOLLYHOCK AND TIN CRYSTALS
(Althaea rosea)
WINE COLOR: ALUMED WOOL; GOOD LIGHTFASTNESS.

TEXTILE
Scoured, presoaked, alum-mordanted wool (1 ounce)

INGREDIENTS
Petals, fresh (4 ounces)

Tin crystals (dissolved in 1 cup of hot water immediately before using) (pinch or 1⁄16 teaspoon)

Cream of tartar (dissolved in 1 cup of hot water) (1 teaspoon)

WATER
Distilled (enough to cover textile)

POT
Nonreacting

METHOD
1. Cover flowers and textile with water.
2. Heat for 15 minutes.
3. Remove textile.
4. Stir in tin and cream of tartar solutions.
5. Reenter textile.
6. Simmer for 30 minutes.
7. Cool overnight in ooze.
8. Rinse thoroughly.
9. Dry in shade.

NOTE: Old petals tend to yield brownish colors.

116 / DEEP-BLUE HYACINTH FLOWERS
(Hyacinthus orientalis)
POWDER BLUE TO MEDIUM BLUE: ALUMED WOOL; FAIR TO GOOD LIGHTFASTNESS.

TEXTILE
Scoured, presoaked, alum-mordanted wool (1 ounce)

INGREDIENTS
Dark-blue hyacinth flowers (6 ounces)

Tin crystals (dissolved in 1 cup of hot water immediately before using) (pinch or 1⁄16 teaspoon)

WATER
Tap (enough to cover textile)

POT
Nonreacting

METHOD
1. Cover flowers and textile with water.
2. Heat.
3. Remove textile.
4. Add tin solution.
5. Reenter textile.
6. Simmer for 30 minutes.
7. Cool overnight in ooze.
8. Rinse thoroughly.
9. Dry in shade.

117/DARK-PURPLE IRIS (Iris spp.)

VARIOUS VIOLET-BLUES: CHROMED WOOL; GOOD LIGHTFASTNESS.

Irises are favorite garden plants grown from bulbs or rhizomes. There are more than 150 species. Several are common in gardens and many are grown by fanciers. There were only a few iris in the old-fashioned garden of fifty years ago, for example, *Iris germanica* and *Iris pallida*. These are of interest because of dyes and orris root which is still made from one or both of the above iris. Orris (corruption of iris) root is used for its violet-like scent in perfumes, sachets, and dentifrices. Tuscany and other parts of Italy have orris plantations and export large quantities for the trade.

Irises are not difficult to grow. I suggest that you grow some of these. After two or three years a plant is mature. Pull out the roots and put them away in a dark, dry place to age. The violet fragrance develops after several years of drying! If you can wait, try the following uses:

1. Chew pieces of dry root to sweeten the breath.
2. Powder the orris and use in rinse water to perfume linens and undergarments.
3. Carve decorations from the orris root and attach to garments. The wearer will be sweetly fragrant a long time.
4. Carve ornaments such as beads or earring drops. So sweet!
5. Said to be used in Russia in a drink flavored with honey and ginger.

WARNING: *Be sure you know your iris species.*

Freshly ground iris root is said to have been used as a cosmetic and freckle remover. A slice held on an aching tooth is said to cure toothache. A black dye is made with ferrous sulfate and iris root. But the greatest surprise of all is the beautiful dye which can be made from the flowers.

TEXTILE
Scoured, presoaked, chrome-mordanted wool (1 ounce)

INGREDIENT
Flowers (6 ounces)

WATER
Distilled (enough to cover textile)

POT
Nonreacting

METHOD
1. Cover flowers and wool with water.
2. Steep several hours.
3. Simmer for 30 minutes.
4. Cool overnight in ooze.
5. Rinse thoroughly.
6. Dry in shade.

NOTE: After a rain, irises are not as full of dye.

118/PURPLE IRIS, FLEUR-DE-LIS AND TIN CRYSTALS (Iris germanica and other Iris spp.)

VARIOUS DARK TO LIGHT BLUES: ALUMED OR CHROMED WOOL; GOOD LIGHTFASTNESS.

TEXTILE
Scoured, presoaked, alum- or chrome-mordanted wool (1 ounce)

INGREDIENTS
Flowers (6 ounces)
Tin crystals (dissolved in 1 cup of hot water immediately before using) (pinch or ⅛ teaspoon)

WATER
Distilled (enough to cover textile)

POT
Nonreacting

METHOD
1. Cover flowers and wool with water.
2. Steep for several hours.
3. Simmer for 20 minutes.
4. Remove wool.

5. Add tin solution.
6. Reenter wool.
7. Simmer for 20 more minutes.
8. Cool overnight in ooze.
9. Rinse thoroughly.
10. Dry in shade.

119/BLUE LOBELIA IN COPPER POT
(Lobelia erinus)

PASTEL GREEN: ALUMED OR CHROMED WOOL; GOOD LIGHTFASTNESS.

Annual. Member of Lobelia Family. Low-growing with deep-blue flowers. One of the commonest plants used for edging and borders.

TEXTILE
Scoured, presoaked, alum- or chrome-mordanted wool (1 ounce)

INGREDIENTS
Blue flowers and stems, torn up (6 ounces)

WATER
Tap (enough to cover textile)

POTS
Step I
Nonreacting

Step II
Unlined copper

METHOD
Step I
1. Cover plants with water in non-reacting pot.
2. Simmer for 20 minutes. Cool.

Step II
1. Transfer ooze to copper pot.
2. Enter wool.
3. Simmer for 20 minutes.
4. Cool overnight in ooze.
5. Rinse thoroughly.
6. Dry in shade.

120/YELLOW MARGUE-RITES, PARIS DAISY
(Chrysanthemum frutescens)

GOLD (STEP I): CHROMED WOOL; GOOD LIGHTFASTNESS.
MUSTARD GREEN (STEP II): CHROMED WOOL; GOOD LIGHTFASTNESS.

Shrubby perennial member of the Sunflower Family.

TEXTILE
Scoured, presoaked, chrome-mor-danted wool (1 ounce)

INGREDIENT
Flower heads (8 ounces)

WATER
Distilled (enough to cover textile)

POTS
Step I
Nonreacting

Step II
Iron

METHOD
Step I
1. Cover plant material and textile with water.
2. Simmer for 1 hour.
3. *For gold:* Cool several hours, rinse thoroughly; and dry in shade.
4. *For green:* Proceed to Step II.

Step II
1. Transfer contents into iron pot.
2. Simmer for 30 minutes.
3. Cool for several hours.
4. Rinse thoroughly.
5. Dry in shade.

121/MARIGOLDS WITH TIN CRYSTALS
(Tagetes sp.)

YELLOW-ORANGE: ALUMED WOOL AND TIN; GOOD LIGHTFASTNESS.
GOLD: ALUMED WOOL; GOOD LIGHTFASTNESS.
DULL GREEN: ALUMED WOOL AND IRON POT; GOOD LIGHTFASTNESS.

Annual, garden favorite. Member of the Sunflower Family. Introduced from Mexico. Easily grown from seed or seedling. The plant was mentioned in herbals as early as 1500. Orange-flowered marigolds were used as a medicine: add one ounce of dried flowers to one pint of boiling water. Doses of one table-spoon, once a day, were prescribed for internal use. The infusion was recommended for external use for bee sting, sprains, body aches, sore eyes, and other infirmities.

The flowers were used in cook-ing, including the flavoring of salads and broth, and for coloring beverages. Cheeses were colored a robust orangish "cheese color" with this popular flower. (What artificial colorant is used to color our cheeses today?)

And, most useful of all for the dissatisfied, a fine yellow hair dye was concocted from dried marigold petals. It follows as no surprise that dyers also are fond of this flower. It is a potent dye—fresh or dried. The flowers are easily dried and keep well.

TEXTILE
Scoured, presoaked, alum-mordanted wool (8 ounces)

INGREDIENTS
Flower heads, torn up (6 ounces)
Tin crystals (dissolved in 1 cup of hot water immediately before using) for yellow-orange only (⅟₁₆ ounce or pinch)
Cream of tartar (dissolved in 1 cup of hot water immediately before using for yellow-orange only) (⅙ ounce or 1 teaspoon)

WATER
Tap (enough to cover textile)

POTS
Nonreacting for gold or yellow-orange (4- to 5-gallon)
Iron for dull green

METHOD
1. *For gold:* Combine flowers, textile, and water in nonreacting pot.
2. Simmer for 30 minutes.
3. Cool overnight in dye bath.
4. Rinse.
5. Dry in shade.
1. *For dull green:* Proceed as above, but use the iron pot instead of the nonreacting pot.
1. *For yellow-orange:* Combine flowers, textile, and water in nonreacting pot.
2. Simmer for 30 minutes.
3. Remove textile.
4. Stir in the tin and cream of tartar solutions.

5. Reenter textile.
6. Simmer for 15 minutes longer.
7. Cool overnight in dye bath.
8. Rinse.
9. Dry in shade.

122/MAROON NICOTIANA AND CUPRIC SULFATE (Nicotiana sp.)
GRAYED GREEN: CHROMED WOOL; GOOD LIGHTFASTNESS.

Also called flowering tobacco. Sweet scented. Related to the commercial tobacco plant. Belongs to the Nightshade Family, which includes eggplant, jimson weed, red pepper, petunia, potato, tomato, and the nightshade for which I have a dye recipe.

TEXTILE
Scoured, presoaked, chrome-mordanted wool (1 ounce)

INGREDIENTS
Flowers (4 ounces)
Alum (dissolved in 1 cup of hot water) (1 teaspoon)
Tin crystals (dissolved in 1 cup of hot water immediately before using) (pinch or ⅟₁₆ teaspoon)
Cupric sulfate (dissolved in 1 cup of hot water) (⅛ teaspoon)

WATER
Distilled (enough to cover textile)

POT
Nonreacting

METHOD
1. Combine flowers, water, alum solution, and textile.
2. Heat.
3. Remove textile and stir in tin solution.
4. Reenter textile.
5. Simmer for 30 minutes.
6. Cool overnight in ooze.
7. Remove plant material from dye bath.
8. Stir in cupric sulfate solution.
9. Heat for 20 minutes.
10. Rinse thoroughly.
11. Dry in shade.

Figure 57 NICOTIANA (*Nicotiana* sp.)

123/PANSY, HEARTS-EASE AND CUPRIC SULFATE
(Viola tricolor)

VARIATIONS OF DEEP YELLOW-GREEN: ALUMED WOOL; FAIR TO GOOD LIGHT-FASTNESS.

Low-growing annual. Violet Family. Originated in Europe. In the thirteenth century, pansies were still a wild flower with a face the size of a fingernail! Weavers and miners of Lancashire formed florists' clubs. They bred and developed certain garden flowers including the pansy. The giant-faced pansy as we know it was developed in 1850 by John Salter. It had become a fashionable flower by 1870.

Full of dye, which easily goes into the dye bath. A heavy rain will leach color out of pansies. Beautiful colors can be achieved with this flower, but lightfastness is a problem. This is why a cupric sulfate afterbath is necessary, even though the color is dulled and darkened. This is a promising flower to experiment with. Dyed yarn can be used for wall hangings.

TEXTILE
Scoured, presoaked, alum-mordanted wool (1 ounce)

INGREDIENTS
Flowers, dark blue or purple (4 ounces)
Cupric sulfate stock solution (in 1 quart of water) (½ ounce or 1 tablespoon)

WATER
Distilled (enough to cover textile)

POT
Nonreacting

METHOD
1. Cover flowers and textile with water.
2. Steep for 3 days.
3. Bring dye bath to simmer and turn heat off.
4. Cool overnight in ooze.
5. Remove textile.
6. Prepare cupric sulfate afterbath.
7. Reenter textile.

8. Heat for 10 minutes.
9. Rinse thoroughly.
10. Dry in shade.

124/DARK-BLUE PANSIES, STEEPED
(Viola tricolor)
BLUE-GREENS: ALUMED WOOL; GOOD LIGHTFASTNESS.

TEXTILE

Scoured, presoaked, alum-mordanted wool (1 ounce)

INGREDIENT

Dark-blue flowers (4 ounces)

WATER

Distilled (enough to cover textile)

POT

Nonreacting

METHOD

1. Cover pansies and wool with water.
2. Steep (just set aside covered) for about 3 days.
3. Bring dye bath to a simmer and turn heat off.
4. Cool overnight in ooze.
5. Save ooze.
6. Remove textile.
7. Rinse thoroughly.
8. Dry in shade.

NOTES: In hot weather, less time is needed for steeping. □ Use leftover ooze for experimenting. Add more water. Try chromed wool and simmer for 20 minutes. See what happens.

125/RED PENSTEMON, ONE-POT AND MORDANT METHOD*
(Penstemon sp.)
TAN TO GOLDEN BROWN: UNMORDANTED WOOL; GOOD LIGHTFASTNESS.

Figwort Family. There are over 200 species of Penstemon native to North America. It is likely that other Penstemon species will yield dye. If you grow them, experiment.

TEXTILE

Scoured, presoaked, unmordanted

Figure 58 PENSTEMON (*Penstemon* sp.)

wool (1 ounce)

INGREDIENTS

Flowers (6 ounces)

Alum (dissolved in 1 cup of hot water) (1 teaspoon)

Cream of tartar (dissolved in 1 cup of hot water) (1 teaspoon)

WATER

Distilled (enough to cover textile)

POT

Nonreacting

METHOD

1. Heat flowers, water, and textile.
2. Remove textile.
3. Add dissolved alum and cream of tartar.
4. Reenter textile.
5. Simmer for 45 minutes.
6. Cool overnight in ooze.
7. Rinse thoroughly.
8. Dry in shade.

126/RED PENSTEMON WITH CUPRIC SULFATE
(Penstemon sp.)
MEDIUM BROWN: ALUMED AND CHROMED WOOL; GOOD LIGHTFASTNESS.

TEXTILE

Scoured, presoaked, alum- or chrome-mordanted wool (1 ounce)

INGREDIENTS

Flowers (4 ounces)
Cupric sulfate (dissolved in 1 cup of hot water) ($\frac{1}{8}$ teaspoon)

WATER

Distilled (enough to cover textile)

POT

Nonreacting

METHOD

1. Heat flowers, water, and textile.
2. Remove textile.
3. Add cupric sulfate solution.
4. Reenter textile.
5. Simmer for 45 minutes.
6. Cool overnight in ooze.
7. Rinse thoroughly.
8. Dry in shade.

127/PURPLE PETUNIAS AND ENGLISH WALNUT LEAVES (Petunia hybrida and Juglans regia)

LIGHT KHAKI GREEN: CHROMED WOOL; GOOD LIGHTFASTNESS.

Annual. Member of the Nightshade Family which includes the tomato, potato, eggplant, and others. Originated in South America. The color of the petunia used in the dye bath seems to affect the outcome. This is not always the case. Zinnias, for example, yield the same dye results irrespective of the color. (White is the exception.)

TEXTILE

Scoured, presoaked, chrome-mordanted wool (1 ounce)

INGREDIENTS

Flowers (about 4 ounces)
Walnut leaves (2 ounces)

WATER

Distilled(enough to cover textile)

POT

Nonreacting

METHOD

1. Combine walnut leaves, petunia flowers, water, and textile.
2. Simmer for 45 minutes.

3. Cool overnight in ooze.
4. Rinse thoroughly.
5. Dry in shade.

128/RED PETUNIAS AND MARIGOLDS (Petunia sp. and Tagetes sp.)

VARIOUS DARK GREENS TO BROWN: CHROMED WOOL; GOOD LIGHTFASTNESS.

TEXTILE

Scoured, presoaked, chrome-mordanted wool (1 ounce)

INGREDIENTS

Petunias (about 4 ounces)
Marigolds (2 ounces)

WATER

Distilled (enough to cover textile)

POT

Nonreacting

METHOD

1. Cover flowers and textile with water.
2. Simmer for 15 minutes for dark green.
3. Cool overnight in ooze.
4. Rinse thoroughly.
5. Dry in shade.

NOTE: Longer cooking yields darker colors: greens and browns.

129/RED ICELAND POPPY (Papaver nudicaule)

LIGHT BRICK RED: ALUMED WOOL; GOOD LIGHTFASTNESS.
BEIGE: STEEPED ALUMED WOOL; GOOD LIGHTFASTNESS.

Perennial. Most poppies are native to Europe but a few originate in Western United States. This one comes from the Arctic regions.

TEXTILE

Scoured, presoaked, alum-mordanted wool (1 ounce)

INGREDIENTS

Petals (6 ounces)
Tin crystals (dissolved in 1 cup of hot water immediately before using) (pinch or $\frac{1}{16}$ teaspoon)
Cream of tartar (dissolved in 1 cup of hot water) (1 teaspoon)

WATER
Distilled (enough to cover textile)

POT
Coffee can

METHOD
1. Cover petals and textile with water.
2. Heat to simmer.
3. Remove textile.
4. Add tin and cream of tartar solutions.
5. Reenter textile.
6. Simmer for 20 minutes.
7. Cool overnight in pot.
8. Rinse thoroughly.
9. Dry in shade.

NOTE: *For beige*: Steep flowers and textile in water for several days. No cooking is necessary.

130/ICELAND POPPY PODS (Papaver nudicaule)

MUSTARD YELLOW: ALUMED WOOL; GOOD LIGHTFASTNESS.
COPPER BROWN: CHROMED WOOL; GOOD LIGHTFASTNESS.
LIGHT BROWN: ALUMED COTTON; GOOD LIGHTFASTNESS.

TEXTILE
Scoured, presoaked, alum- or chrome-mordanted wool or alum-mordanted cotton (1 ounce)

INGREDIENT
Flower pods (6 ounces)

WATER
Distilled (enough to cover textile)

POT
Nonreacting

METHOD
1. Cover flowers and textile with water.
2. Simmer for 15 minutes.
3. Cool overnight in ooze.
4. Rinse thoroughly.
5. Dry in shade.

131/DARK-RED PRIMROSE IN IRON POT (Primula sp.)

GREENISH YELLOW (STEP I): ALUMED WOOL; FAIR LIGHTFASTNESS.
BRIGHT AVOCADO GREEN (STEP II): ALUMED WOOL; FAIR LIGHTFASTNESS.

Low-growing perennial of the Primrose Family. Similar dye results would probably result from most dark-colored primroses. I wonder whether dark-blue flowers would yield a blue or a blue-green? Experiment!

TEXTILE
Scoured, presoaked, alum-mordanted wool (1 ounce)

INGREDIENT
Petals (6 ounces)

WATER
Distilled (enough to cover textile)

POTS
Step I
Nonreacting

Step II
Iron

METHOD
Step I
1. Cover petals and textile with water.
2. Simmer for 30 minutes.

Step II
1. Transfer contents into iron pot.
2. Simmer for 30 minutes.
3. Cool for 1 hour.
4. Rinse thoroughly.
5. Dry in shade.

132/YELLOW LADIES' PURSE (Calceolaria angustifolia)

MAIZE YELLOW TO GOLD: ALUMED WOOL OR JUTE; GOOD LIGHTFASTNESS.
DEEP ORANGE: CHROMED WOOL; GOOD LIGHTFASTNESS.

Shrubby perennial. Odd, showy sac or pouchlike flowers. Originated in Mexico, Peru, and Chile. Grown under glass and planted out, in the San Francisco Bay area. The deer (in *my meadow*—henceforth referred to as "the deer") are not interested. This shrubby perennial belongs to the Figwort Family of plants, which includes the following dye plants (that is, "dye plants" from my own experience): foxglove, mullein, penstemon, snap-

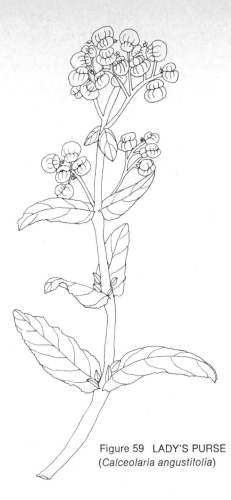

Figure 59 LADY'S PURSE
(*Calceolaria angustifolia*)

dragon. See dye recipes for these. *Calceolaria* is a potent dye plant and holds color well in the sunlight tests. Interestingly, the same can be said for mullein and snapdragon.

TEXTILE
Scoured, presoaked, alum- or chrome-mordanted wool or alum-mordanted jute (1 ounce)

INGREDIENTS
Flower heads (3 ounces)

Alum (1 teaspoon)

Tin crystals (dissolved in 1 cup of hot water immediately before using) (pinch or 1/16 teaspoon)

WATER
Distilled (enough to cover textile)

POT
Nonreacting

METHOD
1. Cover flower heads with water.
2. Stir in the alum.
3. Simmer for 30 minutes.
4. Stir in tin solution. Cool.
5. Enter textile.
6. Simmer for 1 hour.
7. Cool overnight in ooze.
8. Rinse thoroughly.
9. Dry in shade.

133/RUDBECKIA (Rudbeckia sp.)
BRIGHT CHARTREUSE TO DARK GREEN: CHROMED WOOL; GOOD LIGHTFASTNESS.

Mostly perennials, native of North America. Sunflower Family. Easily grown from seed. The variations from chartreuse to dark green in this formula are attributable to *two different* batches of *wool* from the *same* manufacturer. I point this out so that the dyer can appreciate some of the uncontrollable causes of color variation. A similar color variation can also be achieved by using two different mordant batches: one mordant batch aged about two days; the other mordant batch aged about four weeks. Variable color can happen in *any* dye experiment. Expect it, but try to help yourself by guessing why variations occur.

TEXTILE
Scoured, presoaked, chrome-mordanted wool (1 ounce)

INGREDIENT
Flower heads (6 ounces)

WATER
Tap (enough to cover textile)

POT
Nonreacting

METHOD
1. Cover flowers and wool with water.
2. Simmer for 30 minutes.
3. Cool overnight in ooze.

4. Rinse thoroughly.
5. Dry in shade.

134/PURPLISH SCABIOSA, PINCUSHION FLOWER (Scabiosa atropurpurea)

BRIGHT GREEN: ALUMED OR CHROMED WOOL; ACCEPTABLE LIGHTFASTNESS.
DULL DARK BLUE: ALUMED COTTON; POOR LIGHTFASTNESS.

Old-fashioned annual, member of the Teasel Family. Easily grown from seed. Withstands poor growing conditions. Originated in south-

Figure 60 SCABIOSA
(Scabiosa atropurpurea)

ern Europe and was introduced to Britain in 1591. The name *Scabiosa* refers to the belief that the plant was good for healing scabies and other skin diseases. It is unfortunate that so pretty a flower bears a name evocative of unsightly skin eruptions.

The scabiosa is a wonderful, tantalizing, frustrating dye plant. It easily yields a bright, grassy green dye. One can also extract a dull dark blue at times. The problem is that these colors are not as fast as one would hope for. The recipe for bright green is included even though it rates only *acceptable*. This means that fading does occur, but that a reasonably beautiful

color remains. With further experimentation, better results might be obtained. I am including several other scabiosa recipes in which other dye plants were added to improve resistance to fading. Lightfastness was finally achieved— but, alas, we lost our bright green!

TEXTILE
Scoured, presoaked, alum- or chrome-mordanted wool or cotton (1 ounce)

INGREDIENT
Purple or maroon flower heads (1 ounce)

WATER
Distilled (enough to cover textile)

POT
Nonreacting

METHOD
1. Combine flowers, wool, and water.
2. Simmer for 20 minutes.
3. Cool overnight in ooze.
4. Wash thoroughly.
5. Dry in shade.

NOTE: Whole scabiosa plants may be used for the dye bath instead of just flowers. A dull green results, but it is a more permanent dye than the bright green from flowers only.

135/SAGEBRUSH OVER-DYE ON SCABIOSA GREEN (Artemisia tridentata and Scabiosa atropurpurea)

DARK AVOCADO GREEN: CHROMED WOOL; GOOD LIGHTFASTNESS.

This recipe is useful as an example of over-dyeing for the purpose of improving lightfastness. The already dyed textile is dyed again in a sage bath in an iron pot.

TEXTILE
Scoured, presoaked, chrome-mordanted wool dyed scabiosa green (see Recipe 134) (3 ounces)

INGREDIENTS
Sage leaves and stems (about 3 ounces)

WATER
Tap (enough to cover textile)

POTS
Step I
Nonreacting

Step II
Iron

METHOD
Step I
1. Combine water and sage in non-reacting pot.
2. Simmer for 30 minutes.
3. Cool.
4. Enter previously dyed textile in sage ooze.
5. Steep textile overnight in sage ooze.
6. Remove textile.

Step II
1. Transfer sage ooze to iron pot.
2. Simmer for 40 minutes.
3. Cool for about 2 hours.
4. Enter previously dyed textile.
5. Simmer for 10 minutes.
6. Cool for several hours in iron pot.
7. Rinse thoroughly.
8. Dry in shade.

136 / PURPLISH SCABIOSA AND WALNUT LEAVES
(Scabiosa atropurpurea and Juglans spp.)

AVOCADO GREEN: ALUMED WOOL; GOOD LIGHTFASTNESS.
DARK GRAY-GREEN: ALUMED COTTON, LINEN, OR JUTE; GOOD LIGHTFASTNESS.

TEXTILE
Scoured, presoaked, alum-mordanted wool, cotton, linen, or jute (1 ounce)

INGREDIENTS
Walnut leaves (1 ounce)
Scabiosa flowers (3 ounces)

WATER
Tap (enough to cover textile)

POTS
Steps I and II
Nonreacting

Step III
Iron

METHOD
Step I
1. Combine walnut leaves, water, and textile in nonreacting pot.
2. Simmer for 30 minutes.
3. Lift out textile. Discard ooze.

Step II
1. Cover scabiosa flowers and above textile with warm water.
2. Simmer for 30 minutes.
3. Cool overnight in ooze.

Step III
1. Pour textile and ooze into iron pot.
2. Simmer for 5 minutes if dyeing wool or for 30 minutes if dyeing cotton, linen, or jute.
3. Cool overnight in iron pot.
4. Rinse thoroughly.
5. Dry in shade.

NOTE: For dyeing larger quantities of wool use the proportion of about 1:1 e.g., 1 pound of wool to 1 pound of flowers and about 1/3 part walnut leaves. The amount of leaves to use is variable. The textile must not be permitted to get darker than tan color before proceeding to Step II.

137 / DARK-REDDISH SNAPDRAGON*
(Antirrhinum majus)

LIGHT GREEN: UNMORDANTED WOOL; GOOD LIGHTFASTNESS.
DARK GREEN: ALUMED WOOL; GOOD LIGHTFASTNESS.
BROWN: CHROMED WOOL; GOOD LIGHTFASTNESS.

TEXTILE
Scoured, presoaked, unmordanted, alum- or chrome-mordanted wool (1 ounce)

INGREDIENT
Flowers (6 ounces)

WATER
Distilled (enough to cover textile)

POT
Nonreacting

METHOD
1. Cover flowers and textile with water.

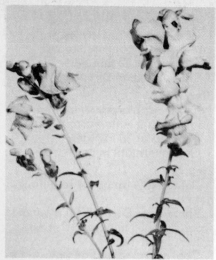

Figure 61 SNAPDRAGON
(*Antirrhinum majus*)

2. Simmer for 30 minutes.
3. Cool overnight in ooze.
4. Rinse thoroughly.
5. Dry in shade.

138/DARK-REDDISH SNAPDRAGON ON PLANT FIBERS
(**Antirrhinum majus**)

PALE GREEN: ALUMED COTTON OR LINEN; GOOD LIGHTFASTNESS.
TANNISH GOLD: ALUMED JUTE; GOOD LIGHTFASTNESS.

Perennial. Member of Figwort Family. Native to Europe. Favorite flower garden subject.

TEXTILE
Scoured, presoaked, alum-mordanted cotton, linen, or jute (1 ounce)

INGREDIENT
Flowers (6 ounces)

WATER
Distilled (enough to cover textile)

POT
Nonreacting

METHOD
1. Cover flowers and textile with water.
2. Simmer for 30 minutes.
3. Cool overnight in ooze.

4. Rinse thoroughly.
5. Dry in shade.

139/PURPLE STOCK
(**Matthiola incana**)

BLUE: ALUMED WOOL; GOOD LIGHTFASTNESS.
TURQUOISE: CHROMED WOOL; GOOD LIGHTFASTNESS.

Annual or perennial member of the Mustard Family (Cruciferae). Sweet smelling. Popular in Europe during the Middle Ages. Present form was developed in Brampton, England, in 1725. Makes a surprisingly strong dye.

TEXTILE
Scoured, presoaked, alum- or chrome-mordanted wool (1 ounce)

INGREDIENT
Flowers, dark-purple (2 ounces)

WATER
Distilled (enough to cover textile)

POT
Nonreacting

METHOD
1. Cover flowers and textile with water.
2. Simmer for 20 minutes.
3. Cool overnight in ooze.
4. Rinse thoroughly.
5. Dry in shade.

NOTE: This dye plant is easily affected by moisture variation.

140/PURPLE STOCK AND TIN CRYSTALS
(**Matthiola incana**)

DARK BLUE: ALUMED WOOL; GOOD LIGHTFASTNESS.
PURPLE: CHROMED WOOL; GOOD LIGHTFASTNESS.

TEXTILE
Scoured, presoaked, alum- or chrome-mordanted wool (1 ounce)

INGREDIENTS
Flowers, dark-purple (about 2 ounces)

Tin crystals (dissolved in 1 cup of hot water immediately before using) (pinch or 1/16 teaspoon)

WATER
Distilled (enough to cover textile)

POT
Nonreacting or tin

METHOD
1. Combine flowers, water, tin solution, and wool.
2. Simmer for 30 minutes.
3. Cool overnight in ooze.
4. Rinse thoroughly.
5. Dry in shade.

141 / SAINT-JOHN'S-WORT
(Hypericum calycinum)

YELLOW-ORANGE: ALUMED WOOL; GOOD LIGHTFASTNESS.
PUMPKIN COLOR: CHROMED WOOL; GOOD LIGHTFASTNESS (DARKENS SLIGHTLY IN SUN).

Saint-John's-Wort Family. Most cultivated kinds, including shrubs, can be used for dye. Even the weedy relative, Klamath weed, is a good dye subject (see weeds). Weedy as well as cultivated species were used to dispel bad spirits. Flowers were hung over beds, doors, and stable gates to protect against accident, sickness, and witchcraft. It was said that if a witch entered the house the flower withered.

Figure 62 SAINT-JOHN'S-WORT
(*Hypericum calycinum*)

TEXTILE
Scoured, presoaked, alum- or chrome-mordanted wool (1 ounce)

INGREDIENTS
Flowers (6 ounces)
Tin crystals (dissolved in 1 cup of hot water immediately before using) (pinch or 1/16 teaspoon)

WATER
Distilled (enough to cover textile)

POT
Nonreacting

METHOD
1. Combine flowers, textile, and water.
2. Simmer for 20 minutes.
3. Remove textile.
4. Add tin solution.
5. Reenter textile.
6. Simmer for 40 minutes.
7. Cool overnight in ooze.
8. Rinse thoroughly.
9. Dry in shade.

14

Wild shrub recipes

142/BLUE OR BLACK ELDERBERRY, ONE-POT AND MORDANT METHOD* (Sambucus sp.)

MAUVE: UNMORDANTED WOOL; FAIR LIGHT-FASTNESS.

One of several species found throughout the United States. Black or blue berries in late summer and early fall were used for jams and pies. Important food source for Indians. Rich in vitamins A and C. Some species are said to be poisonous, but well-documented cases have rarely been recorded. Purgative substances are present.

TEXTILE
Scoured, presoaked, unmordanted wool (1 ounce)

INGREDIENTS
Berries (5 ounces)
Alum (dissolved in 1 cup of hot water) (2 teaspoons)
Cream of tartar (dissolved in 1 cup of hot water) (2 teaspoons)

WATER
Distilled (enough to cover textile)

POT
Nonreacting

METHOD
1. Cover berries and textile with water.
2. Bring to simmer.
3. Remove textile.
4. Add alum and cream of tartar solutions.
5. Reenter textile.
6. Simmer for 20 minutes.
7. Cool overnight in ooze.
8. Rinse thoroughly.
9. Dry in shade.

143/BLUE OR BLACK ELDERBERRY, ONE-POT AND MORDANT METHOD WITH AMMONIA* (Sambucus spp.)

GRAY-BLUE: UNMORDANTED WOOL; FAIR LIGHTFASTNESS.

TEXTILE
Scoured, presoaked, unmordanted wool (1 ounce)

INGREDIENTS
Berries (5 ounces)
Alum (dissolved in 1 cup of hot water) (2 teaspoons)
Cream of tartar (dissolved in 1 cup of hot water) (2 teaspoons)
Ammonia (dissolved in 1 quart of water) (1 teaspoon)

WATER
Distilled (enough to cover textile)

POT
Nonreacting

METHOD
1. Cover berries and textile with water.
2. Bring to simmer.
3. Remove textile.
4. Add alum and cream of tartar solutions.
5. Reenter textile.
6. Simmer for 20 minutes.
7. Cool overnight in ooze.
8. Remove textile.
9. Dip textile into ammonia solution.
10. Rinse thoroughly.
11. Dry in shade.

144/GORSE, FURZE FLOWERS (Ulex europaeus)

ORANGE: CHROMED WOOL; GOOD LIGHTFASTNESS.

Introduced from Europe. Pea Family. Spiney pest of California grazing land. Used in Europe for burning. Soil is improved by ashes from burned-down furze. Horses and cows relish bruised shoots. Pricked fingers from collecting flowers are soon forgotton when the dyed textile is viewed.

TEXTILE
Scoured, presoaked, chrome-mordanted wool (1 ounce)

INGREDIENT
Flowers (6 ounces)

WATER
Distilled (enough to cover textile)

POT
Nonreacting

METHOD
1. Cover flowers and textile with water.
2. Simmer for 30 minutes.
3. Cool overnight in ooze.
4. Rinse thoroughly.
5. Dry in shade.

145 / OREGON GRAPE BERRIES
(Mahonia spp.)
VIOLET: ALUMED WOOL; FAIR LIGHTFASTNESS.
DARK GREEN: ALUMED-WOOL AND AMMONIA; FAIR LIGHTFASTNESS.

Shrub, native to Northwestern United States. Barberry Family. Some species are used as ornamentals. Indians used berries to make a drink and dried the fruits for winter use. Yellow dye was extracted from roots, stem, and leaves and used on baskets and clothing. Colonists used berries for tarts and jellies.

TEXTILE
Scoured, presoaked, alum-mordanted wool (1 ounce)

INGREDIENTS
Berries, mashed (5 ounces)
Ammonia (in quart of water) for dark green only (1 teaspoon)

WATER
Tap (enough to cover textile)

POT
Nonreacting

METHOD
1. Cover berries and textile with water.
2. Simmer for 30 minutes.
3. Cool overnight in ooze.

Figure 63 OREGON GRAPE (*Mahonia* sp.)

4. Rinse thoroughly.
5. *For violet:* Dry in shade.
6. *For dark green:* Dip dyed textile in ammonia solution, rinse thoroughly, and dry in shade.

146 / OREGON GRAPE BERRIES AND TIN CRYSTALS
(Mahonia spp.)
DARK BLUE-PURPLE: ALUMED WOOL; FAIR LIGHTFASTNESS.

TEXTILE
Scoured, presoaked alum-mordanted wool (1 ounce)

INGREDIENTS
Berries, mashed (5 ounces)
Tin crystals (dissolved in 1 cup of hot water immediately before use) (pinch or 1/16 teaspoon)

WATER
Tap (enough to cover textile)

POT
Nonreacting

METHOD
1. Cover berries and textile with water.
2. Heat to simmer.
3. Remove textile.
4. Add tin solution.
5. Reenter textile.
6. Simmer for 30 minutes.
7. Cool overnight in ooze.
8. Rinse thoroughly.
9. Dry in shade.

147/OREGON GRAPE LEAVES AND CUPRIC SULFATE (Mahonia spp.)

LIGHT OLIVE GREEN: ALUMED WOOL; GOOD LIGHTFASTNESS; AROMATIC.
MEDIUM OLIVE GREEN: CHROMED WOOL; GOOD LIGHTFASTNESS; AROMATIC.

TEXTILE
Scoured, presoaked, alum- or chrome-mordanted wool (1 ounce)

INGREDIENTS
Leaves, cut up (6 ounces)
Cupric sulfate stock solution (in 1 quart of water) (½ ounce or 1 table-spoon)

WATER
Distilled (enough to cover textile)

POT
Nonreacting

METHOD
1. Cover leaves and textile with water.
2. Simmer for 30 minutes.
3. Cool overnight in ooze.
4. Transfer textile to cupric sulfate solution.
5. Heat gently for 10 minutes.
6. Rinse thoroughly.
7. Dry in shade.

148/OREGON GRAPE ROOTS* (Mahonia spp.)

OLIVE GREEN: CHROMED WOOL; GOOD LIGHTFASTNESS.
LIGHT GREEN: UNMORDANTED BASKETRY MATERIALS; POOR LIGHTFASTNESS.

TEXTILE
Scoured, presoaked chrome-mor-danted wool or basketry materials (1 ounce)

INGREDIENT
Roots, lightly rinsed (4 ounces)

WATER
Distilled (enough to cover textile)

POT
Nonreacting

METHOD
1. Cover roots and textile with water.
2. Simmer for 1 hour.
3. Cool overnight in ooze.
4. Rinse thoroughly.
5. Dry in shade.

149/BLUE CALIFORNIA LILAC (Ceanothus spp.)

LIGHT TO MEDIUM GREEN: ALUMED WOOL; GOOD LIGHTFASTNESS; AROMATIC.

Member of Buckthorn Family. There are about forty-three species of *Ceanothus* in California. Many are in cultivation. Native Californians (Indians) used the fluffy flowers to make fragrant soapsuds. The deer love to nibble these. Ticks abound in the foliage.

Ceanothus americanus is an Eastern relative known as "red root" or "New Jersey tea." It is common from Canada to the Gulf States. The wild red root was used by native Americans as a leaf tea. It is noted as our best substitute for Oriental tea. The root is the medicinal part and the solvent is boiling water. Tea infusion is thought to be of direct help in despondency and melancholy. Dose: one teaspoon of granulated root to one pint of boiling water. Steep for thirty minutes. Drink 1 cupful of tea before each meal and before bedtime. Or, better still, try some dye experiments with the root.

TEXTILE
Scoured, presoaked, alum-mor-danted wool (1 ounce)

Figure 64 CALIFORNIA LILAC (*Ceanothus* sp.)

INGREDIENTS
Flowers, blue (12 ounces)
Tin crystals (dissolved in 1 cup of
hot water immediately before use)
(pinch or 1/16 teaspoon)

WATER
Distilled (enough to cover textile)

POT
Nonreacting

METHOD
1. Cover flowers with water.
2. Heat for 15 minutes.
3. Stir tin solution into bath.
4. Enter textile.
5. Simmer for 30 minutes.
6. Cool overnight in ooze.
7. Rinse thoroughly.
8. Dry in shade.

150/YELLOW BUSH LUPINE
(Lupinus arboreus)
BRIGHT YELLOW: ALUMED WOOL; GOOD
LIGHTFASTNESS.

Common shrubby lupine found at
Point Reyes and other localities
around the San Francisco Bay area.
This lupine yields a strong yellow
and a very fast color, unlike the
purple lupine which is not as fast.
Pea Family.

TEXTILE
Scoured, presoaked, alum-mordanted wool (1 ounce)

INGREDIENT
Lupine blossoms (about 5 ounces)

WATER
Tap (enough to cover textile)

POT
Tin can

METHOD
1. Combine blossoms, water, and
textile.
2. Simmer for 1 hour.
3. Cool overnight in ooze.
4. Rinse thoroughly.
5. Dry in shade.

151/MANZANITA LEAVES*
(Arctostaphylos spp.)
DEEP CAMEL: UNMORDANTED WOOL; GOOD
LIGHTFASTNESS.
ROSE-BUFF: ALUMED COTTON; GOOD LIGHT-
FASTNESS.

There are nearly fifty species found
throughout the West, mostly in dry
places. Used for food. Berries can
be eaten fresh or made into a spicy
tart lemonade, or jelly. The dried
leaves and bark of several species
were used for Indian tobacco. A
remedy for poison oak was made

from the leaves, heated, and steeped in water. The wood was used for building huts, making small tools, and carving pipes. Heather Family.

TEXTILE
Scoured, presoaked, unmordanted wool or alum-mordanted cotton (1 ounce)

INGREDIENT
Leaves (4 ounces)

WATER
Distilled (enough to cover textile)

POT
Nonreacting

METHOD
1. Cover leaves and textile with water.
2. Boil for 1 hour.
3. Cool overnight in ooze.
4. Rinse thoroughly.
5. Dry in shade.

NOTE: Colors darken in light after about 1 week.

152/WAX-MYRTLE BERRIES (DRY) (Myrica californica)

VARIOUS GRAY-BROWNS: CHROMED WOOL; GOOD LIGHTFASTNESS.

Native wild shrub or small tree of the San Francisco Bay region. Also occurs in other areas of coastal California and northward to Washington. Member of Wax-Myrtle Family. The berries are small and purplish-brown.

TEXTILE
Scoured, presoaked, chrome-mordanted wool (1 ounce)

INGREDIENT
Berries dry (or fresh) (5 ounces)

WATER
Distilled (enough to cover textile)

POT
Nonreacting

METHOD
1. Combine berries, water, and textile.

2. Simmer for 30 minutes.
3. Cool overnight in ooze.
4. Rinse thoroughly.
5. Dry in shade.

153/WAX-MYRTLE BERRIES (DRY) AND TIN CRYSTALS (Myrica californica)

MAROON PURPLE: CHROMED WOOL; GOOD LIGHTFASTNESS.

TEXTILE
Scoured, presoaked, chrome-mordanted wool (1 ounce)

INGREDIENTS
Berries, dry (5 ounces)
Tin crystals (dissolved in 1 cup of hot water immediately before using) (pinch or 1/16 teaspoon)

WATER
Distilled (enough to cover textile)

POT
Nonreacting

METHOD
1. Combine berries, tin solution, water, and wool.
2. Simmer for 30 minutes.
3. Cool overnight in ooze.
4. Rinse thoroughly.
5. Dry in shade.

154/SALAL BERRIES* (Gaultheria shallon)

DARK BLUE: UNMORDANTED WOOL; GOOD LIGHTFASTNESS.

Wild shrub growing in British Columbia and south to California. Heather Family. Berries are eaten raw or cooked. The Eastern aromatic wintergreen is a relative.

TEXTILE
Scoured, presoaked, unmordanted wool (1 ounce)

INGREDIENTS
Berries (4 ounces)
Alum (dissolved in 1 cup of hot water) (1 teaspoon)

WATER
Tap (enough to cover textile)

POT
Nonreacting

Figure 65 SALAL BERRIES (*Gaultheria shallon*)

METHOD
1. Combine berries, alum, water, and textile.
2. Simmer for 20 minutes.
3. Cool overnight in ooze.
4. Rinse thoroughly.
5. Dry in shade.

155/SALAL BERRIES AND CUPRIC SULFATE*
(Gaultheria shallon)
VARIOUS DARK GREENS: UNMORDANTED WOOL; GOOD LIGHTFASTNESS.

TEXTILE
Scoured, presoaked, unmordanted wool (1 ounce)

INGREDIENTS
Berries (4 ounces)
Cupric sulfate stock solution (in 1 quart of water) (½ ounce or 1 tablespoon)
Alum (dissolved in 1 cup hot water) (1 teaspoon)

WATER
Tap (enough to cover textile)

POT
Nonreacting

METHOD
1. Combine berries, alum, water, and textile.
2. Simmer for 20 minutes.

3. Cool overnight in ooze.
4. Prepare copper afterbath.
5. Enter textile and heat for 10 minutes.
6. Rinse thoroughly.
7. Dry in shade.

156/SANDBAR WILLOW IN IRON POT
(Salix hindsiana)

PALE YELLOW (STEP I): ALUMED WOOL; GOOD LIGHTFASTNESS.
GOLD (STEP I): CHROMED WOOL; GOOD LIGHTFASTNESS.
AVOCADO (STEP II): ALUMED WOOL; GOOD LIGHTFASTNESS.
DEEP MUSTARD GREEN (STEP II): CHROMED WOOL; GOOD LIGHTFASTNESS.

Native shrub or small tree of San Francisco Bay region. Also occurs from Oregon south to northern Baja California. Grows in dense thickets in moist places. Willow Family. It is likely that other willows, tree or shrub, yield dye also.

TEXTILE
Scoured, presoaked, alum- or chrome-mordanted wool (1 ounce)

INGREDIENT
Leaves (4 ounces)

WATER
Tap (enough to cover textile)

POTS
Step I
Nonreacting
Step II
Iron

METHOD
Step I
1. Cover plant material and textile with water.
2. Simmer for 30 minutes.
3. *For pale yellow or gold:* Cool overnight in pot. Rinse thoroughly and dry in shade.
4. *For avocado or deep mustard green:* Proceed to Step II.

Step II
1. Transfer contents to iron pot.
2. Simmer for 40 minutes.
3. Cool in ooze about 1 hour.
4. Rinse thoroughly.
5. Dry in shade.

157/SILK-TASSEL SHRUB, FRUITS
(Garrya elliptica)

GRAY TO BLACK: ALUMED WOOL; GOOD LIGHTFASTNESS AND GOOD WASHFASTNESS.

Native shrub of southern Oregon and California. Member of the Silk-Tassel Family. Male and female

Figure 66 SILK TASSEL SHRUB (*Garrya elliptica*)

Figure 67   SPICE BUSH (*Calycanthus occidentalis*)

flowers are on separate plants. The female bears long clusters of purple fruit from June to September. Color obtained from the fruits varies according to time of year. Strangely, the green fruits give better results than the ripe.

TEXTILE
Scoured, presoaked, alum-mordanted wool (1 ounce)

INGREDIENTS
Fruit in pods, opened and crushed (5 ounces)
Iodized salt (1 tablespoon)
Chrome (dissolved in 1 cup of hot water) ($1/4$ teaspoon)

WATER
Tap (enough to cover textile)

POT
Nonreacting

METHOD
1. Cover fruits and salt with water.
2. Simmer for 1 hour.
3. Cool.
4. Stir in chrome solution.
5. Enter textile.
6. Simmer for 1 hour .
7. Cool overnight in ooze.
8. Wash textile in soapy water.
9. Rinse thoroughly.
10. Dry in shade.

NOTE: It is sometimes possible to achieve maroon or brown by substituting cupric sulfate ($1/4$ teaspoon) for the chrome. This is a touchy dye plant so hope, but don't be disappointed, if maroon escapes you.

158 / SPICE-BUSH AND CUPRIC SULFATE (Calycanthus occidentalis)
LIGHT BROWN: ALUMED WOOL; GOOD LIGHTFASTNESS.

Native shrub of the San Francisco Bay region, as well as other parts of California. Calycanthus Family. Relative of the Eastern sweet-shrub. Maroon flowers are somewhat chrysanthemum-shaped. Spicy aroma.

TEXTILE
Scoured, presoaked, alum-mordanted wool (1 ounce)

INGREDIENTS
Flowers (6 ounces)
Cupric sulfate stock solution (in 1 quart water) (½ ounce or 1 tablespoon)

WATER
Distilled (enough to cover textile)

POT
Nonreacting

METHOD
1. Cover flowers and textile with water.
2. Simmer for 20 minutes.
3. Cool overnight in ooze.
4. Remove textile.
5. Prepare cupric sulfate afterbath.
6. Enter textile.
7. Heat gently for 10 minutes.
8. Rinse thoroughly.
9. Dry in shade.

159/TOYON, CHRISTMAS BERRY
(Heteromeles arbutifolia)
GOLDEN BROWN: CHROMED WOOL; GOOD LIGHTFASTNESS.

Native California shrub or small tree with red berries. Member of the Rose Family. Grows at lower elevations from northern California to northern Baja California. Indians ate the berries raw or roasted. Cider is made as follows: heat berries and crush. Add a quart of water to a quart of berries. Steep for several hours and strain. Drink the juice.

TEXTILE
Scoured, presoaked, chrome-mordanted wool (1 ounce)

INGREDIENTS
Leaves and stems (3 ounces)

WATER
Tap (enough to cover textile)

POT
Nonreacting

METHOD
1. Combine plant material, water, and textile.

2. Simmer for 1 hour for yellow or for 3 hours for golden brown.
3. Cool overnight in ooze.
4. Rinse thoroughly.
5. Dry in shade.

160/TOYON, CHRISTMAS BERRY, BERRIES AND LEAVES IN IRON POT
(Heteromeles arbutifolia)
DARK OLIVE GREEN: ALUMED WOOL; GOOD LIGHTFASTNESS.

TEXTILE
Scoured, presoaked, alum-mordanted wool (1 ounce)

INGREDIENTS
Leaves and berries (6 ounces)

WATER
Distilled (enough to cover textile)

POTS
Step I
Nonreacting

Step II
Iron

METHOD
Step I
1. Cover plant material and textile with water.
2. Simmer in nonreacting pot until textile is yellow or tan (about 1 hour).

Step II
1. Transfer contents into iron pot.
2. Simmer for 1 hour.
3. Cool in ooze for about 1 hour.
4. Rinse thoroughly.
5. Dry in shade.

161/TOYON, CHRISTMAS BERRY, BERRIES AND LEAVES, STEEPED
(Heteromeles arbutifolia)
BLACK: ALUMED WOOL; GOOD LIGHTFASTNESS.

TEXTILE
Scoured, presoaked, alum-mordanted wool (1 ounce)

INGREDIENTS
Leaves and berries (6 ounces)

WATER
Distilled (enough to cover textile)

POTS
Step I
Nonreacting

Step II
Iron

METHOD
Step I
1. Cover plant material and textile with water.
2. Simmer until textile is yellow (about 1 hour).

Step II
1. Transfer contents into iron pot.
2. Simmer for 1 hour.
3. Steep for 1 month in iron pot.
4. Rinse thoroughly.
5. Dry in shade.

NOTE: This is a lovely black.

162 / TWINBERRIES AND TIN CRYSTALS*
(Lonicera involucrata)
GRAY: UNMORDANTED WOOL; GOOD LIGHTFASTNESS.

Wild shrub of the Honeysuckle Family. Native to San Francisco Bay region. The berries are black.

TEXTILE
Scoured, presoaked, unmordanted wool (1 ounce)

INGREDIENTS
Berries (4 ounces)

Tin crystals (dissolved in 1 cup of hot water immediately before using) (pinch or ⅟₁₆ teaspoon)

WATER
Distilled (enough to cover textile)

POT
Nonreacting

METHOD
1. Combine berries, tin solution, water, and textile.
2. Simmer for 30 minutes.
3. Cool overnight in ooze.
4. Rinse thoroughly.
5. Dry in shade.

163 / SEASIDE WOOLLYASTER
(Eriophyllum staechadifolium)
BRONZE-GOLD TO GOLDEN BROWN: ALUMED OR CHROMED WOOL; GOOD LIGHTFASTNESS.

TEXTILE
Scoured, presoaked, alum- or chrome-mordanted wool (1 ounce)

INGREDIENTS
Flower heads (4 ounces)

Ammonia, clear (in 1 quart of water) (1 teaspoon)

WATER
Tap (enough to cover textile)

POT
Nonreacting

METHOD
1. Cover flowers and textile with water.
2. Simmer for 30 minutes.
3. Cool overnight in ooze.
4. Remove textile.
5. Dip in ammonia rinse.
6. Rinse thoroughly.
7. Dry in shade.

15

Garden shrub recipes

164/ALTHEA SHRUB OR ROSE OF SHARON
(Hibiscus syriacus)
MEDIUM TO DARK BLUE: ALUMED WOOL; FAIR LIGHTFASTNESS.

Hardy relative of the tropical species of *Hibiscus*. Dies down to the ground in cold climates and comes back in the spring. In California, only the leaves fall off. The deer love this plant and kept mine nibbled down. They love all members of this family—the mallows.

Figure 68 ALTHEA SHRUB
(*Hibiscus syriacus*)

The root juice of the marsh mallow (*Althaea officinalis*) at one time furnished the basis of the well-known confection.

TEXTILE
Scoured, presoaked, alum-mordanted wool (1 ounce)

INGREDIENTS
Flowers (6 ounces)
Tin crystals (dissolved in 1 cup of hot water immediately before using) (pinch or 1/16 teaspoon)
Cream of tartar (dissolved in 1 cup of hot water) (1 teaspoon)
Iodized salt (dissolved in 1 cup of hot water) (1 tablespoon)
Cupric sulfate stock solution (in 1 quart of water) (1/2 ounce or 1 tablespoon)

WATER
Distilled (enough to cover textile)

POT
Nonreacting

METHOD
1. Combine flowers, tin, salt, cream of tartar solutions, water, and textile.
2. Simmer for 35 minutes.
3. Cool overnight in ooze.
4. Remove textile.
5. Prepare cupric sulfate afterbath.
6. Enter textile.
7. Heat for 10 minutes.
8. Rinse thoroughly.
9. Dry in shade.

165/BARBERRY
(Berberis sp.)
OLIVE GREEN: CHROMED WOOL; FAIR LIGHTFASTNESS.

Deciduous shrub. Barberry Family. Leaves turn red in the fall. Wood is yellow. Used for fall color and as traffic regulators. The dye bath color is a deep rosy red. Further experimentation is warranted. Common barberry (*Berberis vulgaris*) is native to Europe and eastern Asia and has become naturalized in the Eastern United States. Its clusters of coral red berries are

used for preserves and jellies. East-
erners should experiment with the
berries for dye. Or, try the purple-
leaved varieties in the recipe
above. The Eastern native barberry
(Berberis canadensis) can be found
from West Virginia to Georgia and
Missouri. Its berries are edible and
worth experimenting with for dye.

TEXTILE
Scoured, presoaked, chrome-mordanted wool (1 ounce)

INGREDIENTS
Leaves and stems (6 ounces)

WATER
Distilled (enough to cover textile)

POT
Nonreacting

METHOD
1. Cover plant material and textile
with water.
2. Simmer for 30 minutes.
3. Cool overnight in ooze.

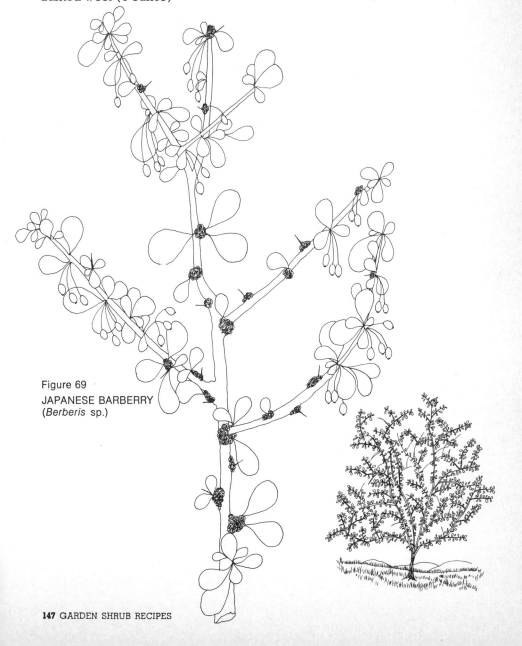

Figure 69
JAPANESE BARBERRY
(Berberis sp.)

4. Rinse thoroughly.
5. Dry in shade.
NOTE: For 1 pound of wool use 2 pounds of barberry.

166 / BARBERRY AND TIN CRYSTALS

TERRA-COTTA BROWN: CHROMED WOOL; FAIR LIGHTFASTNESS.

TEXTILE
Scoured, presoaked, chrome-mordanted wool (1 ounce)

INGREDIENTS
Leaves and stems (6 ounces)
Tin crystals (dissolved in 1 cup of hot water immediately before using) (pinch or 1/16 teaspoon)
Cream of tartar (dissolved in 1 cup of hot water) (1 teaspoon)

WATER
Distilled (enough to cover textile)

POT
Nonreacting

METHOD
1. Cover plant material and textile with water.
2. Bring to simmer.
3. Remove textile.
4. Add tin and cream of tartar solutions to bath.
5. Reenter textile.
6. Simmer for 30 minutes.
7. Cool overnight in ooze.
8. Rinse thoroughly.
9. Dry in shade.

167 / BUTTERFLY BUSH FLOWERS
(Buddleia davidii)

ORANGE-GOLD: ALUMED JUTE; FAIR LIGHTFASTNESS.
GOLD-GREEN: ALUMED WOOL; GOOD LIGHTFASTNESS.
GOLDEN BROWN: CHROMED WOOL; GOOD LIGHTFASTNESS.

Shrub found in old-fashioned gardens. Native of China but has become naturalized in the Eastern United States and California. Member of the Logania Family. Often called "summer lilac." Butterflies collect around the numerous small purplish flowers. This plant yields rich color.

TEXTILE
Scoured, presoaked, alum-mordanted jute or wool, or chrome-mordanted wool (1 ounce)

INGREDIENTS
Flowers (5 ounces)
Iodized salt (dissolved in 1 cup of hot water) (1 teaspoon)
Tin crystals (dissolved in 1 cup of hot water immediately before using) (pinch or 1/16 teaspoon)
Cream of tartar (dissolved in 1 cup of hot water) (1 teaspoon)

WATER
Distilled (enough to cover textile)

POT
Nonreacting

METHOD
1. Combine salt solution, water, flowers, and textile.
2. Heat to simmer.
3. Remove textile.
4. Add tin and cream of tartar solutions to bath.
5. Reenter textile.
6. Simmer for 35 minutes.
7. Rinse thoroughly.
8. Dry in shade.
NOTE: Save ooze for use in Recipe 168.

168 / BUTTERFLY BUSH IN IRON POT
(Buddleia davidii)

VARIOUS GREENS: ALUMED COTTON, LINEN, OR JUTE; GOOD LIGHTFASTNESS.
BLACK: ALUMED OR CHROMED WOOL; GOOD LIGHTFASTNESS.

TEXTILE
Scoured, presoaked, alum-mordanted vegetable fibers or alum- or chrome-mordanted wool (1 ounce)

INGREDIENTS
Flowers, leaves, and stems (or combined ooze saved from Recipes 167 and 169) (5 ounces)

WATER
Distilled (enough to cover textile)

Figure 70 BUTTERFLY BUSH
(*Buddleia davidii*)

POTS
Step I
Nonreacting

Step II
Iron

METHOD
Step I
1. Cover plants with water in non-reacting pot.
2. Boil gently for 30 minutes.

Step II
1. Transfer contents to iron pot.
2. Enter textile.
3. Simmer for 40 minutes.
4. Cool for 1 hour.
5. Rinse thoroughly.
6. Dry in shade.

169 / BUTTERFLY BUSH, LEAVES AND STEMS
(Buddleia davidii)
OLIVE GREEN: CHROMED WOOL; GOOD LIGHTFASTNESS.

TEXTILE
Scoured, presoaked, chrome-mordanted wool (1 ounce)

INGREDIENTS
Stems and leaves (5 ounces)

WATER
Distilled (enough to cover textile)

POT
Coffee can

METHOD
1. Cover plant material with water.
2. Steep for 2 days.
3. Enter textile.
4. Simmer for 20 minutes.
5. Cool overnight in ooze.
6. Rinse thoroughly.
7. Dry in shade.

NOTE: Save ooze for use in Recipe 168.

170 / RED CAMELLIAS IN IRON POT
(Camellia sp.)
MEDIUM GRAY TO DARK GRAY: ALUMED COTTON OR WOOL; FAIR TO GOOD LIGHT-FASTNESS.

TEXTILE
Scoured, presoaked, alum-mordanted wool or cotton (1 ounce)

INGREDIENT
Pink or red flower petals (8 ounces)

WATER
Tap (enough to cover textile)

POT
Iron

METHOD
1. Combine petals and water in iron pot.
2. Simmer for 20 minutes.
3. Steep in iron pot for 2 or 3 days. If weather is hot, 1 day of steeping may be enough.
4. Enter textile into dye bath.
5. Simmer for 30 minutes.
6. *For wool:* Cool overnight in iron pot.
7. *For cotton:* Leave in iron pot for 3 days.
8. Rinse thoroughly.
9. Dry in shade.

NOTE: An ammonia after-rinse darkens the color.

Figure 71 COTONEASTER (*Cotoneaster* sp.)

171/COTONEASTER BERRIES
(Cotoneaster sp.)

ROSE-TAN: ALUMED OR CHROMED WOOL; GOOD LIGHTFASTNESS.

Evergreen shrubs from the Old World. Red or orange-berried fruits. Member of the Rose Family. Robins love the berries. Before the "silent spring" came, robins clustered greedily on the twigs of my cotoneaster. Nowadays I seldom see them.

TEXTILE
Scoured, presoaked, alum- or chrome-mordanted wool (1 ounce)

INGREDIENT
Berries, crushed (4 ounces)

WATER
Distilled (enough to cover textile)

POT
Nonreacting

METHOD
1. Soak crushed berries overnight.
2. Enter textile.
3. Simmer for 30 minutes.
4. Cool overnight in ooze
5. Rinse thoroughly.
6. Dry in shade.

172/NEW ZEALAND FLAX FLOWERS*
(Phormium tenax)

BROWN: UNMORDANTED WOOL; GOOD LIGHTFASTNESS.

Perennial. Member of the Agave Family. *Yucca* is a well-known member of this family. Originated in New Zealand. Treated as a shrub because of its size (up to fifteen feet). Swordlike, stiff green or reddish-brown leaves furnish excellent mat and basketry material. Exotic, birdlike flowers are very rich in tannin. The Maori peoples of New Zealand obtain fibers from the leaves and use these for textile weaving and for cordage. The fibers, being of plant origin, can be dyed like linen and jute.

Figure 72 NEW ZEALAND FLAX (*Phormium tenax*)

TEXTILE
Scoured, presoaked, unmordanted wool (2 ounces)

INGREDIENT
Flowers, cut up or chopped in blender (4 ounces)

WATER
Tap (enough to cover textile)

POT
Nonreacting

METHOD
1. Cover flowers and textile with water.
2. Simmer for 30 minutes.
3. Cool overnight in ooze.
4. Rinse thoroughly.
5. Dry in shade.

173/NEW ZEALAND FLAX SEED PODS
(Phormium tenax)
BRIGHT TERRA-COTTA: ALUMED WOOL; GOOD LIGHTFASTNESS.

TEXTILE
Scoured, presoaked, alum-mordanted wool (2 ounces)

INGREDIENTS
Seed pods, split open (4 ounces, about 90 pods)

Tin crystals (dissolved in 1 cup of hot water immediately before using) (pinch or ¹⁄₁₆ teaspoon)

WATER
Tap (enough to cover textile)

POT
Nonreacting

METHOD
1. Cover pods and textile with water.
2. Simmer for 30 minutes.
3. Remove textile.
4. Add tin solution.
5. Reenter textile.
6. Simmer for 30 minutes.
7. Cool overnight in ooze.
8. Rinse thoroughly.
9. Dry in shade.

174/NEW ZEALAND FLAX SEED PODS AND AMMONIA (Phormium tenax)

MAUVE: ALUMED WOOL; GOOD LIGHT-FASTNESS.

TEXTILE
Scoured, presoaked, alum-mordanted wool (2 ounces)

INGREDIENTS
Seed pods, split open (4 ounces)
Tin crystals (dissolved in 1 cup of hot water immediately before using) (pinch or 1/16 teaspoon)
Ammonia, clear (in 1 quart of water) (1 teaspoon)

WATER
Tap (enough to cover textile)

POT
Nonreacting

METHOD
1. Cover pods and textile with water.
2. Simmer for 30 minutes.
3. Remove textile.
4. Add tin solution.
5. Reenter textile.
6. Simmer for 30 minutes.
7. Cool.
8. Remove plant material and textile from bath.
9. Stir in ammonia solution.
10. Reenter textile.
11. Soak overnight.
12. Rinse thoroughly.
13. Dry in shade.

175/RED HIBISCUS, ROSE MALLOW (Hibiscus spp.)

VARIOUS DARK BLUES: ALUMED WOOL; GOOD LIGHTFASTNESS.
VARIOUS DARK GREENS: CHROMED WOOL; GOOD LIGHTFASTNESS.

Tropical shrubs of the Mallow Family. Grown in protected areas away from the cold. Flowers may be dried and used for coloring beverages.

TEXTILE
Scoured, presoaked, alum- or chrome-mordanted wool (1 ounce)

INGREDIENT
Flowers (2 ounces)

WATER
Distilled (enough to cover textile)

POT
Coffee can or tin pail

METHOD
1. Cover flowers and textile with water.
2. Simmer for 20 minutes.
3. Cool overnight in ooze.
4. Rinse thoroughly.
5. Dry in shade.

NOTE: Variable dye plant. Dye tends toward black with the slightest provocation.

176/RED HIBISCUS AND TIN CRYSTALS

PURPLE: CHROMED WOOL; GOOD LIGHT-FASTNESS.

TEXTILE
Scoured, presoaked, chrome-mordanted wool (1 ounce)

INGREDIENTS
Flowers (2 ounces)
Tin crystals (dissolved in 1 cup of hot water immediately before using) (pinch or 1/16 teaspoon)
Iodized salt (1 teaspoon)

WATER
Distilled (enough to cover textile)

POT
Nonreacting

METHOD
1. Combine flowers, tin solution, salt, water, and wool.
2. Simmer for 20 minutes.
3. Cool overnight in ooze.
4. Rinse thoroughly.
5. Dry in shade.

177/HONEY BUSH AND TIN CRYSTALS

VIOLET: ALUMED WOOL; GOOD LIGHTFASTNESS.

Large-leaved shrub from South Africa. Grown as an ornamental in warm climates. Melianthus Family.

TEXTILE

Scoured, presoaked, alum-mordanted wool (1 ounce)

INGREDIENTS

Flowers (6 ounces)

Tin crystals (dissolved in 1 cup of hot water immediately before using) (pinch or ⅟₁₆ teaspoon)

WATER

Distilled (enough to cover textile).

POT

Nonreacting

METHOD

1. Cover flowers and textile with water.
2. Heat to simmer.
3. Remove textile.
4. Add tin solution.
5. Reenter textile.
6. Simmer for 30 minutes.
7. Cool overnight in ooze.
8. Rinse thoroughly.
9. Dry in shade.

178/INDIA-HAWTHORN (Raphiolepis indica)

DARK BLUE: ALUMED WOOL; FAIR LIGHT-FASTNESS.
TURQUOISE: CHROMED WOOL; FAIR LIGHT-FASTNESS.

Evergreen shrub, four to five feet high, with pinkish flowers and blue-black fruit. Grown for ornament. Member of Rose Family. An interesting dye plant because it yields various blue colors. Variable results, probably due to seasonal changes.

TEXTILE

Scoured, presoaked, alum- or chrome-mordanted wool (1 ounce)

INGREDIENT

Fruit, crushed (4 ounces)

WATER

Distilled (enough to cover textile)

POT

Nonreacting

METHOD

1. Cover fruit with water.
2. Begin simmering.
3. Crush berries in pot with potato masher while simmering.
4. Simmer until bath is dark magenta, about 10 minutes. Cool.
5. Enter textile.
6. Simmer for 20 minutes.
7. Cool overnight in ooze.
8. Rinse thoroughly.
9. Dry in shade.

Figure 73 INDIA-HAWTHORN (*Raphiolepis indica*)

179/INDIA-HAWTHORN AND TIN CRYSTALS
(Raphiolepis indica)
PURPLE: ALUMED WOOL; GOOD LIGHTFAST-NESS.

TEXTILE
Scoured, presoaked, alum-mordanted wool (1 ounce)

INGREDIENTS
Fruit, crushed (4 ounces)
Tin crystals (dissolved in 1 cup of hot water immediately before using) (pinch or 1/16 teaspoon)

WATER
Distilled (enough to cover textile)

POT
Nonreacting

METHOD
1. Cover fruit and textile with water.
2. Heat to simmer.
3. Remove textile.
4. Add tin solution.
5. Reenter textile.
6. Simmer for 20 minutes.
7. Cool overnight in ooze.
8. Rinse thoroughly.
9. Dry in shade.

NOTE: An ammonia afterbath turns the textile green.

180/PURPLE LILAC
(Syringa spp.)
LIGHT GREEN (STEP I): ALUMED WOOL; GOOD LIGHTFASTNESS.
LIGHT BLUE-GREEN (STEP II): ALUMED WOOL; GOOD LIGHTFASTNESS.

One of our oldest garden shrubs, linked romantically with beautiful women. Olive Family. Introduced to Britain during the reign of Henry VII. Growing directions are as follows: "A little sun, a little soil, a little rain, and a little toil." Good vermifuge.

TEXTILE
Scoured, presoaked, alum-mordanted wool (1 ounce)

INGREDIENT
Flowers, fresh (4 ounces)

WATER
Distilled (enough to cover textile)

POT
Nonreacting

METHOD
Step I
1. Cover flowers and textile with water.
2. Simmer for 15 minutes.
For light green color: Remove textile, rinse thoroughly, and dry in shade.
3. *For light blue-green* (obtainable occasionally): Proceed to Step II.

Step II
1. Simmer for 15 minutes longer.
2. Cool overnight in ooze.
3. Rinse thoroughly.
4. Dry in shade.

NOTE: An ammonia after-rinse deepens the green color.

181/PURPLE LILAC, LEAVES IN IRON POT*
(Syringa spp.)
VARIOUS GREENS: UNMORDANTED WOOL, COTTON, JUTE, OR LINEN; GOOD LIGHT-FASTNESS.
DARK GREEN: ALUMED WOOL; GOOD LIGHT-FASTNESS.
DARK BROWN: ALUMED WOOL AND AM-MONIA; GOOD LIGHTFASTNESS.

TEXTILE
Scoured, presoaked, unmordanted fibers, or alum-mordanted wool (1 ounce)

INGREDIENTS
Leaves (5 ounces)
Ammonia, clear (in 1 quart of water) for brown only (1 teaspoon)

WATER
Distilled (enough to cover textile)

POT
Iron

METHOD
1. Cover leaves and textile with water.
2. Simmer for 45 minutes.
3. Remove from pot when cooled.
4. Rinse thoroughly.

5. Dry in shade.
6. *For brown*: Dip dyed alumed wool in ammonia afterbath, rinse thoroughly.
7. Dry in shade.

182 / PURPLE LILAC, TWIGS
(Syringa spp.)
YELLOW-ORANGE: CHROMED WOOL; GOOD LIGHTFASTNESS.

TEXTILE
Scoured, presoaked, chrome-mordanted wool (1 ounce)

INGREDIENT
Twigs, cut up (5 ounces)

WATER
Distilled (enough to cover textile)

POT
Nonreacting

METHOD
1. Cover twigs and wool with water.
2. Simmer for 30 minutes.
3. Cool overnight in ooze.
4. Rinse thoroughly.
5. Dry in shade.

183 / RED FLOWERING MAPLE
(Abutilon hybridum)
NAVY BLUE: ALUMED WOOL; GOOD LIGHT-FASTNESS.

Evergreen, rangy shrub. Large hibiscus-like flowers. Relative of the hibiscus, hollyhock, and other mallows. Has dye properties similar to its relatives.

TEXTILE
Scoured, presoaked, alum-mordanted wool (1 ounce)

INGREDIENTS
Petals and centers (3 ounces)
Tin crystals (dissolved in 1 cup of hot water immediately before using) (pinch or 1/16 teaspoon)
Cream of tartar (dissolved in 1 cup of hot water) (1 teaspoon)
Iodized salt (pinch)

WATER
Distilled (enough to cover textile)

POT
Nonreacting

METHOD
1. Cover plant material and textile with water.
2. Heat gently for 5 minutes.

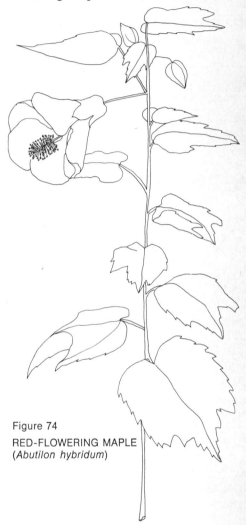

Figure 74

RED-FLOWERING MAPLE
(*Abutilon hybridum*)

3. Remove textile.
4. Stir in tin solution, cream of tartar solution, and salt.
5. Enter textile.
6. Simmer for 45 minutes.
7. Cool overnight in ooze.
8. Rinse thoroughly.
9. Dry in shade.
NOTE: Color varies.

184/DARK-PINK OLEANDER
(Nerium oleander)

LIGHT GRAY-GREEN: ALUMED WOOL; GOOD LIGHTFASTNESS.

MEDIUM GRAY-GREEN: CHROMED WOOL; GOOD LIGHTFASTNESS.

Tough, gray-green shrub. Member of the Dogbane Family. Originated in the Mediterranean region. Periwinkle is a well-known relative. Oleander thrives in heat. Used along driveways and roads in warm climates. Poisonous. Unexpectedly, the flowers yield a fine green dye.

TEXTILE
Scoured, presoaked, alum- or chrome-mordanted wool (1 ounce)

INGREDIENT
Flowers (6 ounces)

WATER
Distilled (enough to cover textile)

POT
Nonreacting

METHOD
1. Cover flowers and textile with water.
2. Simmer for 30 minutes.
3. Cool overnight in ooze.
4. Rinse thoroughly.
5. Dry in shade.

185/POINSETTIA LEAVES
(Euphorbia pulcherrima)

GREENISH BROWN: ALUMED WOOL; FAIR LIGHTFASTNESS.

Euphorbia Family. Originally from Mexico. The Christmas pot plant yields several other colors which are beautiful, but not lightfast. Perhaps further experiment will lead to more stable color. According to the Aztec codices, good dye recipes for this plant were once known.

TEXTILE
Scoured, presoaked, alum-mordanted wool (1 ounce)

INGREDIENTS
Leaves (3 ounces)

Chrome (dissolved in 1 quart of water) ($\frac{1}{8}$ teaspoon)
Iodized salt (1 teaspoon)

WATER
Distilled (enough to cover textile)

POT
Nonreacting

METHOD
1. Cover leaves and textile with water.
2. Add salt.
3. Simmer for 30 minutes.
4. Remove leaves. Textile may now be purple but it is not fast color.
5. Simmer for 30 minutes more.
6. Cool overnight in ooze.
7. Transfer textile to chrome solution.
8. Heat gently for 10 minutes.
9. Rinse thoroughly.
10. Dry in shade.

186/RHODODENDRON
LEAVES IN IRON POT
(Rhododendron spp.)

GRAY-GREEN: ALUMED WOOL; GOOD LIGHTFASTNESS.

There are 800-plus species of *Rhododendron*, mostly from the Himalayas and eastern Asia, a few in North America. Cultivated hybrid varieties abound. Can be found in the wild state and lifted when dormant. Leaves are a good source of gray color. The flowers, colorful and lush as they are, have been disappointing dye subjects.

TEXTILE
Scoured, presoaked, alum-mordanted wool (1 ounce)

INGREDIENT
Leaves (6 ounces)

WATER
Tap (enough to cover textile)

POTS
Step I
Nonreacting

Step II
Iron

METHOD
Step I
1. Cover leaves and textile with water in nonreacting pot.
2. Steep overnight.

Step II
1. Transfer contents to iron pot.
2. Simmer for 30 minutes.
3. Cool for 1 hour.
4. Rinse thoroughly.
5. Dry in shade.

187 / RED-FLOWERED NEW ZEALAND TEA TREE
(Leptospermum scoparium)
MEDIUM YELLOW-GREEN: ALUMED OR CHROMED WOOL; GOOD LIGHTFASTNESS.

Large shrub with tiny leaves and numerous rather small flowers. Belongs to the Myrtle Family. Resists wind. Makes a good hedge. Called "tea tree" because the surgeon on Captain Cook's third voyage in 1773 gave a tea made from leaves of *L. scoparium* to the scurvy-sick crew. Makes a surprisingly lively green dye.

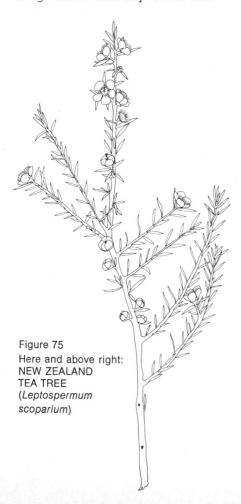

Figure 75
Here and above right:
NEW ZEALAND
TEA TREE
(*Leptospermum scoparium*)

TEXTILE
Scoured, presoaked, alum- or chrome-mordanted wool (1 ounce)

INGREDIENTS
Flowers, branches, leaves (about 5 ounces)
Iodized salt (1 teaspoon)

WATER
Distilled (enough to cover textile)

POT
Tin pail

METHOD
1. Cover plants with water.
2. Heat in pail.
3. Enter wool and salt.
4. Simmer for 20 minutes.
5. Remove wool from dye bath.
6. Rinse thoroughly.
7. Dry in shade.

188 / RED-FLOWERED NEW ZEALAND TEA TREE IN IRON POT
(Leptospermum scoparium)
GREENISH BLACK: ALUMED WOOL; GOOD LIGHTFASTNESS.

TEXTILE
Scoured, presoaked, alum-mordanted wool (1 ounce)

INGREDIENT
Flowers (4 ounces)

WATER
Tap (enough to cover textile)

POTS
Step I
Nonreacting

Step II
Iron

METHOD
Step I
1. Cover flowers and wool with water.
2. Simmer for 30 minutes in non-reacting pot.

Step II
1. Transfer to iron pot.
2. Simmer for 20 minutes.
3. Cool overnight in ooze.
4. Rinse thoroughly.
5. Dry in shade.

16

Tree recipes

189/ ACACIA, FLOWERS
(**Acacia** sp.)
YELLOW: ALUMED WOOL; GOOD LIGHT-FASTNESS.
GRAYED MAIZE YELLOW TO LIGHT GOLDEN BROWN: CHROMED WOOL; GOOD LIGHTFASTNESS.

Member of the Pea Family. Fast-growing tree that has escaped from cultivation. Can be seen as a volunteer in many parts of California. Begins flowering early in the San Francisco Bay area. If you need to dye a lot of wool in midwinter, try the acacia.

TEXTILE
Scoured, presoaked, alum- or chrome-mordanted wool (1 ounce)

INGREDIENTS
Flowers and stems, fresh (6 ounces)
Salt (dissolved in 1 cup of hot water) (2 teaspoons)

WATER
Tap (enough to cover textile)

POT
Nonreacting

METHOD
1. Combine plant material, salt solution, water, and textile.
2. Simmer for 30 minutes.
3. Cool overnight in ooze.
4. Rinse thoroughly.
5. Dry in shade.

190/ ACACIA, PODS
(**Acacia** sp.)
MOSS GREEN OR TAN: ALUMED WOOL; GOOD LIGHTFASTNESS.

TEXTILE
Scoured, presoaked, alum-mordanted wool (1 ounce)

INGREDIENTS
Pods, fresh or dry (6 ounces)
Salt (2 teaspoons)

WATER
Tap (enough to cover textile)

POT
Nonreacting

METHOD
1. Combine plant, water, and textile.
2. Simmer for 30 minutes.
3. Cool overnight in ooze.
4. Rinse thoroughly.
5. Dry in shade.

NOTE: Color varies according to whether pods are fresh or dry, and according to species.

191/ BOTTLE BRUSH, FLOWERS*
(**Callistemon** sp.)
TAN. UNMORDANTED WOOL; FAIR LIGHT-FASTNESS.
GREENISH BEIGE: ALUMED WOOL; FAIR LIGHTFASTNESS.

Australian trees and shrubs. Member of the Myrtle Family. Grown for their showy flower spikes, which resemble bottle brushes. The dye bath is a beautiful magenta and aromatic. It is most frustrating that only beige-tan colors result. Experiment!

TEXTILE
Scoured, presoaked, unmordanted or alum-mordanted wool (1 ounce)

INGREDIENT
Flowers (2 ounces)

WATER
Tap (enough to cover textile)

POT
Nonreacting

METHOD
1. Combine flowers, water, and textile.
2. Simmer for 1 hour.
3. Cool overnight in ooze.
4. Rinse thoroughly.
5. Dry in shade.

Figure 76 BOTTLE BRUSH
(*Callistemon* sp.)

192/BOTTLE BRUSH, LEAVES
(Callistemon sp.)
CINNAMON BROWN: ALUMED WOOL; GOOD LIGHTFASTNESS.

TEXTILE
Scoured, presoaked, alum-mordanted wool (1 ounce)

INGREDIENTS
Leaves (8 ounces)
Chrome (dissolved in 1 cup of hot water) (1/8 teaspoon)

WATER
Tap (enough to cover textile)

POT
Nonreacting

METHOD
1. Boil leaves and water for 1 hour.
2. Cool.
3. Stir in chrome dissolved in 1 cup of hot water.

4. Enter wool and simmer for 45 minutes.
5. Cool overnight in ooze.
6. Rinse thoroughly.
7. Dry in shade.

NOTE: For 1/2 pound of wool use 2 pounds of leaves, 1/4 teaspoon chrome, and 1/2 teaspoon of cream of tartar.

193/CANARY WOOD, STEEPED*
(Morus mesozygia)
MAIZE YELLOW: UNMORDANTED WOOL; GOOD LIGHTFASTNESS (DARKENS SLIGHTLY) AND GOOD WASHFASTNESS.
TURMERIC GOLD: ALUMED WOOL; GOOD LIGHTFASTNESS AND GOOD WASHFASTNESS.

Mulberry Family. Tree, from East Africa. Also known as East African mulberry. The wood is valued for its hardness and color. Used in fine wood art-crafts.

TEXTILE
Scoured, presoaked, unmordanted or alum-mordanted wool (1 ounce)

INGREDIENT
Wood shavings (in net bag if preferred) (about 4 cups or 1 ounce)

WATER
Rain water or distilled (enough to cover textile)

POT
Nonreacting

METHOD
1. Combine shavings and water.
2. Boil for 1 hour. Cool.
3. Enter textile and steep for 1 to 2 days.
4. Rinse thoroughly.
5. Dry in shade.

NOTES: For 1 pound of goods use about 1/2 pound of wood. □ White knitting yarn, unmordanted, dyes a strong lemon yellow.

194/CANARY WOOD
(Morus mesozygia)
TERRA-COTTA: CHROMED WOOL; GOOD LIGHTFASTNESS AND GOOD WASHFASTNESS.
BURNT ORANGE: ALUMED WOOL; GOOD LIGHTFASTNESS AND GOOD WASHFASTNESS.

TEXTILE

Scoured, presoaked, chrome-mordanted wool (1 ounce)

INGREDIENT

Wood shavings (in net bag if preferred) (4 cups or 1 ounce)

WATER

Tap (enough to cover textile)

POT

Nonreacting

METHOD

1. Combine shavings and water.
2. Boil for 1 hour.
3. Cool.
4. Enter textile and simmer for 30 minutes.
5. Cool overnight in ooze.
6. Rinse thoroughly.
7. Dry in shade.

NOTE: For 1 pound of wool use about 1/2 pound of wood.

195/CANARY WOOD AND TIN CRYSTALS
(Morus mesozygia)

PUMPKIN ORANGE: CHROMED WOOL; GOOD LIGHTFASTNESS AND GOOD WASHFASTNESS.

TEXTILE

Scoured, presoaked, chrome-mordanted wool (1 ounce)

INGREDIENTS

Wood shavings (in net bag if preferred) (2 cups or 1 ounce)

Tin crystals (dissolved in 1 cup of hot water immediately before using) (pinch or 1/16 teaspoon)

WATER

Rain water or distilled (enough to cover textile)

POT

Nonreacting

METHOD

1. Combine shavings and water.
2. Boil for 1 hour.
3. Cool.
4. Stir in tin solution.
5. Enter wool and simmer for 30 minutes.
6. Cool overnight in ooze.
7. Rinse thoroughly.

8. Dry in shade.

NOTE: For 1/2 pound of wool use 1/2 pound of wood, 1/6 ounce of tin, and 1/6 ounce of cream of tartar.

196/CORALLINE
(Clutia tranvancorica)

PALE APRICOT: ALUMED COTTON; GOOD LIGHTFASTNESS.
BRILLIANT ORANGE: ALUMED WOOL; GOOD LIGHTFASTNESS.

An exotic hardwood prized for its orange-red color. Some of the exotic woods can be purchased from dealers in fine woods. See listing in Appendix.

TEXTILE

Scoured, presoaked, alum-mordanted cotton or wool (1 ounce)

INGREDIENT

Wood shavings (in net bag if preferred) (1 1/2 ounces)

WATER

Tap (enough to cover textile)

POT

Aluminum

METHOD

1. Combine shavings, water, and textile.
2. Simmer for 30 minutes.
3. Cool overnight in ooze.
4. Rinse thoroughly.
5. Dry in shade.

197/CORALLINE IN IRON POT
(Clutia tranvancorica)

DARK BROWN: ALUMED WOOL; GOOD LIGHTFASTNESS AND GOOD WASHFASTNESS.

TEXTILE

Scoured, presoaked, alum-mordanted wool (1 ounce)

INGREDIENT

Wood shavings (in net bag if preferred) (1 1/2 ounces)

WATER

Tap (enough to cover textile)

POTS

Step I
Nonreacting

Step II
Iron

METHOD
Step I
1. Combine shavings, water, and textile, in nonreacting pot.
2. Simmer for 1 hour.

Step II
1. Pour ooze and textile into iron pot.
2. Simmer until desired shade is achieved.
3. Cool.
4. Rinse thoroughly.
5. Dry in shade.

198/CORALLINE AND TIN CRYSTALS
(Clutia tranvancorica)
BRILLIANT ORANGE-RED TO VERMILION: ALUMED WOOL; GOOD LIGHTFASTNESS.
MAROON-ORANGE: ALUMED GRAY WOOL; GOOD LIGHTFASTNESS AND GOOD WASH-FASTNESS.

TEXTILE
Scoured, presoaked, alum-mordanted wool (natural or gray) (1 ounce)

INGREDIENTS
Wood shavings (in net bag if preferred) (1½ ounces)

Tin crystals (dissolved in 1 cup of hot water immediately before using) (pinch or ⅟₁₆ teaspoon)

WATER
Tap (enough to cover textile)

POT
Nonreacting

METHOD
1. Combine shavings, tin solution, water, and textile.
2. Simmer for 1 hour.
3. Cool overnight in ooze.
4. Rinse thoroughly. Save ooze and use for deeper red.
5. Dry in shade.
6. *For deeper red:* Soak dry dyed textile in water for 1 hour, enter in original ooze, simmer for 45 minutes longer, cool overnight in ooze, rinse thoroughly, and dry in shade.

NOTE: For ½ pound of textile use 6 ounces of wood, ⅙ ounce of tin, and ⅙ ounce of cream of tartar.

199/EUCALYPTUS, SILVER-DOLLAR, AND TIN CRYSTALS*
(Eucalyptus polyanthemos)
VARIOUS BRILLIANT ORANGES: ALUMED WOOL; GOOD LIGHTFASTNESS AND GOOD WASHFASTNESS.
LIGHT ORANGE: UNMORDANTED WOOL; GOOD LIGHTFASTNESS AND GOOD WASH-FASTNESS.

My work, as far as I know, is the first published United States mention of *Eucalyptus polyanthemos* as a source of red and orange dye. Three recipes are included, each demonstrating a variation in technique.

TEXTILE
Scoured, presoaked, unmordanted or alum-mordanted wool (1 ounce)

INGREDIENTS
Leaves (6 ounces)

Tin crystals (dissolved in 1 cup of hot water immediately before using) (pinch or ⅟₁₆ teaspoon)

WATER
Distilled (enough to cover textile)

POT
Nonreacting or tin

METHOD
1. Combine leaves, water, and textile.
2. Simmer for 30 minutes.
3. Remove textile.
4. Stir in tin dissolved in hot water.
5. Reenter textile.
6. Simmer for 15 minutes more.
7. Cool overnight in ooze.
8. Rinse thoroughly.
9. Dry in shade.

200/EUCALYPTUS, SILVER-DOLLAR VARIATION*
(Eucalyptus polyanthemos)
VARIATIONS OF BRILLIANT RED-ORANGE: UNMORDANTED WOOL; GOOD LIGHTFAST-NESS.
ORANGE-RED: CHROMED WOOL; GOOD LIGHTFASTNESS AND GOOD WASHFASTNESS.

This recipe represents the first United States discovery of eucalyptus as a possible source of red dye. Good light and washfastness. Four well-known brands of white two-ply knitting worsted were used. My usual two-ply weaving yarn was also used as a control. Result: three brands dyed almost red, one brand dyed red. Weaving yarn: only a tiny bit redder than the knitting yarn.

TEXTILE
Scoured, presoaked, unmordanted or chrome-mordanted wool (1 ounce)

INGREDIENTS
Leaves (6 ounces)
Tin crystals (dissolved in 1 cup of hot water immediately before using) (pinch or 1/16 teaspoon)

WATER
Tap (enough to cover textile)

POT
Nonreacting or tin

METHOD
1. Cover leaves and textile with water.
2. Boil for 1 hour.
3. Cool.
4. Remove textile from bath.
5. Stir in tin solution.
6. Reenter textile.
7. Simmer for 2 hours.
8. Cool overnight in ooze.
9. Rinse thoroughly.
10. Dry in shade.

201/EUCALYPTUS, SILVER-DOLLAR WITH TIN CRYSTALS AND CHROME*
(Eucalyptus polyanthemos)
RED TO MAROON: UNMORDANTED WOOL; GOOD LIGHTFASTNESS AND GOOD WASHFASTNESS.

TEXTILE
Scoured, presoaked, unmordanted wool (1 ounce)

INGREDIENTS
Young leaves (8 ounces)

Tin crystals (dissolved in 1 cup of hot water) (pinch or 1/16 teaspoon)
Cream of tartar (dissolved in 1 cup of water) (1 tablespoon)
Chrome (dissolved in 1 cup of hot water) (1/4 teaspoon)

WATER
Tap (enough to cover textile)

POT
Nonreacting

METHOD
1. Combine leaves and water.
2. Bring to simmer.
3. Stir in tin and cream of tartar solutions.
4. Boil for 1 hour. Cool.
5. Enter textile.
6. Simmer for 1 1/2 hours longer.
7. Remove textile.
8. Stir in chrome solution. Cool.
9. Reenter textile.
10. Simmer for another 30 minutes (total of 3 hours simmering).
11. Cool overnight in ooze.
12. Rinse thoroughly.
13. Dry in shade.

202/EUCALYPTUS, BLUE-GUM, BARK
(Eucalyptus globulus)
VARIATIONS OF DARK KHAKI GREEN: ALUMED WOOL; GOOD LIGHTFASTNESS.

Australian native of huge size and messy habit. Member of the Myrtle Family. Used as a windbreak in many parts of California and the Southwest. There are 600 or more species of eucalyptus; ninety or so are grown in California. Oil of eucalyptus can be purchased in a pharmacy and is used as an antiseptic. Vapors from dyeing with any *Eucalyptus* can give one a headache, so work in a well-ventilated room or outdoors.

TEXTILE
Scoured, presoaked, alum-mordanted wool (1 ounce)

INGREDIENTS
Young bark, torn up (1 quart)
Ammonia, clear (in 1 quart of

water) (1 teaspoon)

WATER
Tap (enough to cover textile)

POT
Tin can

METHOD
1. Soak bark in water overnight.
2. Boil for 1 hour.
3. Cool.
4. Enter textile and simmer for 1 hour.
5. Cool overnight in ooze.
6. Dip dyed textile in ammonia rinse.
7. Rinse thoroughly.
8. Dry in shade.

203/EUCALYPTUS, BLUE-GUM, LEAVES*
(Eucalyptus globulus)
DEEP CAMEL TAN: UNMORDANTED WOOL; GOOD LIGHTFASTNESS.

The air is fragrant where this euca-lyptus grows. Bees favor the flowers and honey produced in a euca-lyptus area bears a strong flavor. The leaves may be crushed and steeped and used as a medicinal tea. The smoke from dried leaves is said to be of some benefit in asthma.

TEXTILE
Scoured, presoaked, unmordanted wool (1 ounce)

INGREDIENT
Young gray leaves (3 ounces)

WATER
Tap (enough to cover textile)

POT
Nonreacting

METHOD
1. Combine leaves, water, and textile.
2. Steep overnight.
3. Boil gently for 2 hours.
4. Cool overnight in ooze.
5. Rinse thoroughly.
6. Dry in shade.

NOTE: Four brands of knitting wool

(2-ply white) were also tested. The result was a beautiful ocher-camel color.

204/EUCALYPTUS, BLUE-GUM, LEAVES IN IRON POT
(Eucalyptus globulus)
LIGHT TO DARK GREEN: ALUMED WOOL; GOOD LIGHTFASTNESS.
CHARCOAL GRAY: ALUMED COTTON; GOOD LIGHTFASTNESS.

TEXTILE
Scoured, presoaked, alum-mor-danted cotton or wool (1 ounce)

INGREDIENT
New shoots of tree (about 3 ounces)

WATER
Tap (enough to cover textile)

POT
Iron

METHOD
1. Combine shoots, water, and textile.
2. Simmer for 1 hour. Wool is light green at this stage.
3. Simmer for 1 hour more for dark green textile or gray cotton.
4. Cool.
5. Rinse thoroughly.
6. Dry in shade.

205/EUCALYPTUS, TASMANIAN SNOW-GUM
(Eucalyptus cocifera)
MUSTARD GOLD (STEP I): ALUMED WOOL; GOOD LIGHTFASTNESS AND GOOD WASH-FASTNESS.
DARK OLIVE GREEN (STEP II): ALUMED WOOL; GOOD LIGHTFASTNESS AND GOOD WASHFASTNESS.

This is a hardy species from Tas-mania.

TEXTILE
Scoured, presoaked, alum-mor-danted wool (1 ounce)

INGREDIENT
Leaves (6 ounces)

WATER
Tap (enough to cover textile)

POTS
Step I

Nonreacting

Step II

Iron

METHOD

Step I

1. Cover leaves with water in non-reacting pot.
2. Boil for 1 hour.
3. Cool.
4. Enter textile.
5. Simmer for 30 minutes.

Step II

1. Pour ooze and textile into iron pot.
2. Simmer for 30 minutes.
3. Cool.
4. Wash in soapy water.
5. Rinse thoroughly.
6. Dry in shade.

206 / WHITE-IRON BARK EUCALYPTUS, LEAVES AND PODS*
(Eucalyptus leucoxylon)

MEDIUM OR DEEP BURNT ORANGE: ALUMED WOOL; GOOD LIGHTFASTNESS.
DULL ORANGE TO TERRA-COTTA: UNMORDANTED WOOL; GOOD LIGHTFASTNESS.

As far as I know, this recipe represents the first United States discovery of eucalyptus as a source of orange dye. I have been teaching my students this recipe for many years. Recently I read of eucalyptus dye experiments in Australia. It has been found that dye *potency* in leaves is *less* after a rain. Actual color changes occur also.

TEXTILE

Scoured, presoaked, unmordanted or alum-mordanted wool (1 ounce)

INGREDIENTS

Leaves and green pods (about 7 ounces)

WATER

Tap (enough to cover textile)

POT

Nonreacting

METHOD

1. Combine plant material, water, and textile.
2. Simmer for 1½ hours.

3. *For medium orange:* Cool, rinse, and dry at this point.
4. *For deep orange:* Simmer for 1½ hours longer.
5. Cool overnight in ooze.
6. Rinse thoroughly.
7. Dry in shade.

207 / MEALY OR ASHY STRINGYBARK EUCALYPTUS*
(Eucalyptus cinerea)

RED-MAROON: ALUMED WOOL; GOOD LIGHTFASTNESS.
RED-ORANGE: UNMORDANTED WOOL; GOOD LIGHTFASTNESS AND GOOD WASHFASTNESS.

TEXTILE

Scoured, presoaked, alum-mordanted or unmordanted wool (1 ounce)

INGREDIENT

Leaves (7 ounces)

WATER

Tap (enough to cover textile)

POT

Nonreacting

METHOD

1. Combine leaves, water, and textile.
2. Simmer for 3 hours (maroon color appears in last half hour).
3. Cool overnight in ooze.
4. Rinse thoroughly.
5. Dry in shade.

NOTE: Remember that the eucalyptus, as potent as it is, will yield varying results under varying climatic conditions.

208 / CALIFORNIA LAUREL, BAY TREE, FRUIT
(Umbellularia californica)

ROSY BEIGE: ALUMED WOOL; GOOD LIGHTFASTNESS; AROMATIC.
KHAKI GREEN: CHROMED WOOL; GOOD LIGHTFASTNESS; AROMATIC.

Evergreen member of the Laurel Family. Found along Pacific slope from southern Oregon to southern California. Abundant in my meadow—seems as though every other seed takes root! The dried leaves are used in cooking; when I need bay seasoning, I just step outside and pick a leaf off a tree. A medicinal oil is made from the leaves. It is said that the leaves act as flea repellent. I use them as a sinus clearer thus: cover one nostril and hold a crushed, fresh bay leaf to the open nostril. Sniff. Reverse the procedure, covering the other nostril and sniffing. *Easy on the sniff* —the volatile oil is *very* potent.

The dyer and the squirrels can both make use of the bay fruit. The squirrels neatly trim off the pulp surrounding the nut, dropping it to the ground. They store the nut. Good. The dyer needs the fruit without the nut. When the bay fruit is being simmered for dyeing, the kitchen is exquisitely fragrant. The fruit imparts a lasting fragrance to dyed yarn. I have some wool dyed in 1964 that is still fragrant today, November 1973! This is one of the pleasures of dyeing with bay fruit or flowers.

TEXTILE
Scoured, presoaked, alum- or chrome-mordanted wool (1 ounce)

INGREDIENTS
Bay fruit, pits removed (3 cups)
Alum (dissolved in 1 cup of hot water) (1 teaspoon)
Cream of tartar (dissolved in 1 cup of hot water) (1 teaspoon)

WATER
Tap (enough to cover textile)

POT
Nonreacting

METHOD
1. Presoak bay fruit in water overnight.
2. Simmer until fruit is soft.
3. Remove pits.
4. Combine fruit pulp, alum, cream of tartar, and additional water to cover.
5. Enter wool.
6. Simmer for 30 minutes.
7. Cool overnight in ooze.

8. Rinse thoroughly.
9. Dry in shade.

209/CALIFORNIA LAUREL, BAY TREE, FLOWERS (Umbellularia californica)

GREENISH BEIGE: ALUMED WOOL; GOOD LIGHTFASTNESS; AROMATIC.

This recipe is included not because it yields a spectacular color but because of the availability of aromatic plant material to Californians.

TEXTILE
Scoured, presoaked, alum-mordanted wool (1 ounce)

INGREDIENT
Flowers, crushed (4 ounces)

WATER
Tap (enough to cover textile)

POT
Nonreacting

METHOD
1. Combine flowers and water.
2. Soak overnight.
3. Enter textile.
4. Simmer for 30 minutes.
5. Cool overnight in ooze.
6. Rinse thoroughly.
7. Dry in shade.

NOTE: Non-Californian dyers can try spicing their textiles with dried bay leaves. I wish there was time to tell you the story of my aromatic Mexican yarn. If we meet, ask me.

210/HAWTHORN, BLOSSOMS (Crataegus sp.)

VARIATIONS OF YELLOW-GREEN: ALUMED WOOL; GOOD LIGHTFASTNESS.
VARIATIONS OF GOLD-BROWN: CHROMED WOOL; GOOD LIGHTFASTNESS.

Small trees or shrubs. Member of the Rose Family. Richly flowering, followed by small applelike fruit. Used as lawn specimens. Jelly is made from the fruit.

TEXTILE
Scoured, presoaked, alum- or chrome-mordanted wool (1 ounce)

INGREDIENT
Blossoms (8 ounces)

WATER
Tap (enough to cover textile)

POT
Nonreacting

METHOD
1. Combine blossoms, water, and textile.
2. Simmer for 30 minutes.
3. Cool overnight in ooze.
4. Rinse thoroughly.
5. Dry in shade.

211 / MADRONE BARK*
(Arbutus menziesii)

VARIATIONS OF WARM BROWN: ALUMED WOOL; GOOD LIGHTFASTNESS.
VARIATIONS OF GOLD-TAN: UNMORDANTED WOOL; GOOD LIGHTFASTNESS.

Native West Coast tree of the Heath Family. Noted for its smooth, red, terra-cotta flaky bark and hardwood. Tea made from bark was used for stomach aches. Native Americans also prepared a lotion from the bark and leaves for curing cuts and sores. Tools, lodgepoles, and stirrups were made from the wood. As a dye source, use in spring or summer.

TEXTILE
Scoured, presoaked, unmordanted or alum-mordanted wool (1 ounce)

INGREDIENT
Bark, cut up and pounded (4 ounces)

WATER
Tap (enough to cover textile)

POT
Nonreacting

METHOD
1. Soak bark in water overnight.
2. Simmer for 1 hour.
3. Cool.
4. Enter textile.
5. Simmer for 1 hour.
6. Rinse thoroughly.
7. Dry in shade.

NOTE: An ammonia rinse (½ teaspoon in 1 quart of water) darkens the color.

212 / MADRONE BARK ON COTTON AND JUTE*
(Arbutus menziesii)

ROSE-BEIGE: UNMORDANTED COTTON OR LINEN; GOOD LIGHTFASTNESS.
CHESTNUT BROWN: UNMORDANTED JUTE; GOOD LIGHTFASTNESS.

TEXTILE
Scoured, presoaked, unmordanted cotton, linen, or jute (1 ounce)

INGREDIENT
Bark, cut up and pounded (1 ounce)

WATER
Tap (enough to cover textile)

POT
Nonreacting

METHOD
1. Soak bark in water overnight.
2. Simmer for 1 hour.
3. Cool.
4. Enter textile.
5. Simmer for 1 hour.
6. Cool overnight in ooze.
7. Simmer and cool again overnight.
8. Repeat for several days.
9. Rinse thoroughly.
10. Dry in shade.

NOTE: Longer steeping deepens the color.

213 / SILK OAK*
(Grevillea robusta)

INTENSE CANARY YELLOW (STEP I): UNMORDANTED WOOL; GOOD LIGHTFASTNESS.
OLIVE GREEN (STEP II): UNMORDANTED WOOL; GOOD LIGHTFASTNESS.

An Australian tree. Member of the Protea Family. Grown for its fernlike leaves and resistance to dry heat. A spectacular dye plant. Yields beautiful, intense yellows and subtle greens on unmordanted wool.

TEXTILE
Scoured, presoaked, unmordanted wool (2 ounces)

INGREDIENTS
Leaves (3 ounces)

Alum (dissolved in 1 cup of hot water) (1 tablespoon)
Salt (1 tablespoon)
Vinegar (for olive green only) (3 tablespoons)

WATER
Distilled (enough to cover textile)

POTS
Step I
Nonreacting
Step II
Iron

METHOD
Step I
1. Heat leaves and water for 10 minutes in nonreacting pot.
2. Add alum and salt. Cool.
3. Enter textile.
4. Simmer for 30 minutes.
5. Cool overnight.

Step II
1. Add 3 tablespoons of vinegar to iron pot.
2. Transfer contents to iron pot.
3. Simmer for 10 minutes.
4. Cool for 1 hour.
5. Rinse thoroughly.
6. Dry in shade.

214/OSAGE ORANGE
(Maclura pomifera)

INTENSE GREENISH YELLOW: ALUMED WOOL; GOOD LIGHTFASTNESS AND GOOD WASHFASTNESS.
DEEP BURNT ORANGE: CHROMED WOOL; GOOD LIGHTFASTNESS AND GOOD WASH-FASTNESS.

Member of Mulberry Family. Small and medium-sized tree named after Osage Indians of Texas, Oklahoma, and Arkansas. Bows and clubs were made of the wood and also a strong yellow dye. Colonists made fence posts, wagon wheels, and bows of the Osage orange.

TEXTILE
Scoured, presoaked, alum- or chrome-mordanted wool (1 ounce)

INGREDIENT
Wood shavings (in net bag, if preferred) (1 ounce)

WATER
Tap (enough to cover textile)

POT
Nonreacting

METHOD
1. Cover shavings with water.
2. Simmer for 1 hour.
3. Cool.
4. Enter wool.
5. Simmer for 45 minutes.
6. Cool overnight in ooze.
7. Rinse thoroughly.
8. Dry in shade.

NOTES: For 1 pound of wool use ½ pound of Osage wood. □ An Osage dye bath emits a musty odor, somewhat reminiscent of old bars —stale beer and tobacco smoke. The dyed goods smell better eventually. □ Save ooze for use in Recipe 215.

215/OSAGE ORANGE IN IRON POT
(Maclura pomifera)

KHAKI GREEN: ALUMED WOOL; GOOD LIGHTFASTNESS AND GOOD WASHFASTNESS.

TEXTILE
Scoured, presoaked, alum-mordanted wool (1 ounce)

INGREDIENT
Wood shavings (in net bag if preferred) (1 ounce)

WATER
Tap (enough to cover textile)

POTS
Step I
Nonreacting
Step II
Iron

METHOD
Step I
1. Cover shavings with water in nonreacting pot.
2. Simmer for 1 hour.
3. Cool.
4. Enter textile.
5. Simmer for 45 minutes.

Step II
1. Pour ooze and textile into iron pot.

2. Simmer for 30 minutes, or until wool darkens.
3. Cool.
4. Rinse thoroughly.
5. Dry in shade.

NOTE: Old ooze from any Osage orange recipe can be used instead of preparing new dye bath.

216/OSAGE ORANGE ON JUTE AND COTTON
(Maclura pomifera)

INTENSE GREEN GOLD: ALUMED JUTE; GOOD LIGHTFASTNESS.
YELLOW: ALUMED COTTON; GOOD LIGHT-FASTNESS AND GOOD WASHFASTNESS.

TEXTILE
Scoured, presoaked, alum-mordanted jute or cotton (1 ounce)

INGREDIENTS
Wood shavings (in net bag if preferred) (1 ounce)

Chrome-alum (dissolved in 2 quarts of hot water) (1/8 teaspoon)

Vinegar (1 teaspoon)

WATER
Tap (enough to cover textile)

POT
Nonreacting

METHOD
1. Cover shavings with water.
2. Simmer for 1 hour.
3. Cool.
4. Enter textile.
5. Simmer for 45 minutes.
6. Cool overnight in ooze.
7. Bring to simmer and cool overnight again.
8. Remove textile from dye bath.
9. Combine chrome-alum and vinegar for afterbath.
10. Enter textile in afterbath.
11. Simmer for 10 minutes.
12. Cool.
13. Rinse thoroughly.
14. Dry in shade.

217/PADAUK
(Pterocarpus dalbergioides)
SALMON PINK: ALUMED WOOL; GOOD LIGHTFASTNESS.

An exotic hardwood tree of the Pea Family, from the Andaman Islands. The wood is prized for its hardness and brown to violet-red color. Used for fine furniture, bowls, and sculpture.

TEXTILE
Scoured, presoaked, alum-mordanted wool (1 ounce)

INGREDIENT
Wood shavings (in net bag if preferred) (4 ounces)

WATER
Tap (enough to cover textile)

POT
Nonreacting

METHOD
1. Cover shavings with water.
2. Boil for 2 hours.
3. Remove wood shavings.
4. Cool.
5. Enter wool.
6. Simmer for 1 hour.
7. Cool overnight in ooze.
8. Rinse thoroughly.
9. Dry in shade.

218/PADAUK AND CUPRIC SULFATE
(Pterocarpus dalbergioides)
DEEP TERRA-COTTA RED: ALUMED WOOL; GOOD LIGHTFASTNESS.

TEXTILE
Scoured, presoaked, alum-mordanted wool (1 ounce)

INGREDIENTS
Wool shavings (in net bag if preferred) (3 ounces)

Cupric sulfate (dissolved in 1 cup of hot water) (1/4 teaspoon)

WATER
Tap (enough to cover textile)

POT
Nonreacting

METHOD
1. Cover shavings with water.
2. Boil for 1 hour.
3. Remove shavings.
4. Cool.

5. Stir dissolved cupric sulfate into dye bath.
6. Enter wool.
7. Simmer for 30 minutes.
8. Cool overnight in ooze.
9. Rinse thoroughly.
10. Dry in shade.

219/PERNAMBUCO, BRAZILWOOD
(Caesalpinia echinata)

BLOOD RED: ALUMED WOOL; GOOD LIGHT-FASTNESS.

An exotic hardwood tree of the Pea Family from the American tropics. The wood is much prized for its hardness and color. Used for violin bows. Following are three recipes for obtaining red from pernambuco. Each demonstrates a valid technique.

TEXTILE
Scoured, presoaked, alum-mordanted wool (1 ounce)

INGREDIENT
Wood shavings (in net bag if preferred) (2 ounces)

WATER
Tap (enough to cover textile)

POT
Nonreacting

METHOD
1. Cover shavings with water.
2. Soak overnight.
3. Simmer shavings for 1 hour.
4. Soak overnight.
5. Enter textile.
6. Simmer for 45 minutes.
7. Cool overnight in ooze.
8. Rinse thoroughly.
9. Dry in shade.

NOTE: For 1 pound of wool use ½ pound of wood.

220/PERNAMBUCO AND CUPRIC SULFATE
(Caesalpinia echinata)

WINE RED: ALUMED WOOL; GOOD LIGHT-FASTNESS.

TEXTILE
Scoured, presoaked, alum-mordanted wool (1 ounce)

INGREDIENTS
Wood shavings (in net bag if preferred) (2 ounces)
Cupric sulfate (dissolved in 1 cup of hot water) (¼ teaspoon)

WATER
Tap (enough to cover textile)

POT
Nonreacting

METHOD
1. Cover shavings with water.
2. Soak overnight.
3. Simmer shavings for 1 hour.
4. Soak overnight.
5. Enter textile.
6. Simmer for 45 minutes.
7. Remove textile from dye bath.
8. Stir cupric sulfate into dye bath.
9. Reenter textile into dye bath.
10. Heat for 15 minutes.
11. Cool.
12. Rinse thoroughly.
13. Dry in shade.

NOTE: For 1 pound of wool use ½ pound of wood shavings and ¼ ounce of cupric sulfate.

221/PERNAMBUCO AND TIN CRYSTALS
(Caesalpinia echinata)

VERMILION: ALUMED WOOL; GOOD LIGHT-FASTNESS.

TEXTILE
Scoured, presoaked, alum-mordanted wool (1 ounce)

INGREDIENTS
Wood shavings (in net bag if preferred) (2 ounces)
Tin crystals (dissolved in 1 cup of hot water immediately before using) (pinch or 1/16 teaspoon)

WATER
Tap (enough to cover textile)

POT
Nonreacting

METHOD
1. Cover shavings with water.
2. Soak overnight.

3. Simmer shavings for 1 hour.
4. Soak overnight.
5. Stir in tin solution.
6. Enter textile.
7. Simmer for 45 minutes.
8. Cool overnight in ooze.
9. Rinse thoroughly.
10. Dry in shade.

NOTE: For 1 pound of wool use ½ pound of wood, ⅙ ounce of tin and ⅙ ounce of cream of tartar.

222 / PINE NEEDLES IN IRON POT
(Pinus sp.)
OLIVE GREEN: ALUMED WOOL OR COTTON; GOOD LIGHTFASTNESS; AROMATIC

Pine bark was used extensively by Indians as food. The inner bark is especially nutritious. Pine needles have many uses, including basketry and weaving. In Guatemala, pine needles are strewn thickly on the floor, thus giving carpetlike resilience.

TEXTILE
Scoured, presoaked, alum-mordanted cotton or wool (2 ounces)

INGREDIENT
Pine needles, fresh (6 ounces)

WATER
Distilled (enough to cover textile)

POT
Iron

METHOD
1. Cover pine needles with water.
2. Boil for 45 minutes.
3. Cool overnight.
4. Enter textile.
5. Simmer for 45 minutes.
6. Cool for several hours.
7. Rinse thoroughly.
8. Dry in shade.

NOTE: If a nonreacting dye pot is used instead of an iron pot, a tan dye results.

223 / PITTOSPORUM SEEDS
(Pittosporum crassifolium)
DARK BLUE: ALUMED WOOL; FAIR LIGHTFASTNESS.

Tall shrub or small tree. Member of the Pittosporum Family. From the Greek *pittos* for "pitch" and *porum* for "seed." The pitch around the seed may well add to the dye substance. Seen often in San Francisco as garden windbreak or hedge. Has tiny purple flowers and large seed pods. For dyeing, the pods are opened and the sticky dark seeds are scraped out. It is a slow job. This is a tempermental dye plant.

TEXTILE
Scoured, presoaked, alum-mordanted wool (1 ounce)

INGREDIENT
Seeds separated from pods (½ ounce seeds, about 12 pods)

WATER
Tap (enough to cover textile)

POT
Nonreacting

METHOD
1. Cover seeds with water.
2. Simmer for 30 minutes. Cool.
3. Enter wool.
4. Simmer for 1 hour.
5. Cool overnight in ooze.
6. Wash wool in soap and water.
7. Rinse thoroughly.
8. Dry in shade.

NOTE: Save ooze for Recipe 224.

224 / PITTOSPORUM SEEDS, STEEPED
(Pittosporum crassifolium)
DARK BLUE: ALUMED WOOL; GOOD LIGHTFASTNESS.

TEXTILE
Scoured, presoaked, alum-mordanted wool (1 ounce)

INGREDIENT
Old ooze from Recipe 223, adding water to cover if necessary, or, make a fresh dye bath by simmering seeds in water for 1 hour (1 quart or more, or ½ ounce seeds)

Figure 77   PITTOSPORUM (*Pittosporum crassifolium*)

METHOD
1. Enter textile in ooze.
2. Set aside to steep for about 1 week.
3. Wash textile in soap and water.
4. Rinse thoroughly.
5. Dry in shade.

225/PRIVET BERRIES IN ALUMINUM POT
(Ligustrum sp.)
GRASS GREEN: CHROMED WOOL; ACCEPTABLE LIGHTFASTNESS.

One tree and several shrubby species are grown in gardens. A member of the Olive Family. Common privet is used as a hedge in Eastern United States. The dark blue berries are tantalizing dye subjects. They promise much. Interesting blues and greens are obtained, but end up being less fast than one would wish. Variable.

TEXTILE
Scoured, presoaked, chrome-mordanted wool (1 ounce)

INGREDIENTS
Berries, stems, mashed (13 ounces)
Ammonia, clear (in 1 quart of water) (½ teaspoon)

WATER
Tap (enough to cover textile)

POT
Aluminum

METHOD
1. Combine plant material, berries, water, and textile.
2. Simmer for 25 minutes.
3. Cool overnight in ooze.
4. Remove textile.
5. Prepare ammonia afterbath and dip textile.
6. Rinse thoroughly in fresh water.
7. Dry in shade.

226 / PRIVET BERRIES IN IRON POT
(Ligustrum sp.)
DARK BLUE GRAY: ALUMED WOOL; GOOD LIGHTFASTNESS.

TEXTILE
Scoured, presoaked, alum-mordanted wool (1 ounce)

INGREDIENT
Berries, mashed (13 ounces)

WATER
Tap (enough to cover textile)

POT
Iron

METHOD
1. Combine berries, water, and wool.
2. Simmer for 1 hour.
.3. Cool.
4. Rinse thoroughly.
5. Dry in shade.

NOTE: Cooking in an iron pot improves lightfastness and washfastness, and darkens and cools color.

227 / PRIVET LEAVES
(Ligustrum sp.)
YELLOW (STEP I): ALUMED WOOL; GOOD LIGHTFASTNESS.
DARK KHAKI GREEN (STEP II): ALUMED WOOL; GOOD LIGHTFASTNESS.

TEXTILE
Scoured, presoaked, alum-mordanted wool (1 ounce)

INGREDIENTS
Leaves and stems (10 ounces)
Vinegar (4 teaspoons)

WATER
Tap (enough to cover textile)

POTS
Step I
Nonreacting

Step II
Iron

METHOD
Step I
1. Cover plant material with water, in nonreacting pot.
2. Simmer for 1 hour.
3. Cool.
4. Enter textile.
5. Simmer for 45 minutes.

Step II
1. Pour ooze and textile into iron pot.
2. Add vinegar.
3. Simmer for 40 minutes.
4. Rinse thoroughly.
5. Dry in shade.

228 / CALIFORNIA REDWOOD BARK
(Sequoia spp.)
TAN: ALUMED WOOL; GOOD LIGHTFASTNESS AND GOOD WASHFASTNESS.
LIGHT GOLDEN BROWN TO TERRA-COTTA: CHROMED WOOL; GOOD LIGHTFASTNESS AND GOOD WASHFASTNESS.

Native California trees described as the oldest, tallest, and most magnificent in the world. Once inhabited parts of Asia, Europe, and North America. Excellent source of tannin colors.

TEXTILE
Scoured, presoaked alum- or chrome-mordanted wool (2 ounces)

INGREDIENT
Redwood bark, shredded (8 ounces)

WATER
Tap (enough to cover textile)

POT
Nonreacting

METHOD
1. Cover bark with water and boil for 1 hour.
2. Cool.

3. Enter textile.
4. Simmer for 1 hour.
5. Cool overnight in dye bath.
6. Rinse thoroughly.
7. Dry in shade.

NOTE: The inner layer (red fiber) of redwood roots yields a beautiful terra-cotta dye. Follow above recipe but use twice as much wood as wool, by weight. Try an ammonia afterbath.

17

Food and food-related plant recipes

229/DRY RED BEANS (Phaseolus vulgaris)

TERRA-COTTA BROWN: ALUMED WOOL; GOOD LIGHTFASTNESS.

Pea Family. Use the common dry red kidney bean sold in groceries. Only the bean liquor is used for dyeing. Leftover beans can be eaten. This recipe is an example of having your beans and eating them also! If you don't intend to make a meal of the beans, ignore this one.

TEXTILE
Scoured, presoaked, alum-mordanted wool (1 ounce)

INGREDIENTS
Beans (½ pound)
Iodized salt (1 tablespoon)

WATER
Distilled (enough to cover textile)

POT
Iron

METHOD
1. Cover beans with water.
2. Simmer for 30 minutes.
3. Strain beans out. Use them for food later if desired.
4. Enter wool in bean liquor.
5. Simmer for 45 minutes.

6. Cool in pot.
7. Rinse thoroughly.
8. Dry in shade.

230/BLACKBERRIES IN IRON POT (Rubus sp.)

PURPLE TO DULL BLUE: ALUMED WOOL; GOOD LIGHTFASTNESS AND GOOD WASH-FASTNESS.

Rose Family.

TEXTILE
Scoured, presoaked, alum-mordanted wool (1 ounce)

INGREDIENTS
Berries (2 to 4 cups)
Flour (1 tablespoon)
Sugar (1 tablespoon)
Tin crystals (dissolved in 1 cup of hot water immediately before using) (pinch or ¹⁄₁₆ teaspoon)

WATER
Distilled (enough to cover textile)

POT
Iron

METHOD
1. Cover berries with water.
2. Blend in flour, sugar, and tin solution.
3. Enter textile.
4. Simmer for 1 hour.
5. Cool in bath.
6. Rinse thoroughly to prevent stickiness.
7. Dry in shade.

NOTE: For 1 pound of wool use 1 pound of berries, 3 tablespoons of flour, and 3 tablespoons of sugar.

231/PURPLE CABBAGE (Brassica oleracea var. capitata)

VARIOUS BLUES AND LAVENDERS: ALUMED WOOL, COTTON, OR JUTE; GOOD LIGHT-FASTNESS.

Mustard Family.

TEXTILE
Scoured, presoaked, alum-mordanted wool, cotton, or jute (3 ounces)

INGREDIENTS

Outer cabbage leaves (use the darkest colored leaves) (1½ pounds)

Tin crystals (dissolved in 1 cup of hot water immediately before using) (pinch or 1/16 teaspoon)

WATER

Distilled (enough to cover textile)

POT

Nonreacting

METHOD

1. Cover leaves with water.
2. Simmer carefully for 1 hour. Do not boil.
3. Remove leaves. Cool.
4. Stir in tin solution.
5. Enter textile.
6. Simmer for 45 minutes.
7. Cool overnight in dye bath.
8. Rinse thoroughly.
9. Dry in shade.

NOTES: Color comes after overnight steeping. □ Purple cabbage-leaf trimmings are sometimes available for the asking in supermarkets.

232/PURPLE CABBAGE, ALTERNATE
(Brassica oleracea var. capitata)

VARIOUS BLUES AND LAVENDERS: ALUMED WOOL, COTTON, OR JUTE; GOOD LIGHTFASTNESS.

Mustard Family.

TEXTILE

Scoured, presoaked, alum-mordanted wool, cotton, or jute (1 ounce)

INGREDIENTS

Outer cabbage leaves (8 ounces)
Iodized salt (1 teaspoon)

WATER

Distilled (enough to cover textile)

POT

Nonreacting

METHOD

1. Soak leaves and textile in water overnight.

2. Remove textile.
3. Stir in salt.
4. Reenter textile.
5. Simmer for 30 minutes.
6. Cool overnight in dye bath.
7. Rinse thoroughly.
8. Dry in shade.

233/CHAMOMILE
(Anthemis nobilis)

VARIOUS GOLD-YELLOWS: CHROMED WOOL; GOOD LIGHTFASTNESS.

Perennial. Member of Sunflower Family. Introduced from Europe. Used in medieval times as strewing herb in the streets and at public gatherings to cover up stench. Was also planted in gardens to promote health of other plants. For medicinal purposes: pour 1 pint of boiling water over 1 ounce of flowers and steep covered for 10 minutes. Use 1 teaspoon of the brew to 1 cup water or other liquid. Said to be soothing, a sedative, and a nightmare preventative. Said to make a fine hair rinse for blondes and also a hair dye if prepared in more concentrated form. Yes, it is a good textile dye!

TEXTILE

Scoured, presoaked, chrome-mordanted wool (1 ounce)

INGREDIENT

Chamomile flowers (4 ounces)

WATER

Tap (enough to cover textile)

POT

Nonreacting

METHOD

1. Cover plants with water and steep overnight.
2. Enter textile and simmer for 40 minutes.
3. Cool overnight in ooze.
4. Rinse thoroughly.
5. Dry in shade.

NOTES: For 1 pound of wool, use 1 pound of flowers. □ Alumed jute can be steeped in the leftover dye bath from fetid or garden chamomile. A deep gold color is obtained. Fair lightfastness.

234 / PURPLE INDIAN CORN
(Zea mays)
DARK PURPLE TO MAROON: ALUMED WOOL; GOOD LIGHTFASTNESS.

Member of the Grass Family, like all corn. The Hopi name is "koko'ma." Not used for food because it stains the mouth. Body paint for kachina dances is made from a mixture of white clay and liquor from the boiled purple corn with sumac berries. Used for dye if both corn *and cob* are purple. The Hopi dye basketry materials, wool, and cotton various maroons, deep red, or pink with the purple corn. It is difficult to achieve a fast-color by our usual methods, the exception being the formula which follows.

TEXTILE
Scoured, presoaked, alum-mordanted wool (2 ounces)

INGREDIENT
Shelled corn (1 pound, about 3 purple cobs)

WATER
Distilled (to cover)

POT
Nonreacting

METHOD
1. Bring corn and water to boil.
2. Simmer for 60 minutes or until corn begins to crack.
3. Strain out corn kernels. Cool.
4. Enter wool in dye liquor.
5. Simmer for 40 minutes.
6. Cool overnight in dye bath.
7. Rinse thoroughly.
8. Dry in shade.

235 / GRAPE LEAVES, ONE-POT AND MORDANT METHOD*
(Vitis spp.)
INTENSE YELLOW: UNMORDANTED WOOL; GOOD LIGHTFASTNESS.

Member of Grape Family. Any variety will do. Persian rug weavers have used grape leaves as one source of yellow on rug yarn for centuries. The leaves are collected, dried, and stored for future use. Fresh leaves may also be used.

TEXTILE
Scoured, presoaked, unmordanted wool (1 ounce)

INGREDIENTS
Leaves (3 to 6 ounces)
Alum (dissolved in 1 cup of hot water) (2 teaspoons)
Cream of tartar (dissolved in 1 cup of hot water) (1 teaspoon)
Ammonia, clear (in 1 quart of water) (1 teaspoon)

WATER
Tap (enough to cover textile)

POT
Nonreacting

METHOD
1. Cover leaves with water and soak overnight.
2. Simmer leaves for 30 minutes.
3. Cool.
4. Enter wool.
5. Simmer for 1 hour.
6. Steep wool in ooze for 48 hours.
7. Dip in ammonia rinse.
8. Rinse thoroughly in water.
9. Dry in shade.

NOTE: For 1 pound of wool, 2 pounds of leaves are usually enough.

236 / CONCORD-TYPE GRAPE, SKINS AND AMMONIA
(Vitis labruscana)
DARK GREENISH BLUE: CHROMED WOOL; GOOD LIGHTFASTNESS.

Grape Family.

TEXTILE
Scoured, presoaked, chrome-mordanted wool (1 ounce)

INGREDIENTS
Grape skins, from about 1 pound of grapes (about 4 ounces)

Ammonia, clear (in 1 quart water)
(1 teaspoon)

WATER
Tap (enough to cover textile)

POT
Nonreacting

METHOD
1. Combine skins, wool, and water.
2. Simmer for 30 minutes.
3. Cool overnight in ooze.
4. Remove textile.
5. Dip in ammonia afterbath until color changes.
6. Rinse thoroughly.
7. Dry in shade.

237 / CONCORD-TYPE GRAPE, SKINS AND CUPRIC SULFATE (Vitis labruscana)
DARK BLUE: CHROMED WOOL; GOOD LIGHT-FASTNESS.

Grape Family.

TEXTILE
Scoured, presoaked, chrome-mordanted wool (1 ounce)

INGREDIENTS
Grape skins from about 1 pound of grapes (about 4 ounces)

Cupric sulfate stock solution (in 1 quart of water) ($\frac{1}{2}$ ounce or 1 tablespoon)

WATER
Tap (enough to cover textile)

POT
Nonreacting

METHOD
1. Combine skins, wool, and water.
2. Simmer for 30 minutes.
3. Cool overnight in ooze.
4. Remove wool.
5. Enter wool in cupric sulfate afterbath.
6. Heat for 10 minutes.
7. Remove wool.
8. Rinse thoroughly.
9. Dry in shade.

NOTES: For 1 pound of wool use about 2 pounds of skins (about 8

pounds of grapes). ☐ 1 pound of grapes yields about 4 to 6 ounces of skins. Grape skin recipes are handy for people who relish grape *pulp* but spit out the skins!

238 / CONCORD-TYPE GRAPE, SKINS AND FERROUS SULFATE (Vitis labruscana)
DARK BLUE: CHROMED WOOL; GOOD LIGHTFASTNESS.

Grape Family. Ferrous sulfate is used in this recipe instead of cupric sulfate as an alternate method. The iron salts are used to improve fastness. The color is not as bright with iron, but iron salts are cheaper and not poisonous.

TEXTILE
Scoured, presoaked, chrome-mordanted wool (1 ounce)

INGREDIENTS
Grape skins, from about 1 pound of grapes (about 4 ounces)

Ferrous sulfate (dissolved in 1 quart of hot water) (pinch or $\frac{1}{16}$ teaspoon)

WATER
Tap (enough to cover textile)

POT
Nonreacting

METHOD
1. Combine skins, wool, and water.
2. Simmer for 30 minutes.
3. Cool overnight in ooze.
4. Remove wool.
5. Enter wool in ferrous sulfate afterbath.
6. Heat for 10 minutes.
7. Remove wool.
8. Rinse thoroughly.
9. Dry in shade.

NOTE: For 1 pound of wool use about 2 pounds of skins.

239 / BLACK MULBERRY TREE, BERRIES (Morus nigra)
INTENSE RED-VIOLET TO DARK PURPLE:

ALUMED WOOL; GOOD LIGHTFASTNESS.
PURPLE: JUTE AND REED; FADES BUT RE-
MAINS PLEASANTLY COLORED.

Old favorite. Tree grown for its fruit. Member of the Mulberry Family, which includes many horticultural subjects and products of economic importance. Some products of the family include hemp fiber, rubber, food for silk worms, hops, bread fruit, figs, and mulberries. The Osage orange tree is in this family as is the paper mulberry and cannabis. A fine dye subject.

TEXTILE
Scoured, presoaked, alum-mordanted wool (1 ounce)

INGREDIENTS
Ripe fruit (berries) (about 3 ounces)
Tin crystals (dissolved in 1 cup of hot water immediately before using) (pinch or $\frac{1}{16}$ teaspoon)
Cream of tartar (dissolved in 1 cup of hot water immediately before using) (1 tablespoon)

WATER
Distilled (enough to cover textile)

POT
Nonreacting

METHOD
1. Cover berries with water.
2. Heat.
3. Stir in tin and cream of tartar solutions. Cool.
4. Enter textile.
5. Simmer for 30 minutes.
6. Cool overnight in ooze.
7. Rinse thoroughly.
8. Dry in shade.

NOTE: For 1 pound of wool use about 1½ pounds of mulberries.

240/MULBERRY LEAVES IN IRON POT
(Morus nigra)
YELLOW-GREEN: ALUMED WOOL; GOOD
LIGHTFASTNESS.

TEXTILE
Scoured, presoaked, alum-mordanted wool (1 ounce)

INGREDIENT
Leaves (4 ounces)

WATER
Distilled (enough to cover textile)

POTS
Step I
Nonreacting

Step II
Iron

METHOD
Step I
1. Combine leaves, water, and wool in nonreacting pot.
2. Simmer for 30 minutes.
3. Cool overnight in ooze.

Step II
1. Transfer contents to iron pot.
2. Simmer for 30 minutes.
3. Cool.
4. Rinse thoroughly.
5. Dry in shade.

241/RAW OLIVES
(Olea europaea)
VARIATIONS OF MAROON: ALUMED WOOL;
GOOD LIGHTFASTNESS.

Olive Family. Four recipes are given because the olive is potent and subject to experimental variations.

TEXTILE
Scoured, presoaked, alum-mordanted wool (1 ounce)

INGREDIENT
Raw ripe olives, pitted and mashed (4 ounces)

WATER
Distilled (enough to cover textile)

POT
Nonreacting

METHOD
1. Cover olives and wool with water.
2. Simmer for 30 minutes. The ooze will be oily.
3. Cool overnight in ooze.
4. Rinse thoroughly.
5. Dry in shade.

NOTE: Ripe raw olives are a purplish color. Processed olives are an unsuitable dye source.

Figure 78 OLIVE (*Olea europaea*)

242/RAW OLIVE SKINS
(Olea europaea)

VARIATIONS OF LAVENDER: ALUMED WOOL;
GOOD LIGHTFASTNESS.
VARIATIONS OF BLUE-GREEN: CHROMED
WOOL; GOOD LIGHTFASTNESS.

Olive Family.

TEXTILE
Scoured, presoaked, alum- or
chrome-mordanted wool (1 ounce)

INGREDIENT
Skins from ripe olives (30 olives)

WATER
Distilled (enough to cover textile)

POT
Nonreacting

METHOD
1. Combine skins, wool, and water.
2. Simmer for 15 minutes.
3. Cool in ooze for 3 hours.
4. Rinse thoroughly.
5. Dry in shade.

243/RAW OLIVE SKINS
AND CUPRIC SULFATE
(Olea europaea)

BLUE-GRAY: ALUMED WOOL; GOOD LIGHT-
FASTNESS.
BLACK: CHROMED WOOL; GOOD LIGHT-
FASTNESS.

Olive Family.

TEXTILE
Scoured, presoaked, alum- or
chrome-mordanted wool (1 ounce)

INGREDIENTS
Skins from ripe olives (30 olives)
Cupric sulfate stock solution (in 1
quart of water) ($\frac{1}{2}$ ounce or 1
tablespoon)

WATER
Distilled (enough to cover textile)

POT
Nonreacting

METHOD
1. Combine skins, wool, and water.
2. Simmer for 15 minutes.
3. Cool.
4. Remove wool.
5. Enter wool in cupric sulfate afterbath.
6. Heat for 10 minutes.
7. Rinse thoroughly.
8. Dry in shade.

244 / RAW WHOLE OLIVES ON JUTE IN ALUMINUM POT
(Olea europaea)
DEEP PURPLE: ALUMED JUTE; FAIR LIGHT-FASTNESS.

Olive Family.

TEXTILE
Scoured, presoaked, alum-mordanted jute (1 ounce)

INGREDIENT
Whole raw ripe olives (about 4 ounces)

WATER
Tap (enough to cover textile)

POT
Aluminum

METHOD
1. Cover olives and textile with water.
2. Simmer for 30 minutes.
3. Cool overnight in ooze.
4. Rinse thoroughly.
5. Dry in shade.

NOTE: Use about 2 pounds of olives for 1 pound of jute.

245 / OLIVE TREE LEAVES IN IRON POT
(Olea europaea)
BRIGHT YELLOW (STEP I): ALUMED WOOL; GOOD LIGHTFASTNESS.
OLIVE GREEN (STEP II): ALUMED WOOL; GOOD LIGHTFASTNESS.

Olive Family.

TEXTILE
Scoured, presoaked, alum-mordanted wool (1 ounce)

INGREDIENT
Olive leaves (6 ounces)

WATER
Tap (enough to cover textile)

POTS
Step I
Nonreacting

Step II
Iron

METHOD
Step I
1. Combine leaves, textile, and water in nonreacting pot.
2. Simmer for 30 minutes.
3. *For bright yellow*: Cool overnight, rinse thoroughly, and dry in shade.
4. *For olive green*: Continue to Step II.

Step II
1. Pour contents of nonreacting pot into iron pot.
2. Simmer for 30 minutes.
3. Cool for 1 hour.
4. Rinse thoroughly.
5. Dry in shade.

246 / YELLOW ONION SKINS IN IRON POT
(Allium sp.)
YELLOW-BROWN: ALUMED WOOL OR COTTON; FAIR TO GOOD LIGHTFASTNESS.

TEXTILE
Scoured, presoaked, alum-mordanted wool or cotton (1 ounce)

INGREDIENT
Onion skins (1 ounce)

WATER
Tap (enough to cover textile)

POT
Iron

METHOD
1. Soak skins and textile in water in a bowl.
2. Pour into iron pot.
3. Simmer for 1 hour.

4. Cool overnight in ooze.
5. Rinse thoroughly.
6. Dry in shade.

247/YELLOW ONION SKINS AND TIN CRYSTALS (Allium sp.)

TAN-ORANGE: ALUMED WOOL, COTTON, OR JUTE; FAIR LIGHTFASTNESS.

TEXTILE
Scoured, presoaked, alum-mordanted wool, cotton, or jute (1 ounce)

INGREDIENTS
Onion skins (4 ounces)

Tin crystals (dissolved in 1 cup of hot water immediately before using) (pinch or 1/16 teaspoon)

WATER
Tap (enough to cover textile)

POT
Nonreacting

METHOD
1. Cover skins and wool with water.
2. Heat.
3. Remove wool.
4. Add tin solution.
5. Reenter wool.
6. Simmer for 30 minutes.
7. Cool overnight in ooze.
8. Rinse thoroughly.
9. Dry in shade.

248/RED ONION SKINS AND TIN CRYSTALS (Allium sp.)

KHAKI TO OLIVE GREEN: ALUMED WOOL OR COTTON; FAIR TO GOOD LIGHTFASTNESS.

TEXTILE
Scoured, presoaked, alum-mordanted wool or cotton (1 ounce)

INGREDIENTS
Onion skins (1 ounce)

Ammonia, clear (in 1 quart of water) (1 teaspoon)

WATER
Tap (enough to cover textile)

POT
Tin pail or coffee tin

METHOD
1. Cover onion skins and textile with water.
2. Simmer for 30 minutes.
3. Cool overnight in ooze.
4. Dip wool in ammonia rinse.
5. Rinse thoroughly in fresh water.
6. Dry in shade.

NOTE: Alas. Even onion skins are not as dependable as they once were. Some onions are now treated with a chemical which retards sprouting! This substance can affect dye results.

249/GREEN PLUM LEAVES AND CUPRIC SULFATE (Prunus sp.)

LIGHT GREEN: ALUMED WOOL; GOOD LIGHTFASTNESS.
YELLOW-GREEN: CHROMED WOOL; GOOD LIGHTFASTNESS.

Recipe 250, Plum Leaves in an Iron Pot, yields a green similar to this recipe. The dyer should choose the method that suits his temperament and ability best.

TEXTILE
Scoured, presoaked, alum- or chrome-mordanted wool (1 ounce)

INGREDIENTS
Green leaves, fresh (about 4 ounces)

Cupric sulfate stock solution (in 1 quart of water) (1/2 ounce or 1 tablespoon)

WATER
Distilled (enough to cover textile)

POT
Nonreacting

METHOD
1. Cover leaves and textile with water and soak overnight.
2. Simmer for 30 minutes.
3. Cool overnight in ooze.
4. Remove textile.
5. Enter textile in cupric sulfate afterbath.
6. Heat for 10 minutes.
7. Rinse thoroughly.
8. Dry in shade.

250/GREEN PLUM LEAVES IN IRON POT
(Prunus sp.)

YELLOW-GREEN: CHROMED WOOL; GOOD LIGHTFASTNESS.

Rose Family.

TEXTILE
Scoured, presoaked, chrome-mordanted wool (1 ounce)

INGREDIENT
Green leaves, fresh (about 4 ounces)

WATER
Distilled (enough to cover textile)

POTS
Step I
Nonreacting

Step II
Iron

METHOD
Step I
1. Combine leaves, water, and textile in nonreacting pot.
2. Simmer for 30 minutes.
3. Cool overnight in ooze.

Step II
1. Pour dye pot contents into iron pot.
2. Simmer for 45 minutes.
3. Remove textile.
4. Rinse thoroughly.
5. Dry in shade.

251/RED PLUM FRUIT AND AMMONIA
(Prunus sp.)

VARIATIONS OF DARK OLIVE GREEN: CHROMED WOOL; GOOD LIGHTFASTNESS.

TEXTILE
Scoured, presoaked, chrome-mordanted wool (2 ounces)

INGREDIENTS
Plum fruit (4 cups cooked and pitted)

Ammonia, clear (in 1 quart of water) (1 teaspoon)

WATER
Tap (enough to cover textile)

POT
Nonreacting or tin can (better)

METHOD
1. Cover plums with water.
2. Heat until soft.
3. Pit and measure out 4 cups of plum pulp.
4. Cover plums and textile with water.
5. Simmer for 30 minutes.
6. Cool in ooze.
7. Rinse thoroughly.
8. Dip textile into ammonia rinse until color changes to green.
9. Rinse thoroughly in fresh water.
10. Dry in shade.

252/RED PLUM FRUIT IN IRON POT
(Prunus sp.)

VARIATIONS OF DARK GRAY-GREEN TO DARK GRAY: ALUMED WOOL; GOOD LIGHTFASTNESS.

Rose Family. Any dark plums can be used.

TEXTILE
Scoured, presoaked, alum-mordanted wool (1 ounce)

INGREDIENTS
Fruit, pitted (4 cups cooked and pitted, 1½ pounds)

Flour (1 tablespoon)

Sugar (1 tablespoon)

Lemon juice (1 tablespoon)

WATER
Tap (enough to cover textile)

POTS
Step I
Nonreacting

Step II
Iron

METHOD
Step I
1. Cover plums with water.
2. Simmer in nonreacting pot until barely soft.
3. Remove pits, measuring out 4 cups of pulp.

Step II
1. Combine fruit, flour, sugar, and lemon juice in iron pot.
2. Enter textile and water to cover.
3. Simmer for 1 hour.

4. Cool.
5. Simmer for another 30 minutes.
6. Rinse thoroughly.
7. Dry in shade.

253/RED PLUM FRUIT AND TIN CRYSTALS
(Prunus sp.)

VIOLET: CHROMED WOOL; FAIR LIGHT-FASTNESS.

Rose Family. Any red plums can be used.

TEXTILE

Scoured, presoaked, chrome-mordanted wool (2 ounces)

INGREDIENTS

Fruit (4 cups cooked and pitted, 1½ pounds)

Tin crystals (dissolved in 1 cup of hot water immediately before using) (pinch or ¹⁄₁₆ teaspoon)

WATER

Tap (enough to cover textile)

POT

Nonreacting

METHOD

1. Cover plums with water.
2. Simmer until soft.
3. Pit plums and measure out 4 cups of pulp.
4. Add tin solution to dye bath.
5. Enter textile and cover with water.
6. Simmer for 30 minutes.
7. Cool overnight in ooze.
8. Rinse thoroughly.
9. Dry in shade.

254/DARK RED PLUM LEAVES, ONE-POT METHOD*
(Prunus sp.)

OLIVE GREEN: UNMORDANTED WOOL; GOOD LIGHTFASTNESS.

Any dark red-leaved variety will probably yield similar results.

TEXTILE

Scoured, presoaked, unmordanted wool (1 ounce)

INGREDIENTS

Plum leaves (about 4 ounces)

Alum (dissolved in 1 cup of hot water) (1 tablespoon)

Cream of tartar (dissolved in 1 cup of hot water) (1 teaspoon)

WATER

Tap (enough to cover textile)

POT

Tin can or bucket

METHOD

1. Cover wool and leaves with water.
2. Heat.
3. Remove wool.
4. Stir in alum and cream of tartar solutions.
5. Reenter wool.
6. Simmer for 30 minutes.
7. Cool overnight in ooze.
8. Rinse thoroughly.
9. Dry in shade.

NOTE: An ammonia after-rinse will brighten the green.

255/DARK RED PLUM LEAVES AND TIN CRYSTALS
(Prunus sp.)

VIOLET TO PURPLE: ALUMED WOOL; GOOD LIGHTFASTNESS.
LAVENDER: ALUMED COTTON, LINEN, OR JUTE; FAIR LIGHTFASTNESS.

Rose Family.

TEXTILE

Scoured, presoaked, alum-mordanted wool, jute, cotton, or linen (1 ounce)

INGREDIENTS

Leaves (about 4 ounces)

Tin crystals (dissolved in 1 cup of hot water immediately before using) (pinch or ¹⁄₁₆ teaspoon)

Iodized salt (dissolved in 1 cup of hot water) (1 tablespoon)

WATER

Distilled (enough to cover textile)

POT

Tin pail or coffee tin (for smaller amounts)

METHOD

1. Combine salt, water, leaves, and textile.

2. Heat for 20 minutes.
3. Remove textile.
4. Stir in tin solution.
5. Reenter textile.
6. Simmer for 30 minutes.
7. Cool overnight in ooze.
8. Rinse thoroughly.
9. Dry in shade.

256/POMEGRANATE FLOWERS*
(Punica granatum)

COPPERY BROWN: UNMORDANTED WOOL; GOOD LIGHTFASTNESS.
TAN: ALUMED COTTON; GOOD LIGHTFASTNESS.

Dwarf shrub or tree.

TEXTILE
Scoured, presoaked, unmordanted wool or alum-mordanted cotton (1 ounce)

INGREDIENT
Flowers (about 3 ounces)

WATER
Distilled (enough to cover textile)

POT
Nonreacting

METHOD
1. Enter plants, textile and water.
2. Simmer for 30 minutes.
3. Cool overnight in ooze.
4. Rinse thoroughly.
5. Dry in shade.

NOTE: For 1 pound of wool use 1 pound of flowers.

257/POMEGRANATE SKINS, QUANTITY RECIPE*
(Punica granatum)

DARK BROWN OR BLACK: UNMORDANTED WOOL; GOOD LIGHTFASTNESS AND GOOD WASHFASTNESS.
GRAY: UNMORDANTED COTTON, SISAL, OR JUTE; GOOD LIGHTFASTNESS AND GOOD WASHFASTNESS.

TEXTILE
Scoured, presoaked, unmordanted wool, cotton, sisal, or jute (6 to 8 ounces)

INGREDIENT
Skins of pomegranate, well chopped up or ground (about 12 fruits)

WATER
Tap (enough to cover textile)

POT
Iron

METHOD
1. Cover fruit skins with water in iron pot.
2. Simmer for 45 minutes.
3. Cool.
4. Enter textile.
5. Simmer for 1 hour.
6. Cool overnight in ooze.
7. Rinse thoroughly.
8. Dry in shade.

NOTES: Use less fruit for smaller amounts of textile. □ Less cooking yields lighter colors. □ Save ooze from dye pot. Store in jar or crock. Can be reused (see Recipe 258).

258/POMEGRANATE OOZE*
(Punica granatum)

BLACK: UNMORDANTED WOOL, COTTON, JUTE, OR SISAL; GOOD LIGHTFASTNESS.

TEXTILE
Scoured, presoaked, unmordanted wool, cotton, jute, or sisal (1 ounce)

INGREDIENT
Old pomegranate ooze (2 quarts)

WATER
Tap (enough to cover textile)

POT
Nonreacting

METHOD
1. Cover textile with old ooze.
2. Dilute with tap water if ooze is too thick.
3. Simmer for 30 minutes.
4. Cool overnight in ooze.
5. Rinse thoroughly.
6. Dry in shade.

259/RAW POMEGRANATE SKIN AND SEEDS, STEEPED*
(Punica granatum)

BEIGE TO APRICOT: UNMORDANTED WOOL; GOOD LIGHTFASTNESS AND GOOD WASHFASTNESS.

TEXTILE
Scoured, presoaked, unmordanted wool (1 ounce)

INGREDIENTS
Rinds and seeds (about 4 fruits)

WATER
Tap (enough to cover textile)

POT
Jar with lid

METHOD
1. Combine rind, seeds, textile, and water in jar.
2. Cover loosely.
3. Steep in warm place, turning textile occasionally.
4. Check color every few days. When rinsed yarn holds color, the textile is dyed.

NOTES: For deeper color, allow more time for steeping. □ Ooze from any of the pomegranate recipes can be kept for a year or more and used as needed. The odor of the ooze is strong, but who cares, so long as it makes a dye!

260/POMEGRANATE SKINS, NORTH AFRICAN ONE-POT METHOD*
(Punica granatum)
DARK BROWN: UNMORDANTED WOOL; GOOD LIGHTFASTNESS AND GOOD WASHFASTNESS.

This is an old recipe used by North African rug weavers. I have included it because the method is craftsmanlike and traditional. The procedures are not unlike those used in this book except that larger quantities of textile and plant are employed. The *presoaking* of *wool* in an *alkaline bath* (limewater) is an excellent idea (see Appendix E). The addition of ferrous sulfate to the dye bath is a traditional method. In most of the recipes that require iron, I have substituted cooking in an *iron pot instead* of adding *ferrous sulfate* crystals. For large quantity dyeing it is more convenient to use ferrous sulfate than an iron pot.

TEXTILE
Scoured, presoaked, unmordanted wool (2 pounds)

INGREDIENTS
Pomegranate skins (2 pounds)
Ferrous sulfate (dissolved in 3 gallons of water) ($\frac{1}{2}$ ounce)
Lime powder for alkaline dip (stir into 5 gallons of water and set aside for special use) (3 ounces)

POTS
Step I
Jar or dishpan (for alkaline dip) (12-gallon)

Step II
Any kind of pot (for dye bath)

WATER
Tap (enough to cover textile or about 9 gallons)

METHOD
Step I
1. Prepare alkaline dip by mixing lime powder into water.
2. Dip wet wool into alkaline bath and set aside for 10 minutes.
3. Remove wool and squeeze out water.

Step II
1. Pound up pomegranate skins.
2. Stir into ferrous sulfate solution.
3. Enter skins and ferrous sulfate solution into larger dye pot.
4. Boil for 1 hour.
5. Cool.
6. Enter wool into dye bath.
7. Add additional water to dye bath (about 6 more gallons).
8. Simmer for 4 hours, stirring occasionally.
9. Cool.
10. Remove wool from dye pot.
11. Dip in alkaline dip (see Step I).
12. Rinse thoroughly.
13. Dry in shade.

261/ROSEMARY
(Rosmarinus officinalis)
VARIOUS YELLOW-GREENS: ALUMED WOOL; GOOD LIGHTFASTNESS.

Culinary herb of shrubby growth. Member of the Mint Family. Thought to be a gentle stimulant: cut a teaspoonful of the tops and cover with a cup of boiling water.

Drink 1 cupful cold, by the large mouthful. Mind you, only once a day!

TEXTILE
Scoured, presoaked, alum-mordanted wool (1 ounce)

INGREDIENTS
Leaves and flowers (8 ounces)

WATER
Tap (enough to cover textile)

POT
Nonreacting

METHOD
1. Soak plant material overnight in water.
2. Enter wool.
3. Simmer for 1 hour.
4. Cool overnight in ooze.
5. Rinse thoroughly.
6. Dry in shade.

NOTE: Other seasoning herbs and teas—costmary, oregano, tansy, thyme—can be used for dye, either fresh or dried. Most yield a yellow color.

262 / SANTOLINA, LAVENDER COTTON, FRENCH LAVENDER (Santolina chamaecyparissus)

SIENNA GOLD: CHROMED WOOL; GOOD LIGHTFASTNESS.
YELLOW: ALUMED WOOL; GOOD LIGHTFASTNESS.

Member of the Sunflower Family. Silvery gray plant used in old-fashioned gardens as background or border outline. Aroma similar to chamomile. Dried bouquets were kept with linens during colonial times.

TEXTILE
Scoured, presoaked, alum- or chrome-mordanted wool (1 ounce)

INGREDIENTS
Leaves and flowers (about 4 ounces)

WATER
Tap (enough to cover textile)

POT
Nonreacting

METHOD
1. Combine plants, wool, and water.
2. Soak overnight.
3. Simmer for 30 minutes.

Figure 79 SANTOLINA
(*Santolina chamaecyparissus*)

4. Cool overnight in ooze.
5. Rinse thoroughly.
6. Dry in shade.

NOTE: Use about 1 pound of plant material for 1 pound of wool.

263 / SANTOLINA AND CUPRIC SULFATE (Santolina chamaecyparissus)

PEA GREEN: ALUMED WOOL; GOOD LIGHTFASTNESS.
GREEN-BROWN: CHROMED WOOL; GOOD LIGHTFASTNESS.

TEXTILE
Scoured, presoaked, alum- or chrome-mordanted wool (1 ounce)

INGREDIENTS
Leaves (about 4 ounces)
Cupric sulfate stock solution (in 1 quart of water) (1/2 ounce or 1 tablespoon)

WATER
Tap (enough to cover textile)

POT
Nonreacting or unlined copper

METHOD
1. Soak plants and textile in water overnight.
2. Simmer for 30 minutes.
3. Cool overnight in ooze.
4. Remove textile.
5. Enter textile in cupric sulfate afterbath.
6. Heat for 10 minutes.
7. Rinse thoroughly.
8. Dry in shade.

NOTE: Omit cupric sulfate afterbath if a copper pot is used.

264/SASSAFRAS BARK TEA (PURCHASED)
(Sassafras albidum)
LIGHT TERRA-COTTA TO ORANGE-TAN: ALUMED WOOL; GOOD LIGHTFASTNESS.

Tree of the Laurel Family, indigenous to North America. Tea made from the root bark has a fresh, invigorating fragrance. Best to drink the tea in springtime as the Indians believed.

TEXTILE
Scoured, presoaked, alum-mordanted wool (1 ounce)

INGREDIENTS
Bark (about 4 cups or 4 ounces)
Ammonia, clear (in 1 quart of water) (1 teaspoon)

WATER
Tap (enough to cover textile)

POT
Nonreacting

METHOD
1. Cover bark with water and soak for 24 hours.
2. Enter wool.
3. Simmer for 3 hours.
4. Steep for several days in ooze.
5. Simmer again for 2 hours.
6. Cool.
7. Dip in ammonia afterbath.

8. Rinse thoroughly.
9. Dry in shade.

265/BLACK WALNUT LEAVES*
(Juglans nigra)
CINNAMON TO DARK BROWN: UNMORDANTED WOOL; GOOD LIGHTFASTNESS.
TAN TO BROWN: UNMORDANTED COTTON OR JUTE; GOOD LIGHTFASTNESS.

Walnut Family.

TEXTILE
Scoured, presoaked, unmordanted wool, cotton, or jute (4 ounces)

INGREDIENTS
Leaves and stems, torn up (8 ounces)

WATER
Tap (enough to cover textile)

POT
Nonreacting

METHOD
1. Cover leaves with water.
2. Boil for 1 hour. Cool.
3. Enter textile.
4. Simmer for 1 hour more.
5. Cool overnight in ooze.
6. Rinse thoroughly.
7. Dry in shade.

NOTES: English walnut leaves may be used instead of black. Increase proportion from 1:2 to 1:4 (wool: leaves). □ Black dye can be obtained by using an iron pot.

266/BLACK WALNUT LEAVES, STEEPED*
(Juglans nigra)
ALMOST BLACK: UNMORDANTED WOOL (NATURAL DARK-GRAY); GOOD LIGHTFASTNESS AND GOOD WASHFASTNESS.
LIGHT BROWN: UNMORDANTED COTTON; GOOD LIGHTFASTNESS AND GOOD WASHFASTNESS.
BROWN: UNMORDANTED JUTE; GOOD LIGHTFASTNESS AND GOOD WASHFASTNESS.

TEXTILE
Scoured, presoaked, unmordanted natural dark-gray wool, cotton, or jute (1 ounce)

INGREDIENTS
Leaves and stems, torn up (4 quarts or 4 ounces)

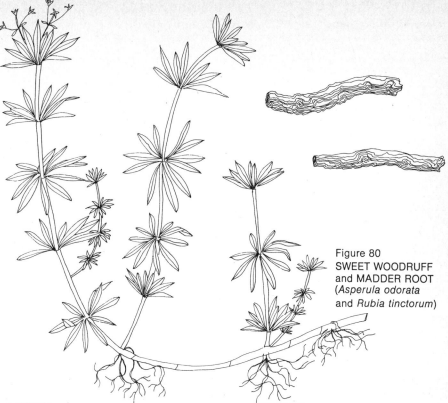

Figure 80
SWEET WOODRUFF
and MADDER ROOT
(*Asperula odorata*
and *Rubia tinctorum*)

WATER
Tap (enough to cover textile)

POT
Nonreacting

METHOD
1. Cover plant material and textile with water.
2. Simmer for 2 hours.
3. Steep (leave in ooze) for 2 days.
4. Rinse thoroughly.
5. Dry in shade.

NOTES: Ooze from black walnuts can be kept indefinitely. The odor is rank, but oh, the color! □ Walnut husks and shells can be substituted for leaves in this recipe and in Recipe 265.

267/ENGLISH WALNUT CATKINS*
(Juglans regia)
LIGHT GOLDEN BROWN: UNMORDANTED WOOL; GOOD LIGHTFASTNESS.

Walnut Family.

TEXTILE
Scoured, presoaked, unmordanted wool (1 ounce)

INGREDIENT
Catkins, cut up (about 5 ounces)

WATER
Tap (enough to cover textile)

POT
Nonreacting

METHOD
1. Combine plant, wool, and water.
2. Simmer for 1 hour.
3. Cool overnight in ooze.
4. Rinse thoroughly.
5. Dry in shade.

268/SWEET WOODRUFF
(Asperula odorata)
SOFT TAN: ALUMED WOOL; GOOD LIGHT-FASTNESS.
GRAY-GREEN: ALUMED WOOL IN IRON POT; GOOD LIGHTFASTNESS.

Madder Family.

TEXTILE

Scoured, presoaked, alum-mordanted wool (1 ounce)

INGREDIENTS

Stems and leaves (5 ounces)

WATER

Distilled (enough to cover textile)

POTS

Step I
Nonreacting

Step II
Iron

METHOD

Step I

1. Cover plant material and textile
with water.
2. Simmer for 15 minutes.
3. *For soft tan:* Cool, rinse thoroughly, and dry in shade.
4. *For gray-green:* Proceed to
Step II.

Step II

1. Transfer ooze and textile to iron
pot.
2. Simmer for 15 minutes.
3. Cool for 1 hour.
4. Rinse thoroughly.
5. Dry in shade.

NOTE: The roots of woodruff yield
a red dye. See Recipe 12 for
method.

Appendices

Decreasing and increasing ingredient amounts in a recipe

DECREASING

Most of the recipes in this book are written for one ounce of yarn. For smaller amounts, decrease the ingredients proportionally. Speaking of small amounts, how does one measure out *one-half pinch* of tin crystals? Let us say that a pinch is four or five crystals. One half of this amount is two or three crystals. Very small amounts can also be divided by "eyeball;" that is, dividing the amount by *sighting* or *as it appears to the eye.*

INCREASING

As mentioned previously, the recipes in this book are usually written for one ounce of textile. This in no way prevents the dyer from working with other textile amounts if she wishes. A convenient method of increasing amounts is simply by proportion. Here is an example:

The recipe requires one ounce of textile and five ounces of plant. The dyer needs six times as much tex-

TABLE I/ESTIMATED PLANT REQUIREMENTS ACCORDING TO PLANT POTENCY

DYE PLANT	PROPORTION OF PLANT TO TEXTILE BY WEIGHT	PLANT AMOUNTS FOR 1/2 POUND OF TEXTILE (8 OUNCES)
Strong dye plant such as bark, lichens, coreopsis, marigold	1 part plant to 1 part textile	Use same weight of plant (1/2 pound) as textile (1/2 pound)
Average dye plant	3 parts plant to 1 part textile *or* 2 parts plant to 1 part textile	Use 3 times as much plant (1 1/2 pounds) as textile (1/2 pound) Use 2 times as much plant (1 pound) as textile (1/2 pound)
Weak dye plant	4 parts plant to 1 part textile	Use 4 times as much plant (2 pounds) as textile (1/2 pound)

NOTES: Some experience with dye plants is required before the above table can be used: the dyer needs to know whether a dye plant is potent or not. ☐ 16 ounces = 1 pound. ☐ See Rule of Thumb Method, Appendix C.

tile. *We must therefore use six times as much plant material; that is, six times five ounces, or 30 ounces of plant material.*

This method is easy and direct. However, as textile amounts increase, *plant requirements become excessive.* If large quantities of plant material are available, the above method presents no problem.

What if plant sources are limited? I suggest the following alternatives: use another recipe for which dye plant material is available. Or, follow a sliding scale of plant increase according to the Table I.

Percentage method of calculating recipe amounts

There is another way of calculating a proportional change of ingredient amounts. It is more precise and allows for more flexibility. A dye-craftsman, set up for business, or a recipe-formula writer usually works this way. The basis of calculation is the *dry weight* of the textile. The remaining ingredients —including dyestuff, mordant, and other chemicals—are written in percentages. These are used to calculate recipe amounts.

The home dyer does not have to work this way. As a matter of fact, many studio dyers work from a favorite recipe and then experiment. For the sake of completeness I have included percentage tables. Who knows, you may want to set up a dyer's shop. Three percentage tables follow:

Table II—Chemicals Used in Dye Recipes: Percentage Amounts
Table III—Chemicals Used for Pre-Mordanting: Fixed Percentages
Table IV—Exotic Dye Requirements

for Recipes: Percentage Amounts

In each of the tables, sample calculations are shown. Amounts needed for eight ounces of textile are given in *grams*, approximate *ounces*, and approximate *kitchen measure*. Kitchen measure can be used if no scale is available. For measuring fractional amounts by kitchen measure use:

Plastic tablespoon, teaspoon, 3/4-teaspoon, 1/2-teaspoon, and 1/4-teaspoon measures.

For amounts less than 1/4-teaspoon follow the "eyeball system" (divide visually). It is better to use a scale for chemicals.

TABLE II / CHEMICALS USED IN DYE RECIPES: PERCENTAGE AMOUNTS
(Chemicals used in dye bath or afterbath)

CHEMICAL	PERCENTAGE TO TRY	CALCULATIONS	GRAM EQUIVALENT PER 8 OUNCES OF TEXTILE	APPROXIMATE OUNCES PER 8 OUNCES OF TEXTILE	APPROXIMATE KITCHEN MEASURE PER 8 OUNCES OF TEXTILE
Alum (potassium alum)	25%	.25 × textile weight	56.7 grams	2 ounces	4 tablespoons
with cream of tartar	6%	.06 × textile weight	13.6 grams	1/2 ounce	1 tablespoons
Chrome (potassium dichromate) (1½–4%)*	1½%	.015 × textile weight	3.4 grams	1/8 ounce	1/2 teaspoon
with cream of tartar	1½%	.015 × textile weight	3.4 grams	1/8 ounce	3/4 teaspoon
Chrome-alum (2–4%)	2%	.02 × textile weight	4.5 grams	1/5 ounce	3/4 teaspoon
with cream of tartar	2%	.02 × textile weight	4.5 grams	1/5 ounce	1 teaspoon
Copper (cupric sulfate) (1–4%)	1½%	.015 × textile weight	3.4 grams	1/10 ounce	3/4 teaspoon
with cream of tartar	3%	.03 × textile weight	6.8 grams	1/4 ounce	1½ teaspoons
Iron (ferrous sulfate) (4–8%)	4%	.04 × textile weight	9.1 grams	1/3 ounce	1 teaspoon
with cream of tartar	6%	.06 × textile weight	13.6 grams	1/2 ounce	1 tablespoon
Salt (table or Glauber's)	20%	.20 × textile weight	45.4 grams	1½ ounces	2 tablespoons
Tin (stannous chloride)	2%	.02 × textile weight	4.5 grams	1/5 ounce	3/4 teaspoon
with cream of tartar	2%	.02 × textile weight	4.5 grams	1/5 ounce	1 teaspoon

NOTES: *1½–4% means that a range of choices may be made, from 1½% to 4% chemical. □ 1 ounce ≡ 28.35 grams. □ Kitchen measure can be used if no scale is available. The above kitchen measure applies only for granular alum, chrome, chrome-alum, iron, and salt. The tin is in crystal form and the cream of tartar is powdered. If the alum is in lump or powder form, it must be weighed, not measured.

TABLE III/CHEMICALS USED FOR PRE-MORDANTING: FIXED PERCENTAGES

CHEMICAL	PERCENTAGE TO TRY	CALCULATIONS	GRAM EQUIVALENT PER 8 OUNCES OF TEXTILE	APPROXIMATE OUNCES PER 8 OUNCES OF TEXTILE	APPROXIMATE KITCHEN MEASURE PER 8 OUNCES OF TEXTILE
Alum (potassium alum) (15–25%)*	25%	.25 × textile weight	56.7 grams	2 ounces	4 tablespoons
with cream of tartar	6%	.06 × textile weight	13.6 grams	1/2 ounce	1 tablespoon
Chrome (potassium dichromate) (2–4%)	3%	.03 × textile weight	6.8 grams	1/4 ounce	1 teaspoon
with cream of tartar	3%	.03 × textile weight	6.8 grams	1/4 ounce	1½ teaspoons
Copper (cupric sulfate) (1–4%)	3%	.03 × textile weight	6.8 grams	1/4 ounce	1¾ teaspoons
with cream of tartar	3%	.03 × textile weight	6.8 grams	1/4 ounce	1½ teaspoons
Iron (ferrous sulfate) (4–6%)	5%	.05 × textile weight	11.3 grams	2/5 ounce	1½ teaspoons
with cream of tartar (10–12%)	10%	.10 × textile weight	22.7 grams	4/5 ounce	4 teaspoons
Tannin	12%	.12 × textile weight	27.2 grams	1 ounce	5 tablespoons
Tin (stannous chloride) (4–6%)	4%	.04 × textile weight	9.1 grams	1/3 ounce	1¼ teaspoons
with cream of tartar	2%	.02 × textile weight	4.5 grams	1/5 ounce	1 teaspoon

NOTES: *15-25% means that a range of choices may be made, from 15% to 25% chemical. □ 1 ounce = 28.35 grams. □ See Notes for Table II.

TABLE IV/"EXOTIC" DYE REQUIREMENTS FOR RECIPES: PERCENTAGE AMOUNTS

EXOTIC DYE	PERCENTAGE TO TRY	CALCULATIONS	GRAM EQUIVALENT PER 8 OUNCES OF TEXTILE	APPROXIMATE OUNCES PER 8 OUNCES OF TEXTILE
Cochineal (for crimson)				
on alumed wool (8–15%)	10%	.10 × textile weight	22.7 grams	4/5 ounce
on alumed silk	40%	.40 × textile weight	90.7 grams	3 1/5 ounces
Cochineal (for scarlet) (5–12%)	8%	.08 × textile weight	18.1 grams	3/5 ounce
with stannous chloride	6%	.06 × textile weight	13.6 grams	1/2 ounce
with cream of tartar (6–8%)	7%	.07 × textile weight	13.6 grams	1/2 ounce
Indigo Crystals (50–100%)	50%	.50 × textile weight	113.4 grams	4 ounces
Indigo extract	3%	.03 × textile weight	6.8 grams	1/4 ounce
Logwood (for blue)				
on chromed cotton	30%	.30 × textile weight	68.0 grams	2 2/5 ounces
with cupric sulfate	2%	.02 × textile weight	4.5 grams	1/5 ounce
with chalk (3% of dye weight)	3%	.03 × 2 2/5 ounces dye	2.0 grams	1/10 ounce
Logwood (for purple)	30%	.30 × textile weight	68.0 grams	2 2/5 ounces
use wool or cotton pre-mordanted				
with tin and cream of tartar				
Madder (40–60%)	40%	.40 × textile weight	90.7 grams	3 1/5 ounces
with chalk (1–2%)	1%	.01 × 3 1/5 ounces dye	.90 grams	Pinch or 3/100 ounce
Osage orange	50%	.50 × textile weight	113.4 grams	4 ounces
Weld	60%	.60 × textile weight	136.0 grams	5 ounces
with chalk (4% of dye weight)	4%	.04 × 5 ounces dye	5.7 grams	1/5 ounce
Woad crystals (50–100%)	50%	.50 × textile weight	113.4 grams	4 ounces

2. *Rule of the plant*: Weigh or measure out plant material at hand. Let this amount determine how much textile can be dyed. Proceed as usual.

Rule-of-thumb estimate of dye plant amounts

There are ways of achieving dye results which are based on experience and so-called "common sense." However, I would guess there is no such thing as common sense without experience or tradition. It is my feeling that successful rule-of-thumb cooking can only be done by practiced cooks. The same for rule-of-thumb dyeing. It takes dyeing practice to proceed in a seemingly free and easy way.

Here are several variations on rule-of-thumb dyeing:

1. *Rule of the pot*: Enter as much plant material, textile, and water as your dye pot will hold without crowding the textile. Proceed as usual, or according to recipe. Or, crowd as much plant material and water as your dye pot will hold; extract dye by heating; strain out plants, and proceed as usual.

D

Iron buff as a mordant for cotton

The iron-buff dye method can also be considered a form of mordanting. Cotton takes certain dyes better when previously mordanted (dyed) with ferrous sulfate followed by an alkaline dip. The cotton turns orange as a result of the process, thus limiting further color effects. Any dye used subsequently on an iron-dyed textile must be compatible visually and chemically. The use of tannin as a mordant presents a similar problem in that the textile is dyed a tan color by the mordant.

TEXTILE
Scoured, presoaked cotton or jute (8 ounces)

INGREDIENTS
Ferrous sulfate (5%—dissolved in 2 gallons of cold water) (11 grams or ⁴⁄₁₀ ounces)

Washing soda (5%—dissolved in 1 gallon of water) (11 grams or ⁴⁄₁₀ ounces)

WATER
Tap

POTS
Step I
Nonreacting pan or plastic dish pan for iron bath

Step II
Nonreacting pot for alkaline dip

METHOD
Step I
1. Enter textile in iron solution in pan.
2. Move textile about in iron solution for 30 minutes.
3. Remove textile and squeeze.

Step II
1. Dip textile in washing soda solution in pot.
2. Heat to 180°F (82°C) for 15 minutes.
3. Wash in dilute soapy bath.
4. Rinse thoroughly.
5. Dry for storage or proceed to over-dye procedure (see Appendix F).

E

Neutralizing machine-spun yarn before mordanting

I have encountered the following problem. Dye variations occur in skeins of the same type of white wool from the same manufacturer even though they were pre-mordanted together and later dyed together. The skeins vary in ability to receive dye, even though they receive exactly the same treatment at the same time *in my workshop*. I finally realized that the difference between one skein which dyed pastel and another which dyed dark was *factory batch*.

It would appear that variable "dye take" is due to a factory process called carbonizing followed by incomplete neutralizing. Thus, one batch of wool may be left more acid than another. Carbonizing involves the use of acid to burn out vegetable contamination present in some grades of loose wool. The spinner (the factory) should wash and neutralize the carbonized wool with an alkaline substance to remove any acidity. If this is not done, trouble occurs at the dyeing stage.

I now routinely neutralize any factory-spun yarn before mordanting. This can be conveniently combined with presoaking. Prepare a bath of one-quarter ounce of baking soda to one quart of water. Soak skeined wool twenty-four hours in this alkaline bath. Rinse wool thoroughly and proceed to mordanting or dye process. It is not necessary to neutralize handspun or any yarn which gives uniform results.

NOTE: For 1 ounce of wool use 1 quart of water and $\frac{1}{4}$ ounce of baking soda. For 16 ounces of wool use 4 gallons of water and 4 ounces of baking soda.

F

Over-dyeing

Over-dyeing is achieved by dyeing one color over another. Certain colors can only be achieved in this way. Bright hard greens are rarely achieved from natural sources except by dyeing first with a clear intense yellow and over-dyeing with indigo. Brilliant yellow-reds are obtained by over-dyeing with madder on a clear bright yellow. The practice of over-dyeing is more successful with exotic dyes, the reason being that such dyes are clear and intense.

I have seldom found it necessary to use this method for the following reasons: first of all, I use country-side plants much of the time. Dyes obtained from these plants are usually neither pure enough, nor clear enough to lend themselves to blending. Secondly (and more important), I am satisfied with the range of color obtained and feel no need for the effects of over-dye.

It is an interesting technique, nonetheless. Should one wish to experiment, remember to choose dyes which are clear and bright. This method is especially useful in brightening fabrics dulled by much use. In certain sections of Nigeria, worn, light-colored work garments were freshened by over-dyeing with indigo blue.

linen cloth.

10. Pour into little bottles and cover tightly.

NOTE: Natural fragrance can be added to the brew before straining; for example, juice from simmered bay fruit.

Country-style black ink (Adapted from J. & R. Bronson).

INGREDIENTS
Oak galls, powdered (4 ounces)
Ferrous sulfate (2 ounces)
Gum arabic (dissolved in 1 cup of boiling water) (1¼ ounces)
Alum (½ ounce)

WATER
Tap (5 cups)

POT
Jar with lid (2-quart)

CONTAINERS
Several small, labeled bottles

METHOD
1. Pour 4 cups of boiling water over powdered galls in jar.
2. Cover jar tightly.
3. Set aside to steep for 3 or so days.
4. Add ferrous sulfate to jar and stir with wooden spoon.
5. Cover.
6. Set aside to steep for several more days, stirring every day.
7. Add gum arabic solution.
8. Stir in the alum.
9. Strain mixture through a coarse

H

Cosmetic recipes

The recipes which follow are intended to demonstrate how natural dyes are used in self-beautification. The concoctions tend to be oily, grainy, or lumpy, and sometimes pungent, as one would expect from simple methods. Here again, a professional concocter would patiently compound and produce more accomplished results. Practice helps. There is, nonetheless, a *real* difference between freshly picked, lumpy chamomile flower hair pack and the smooth, creamy, seductive shampoo which wells up from a plastic tube. One has to take sides.

NOTE: Always consult your physician before using any of the following concoctions for the hair or face.

EGYPTIAN HENNA BRILLIANTINE FOR THE HAIR

Henna is one of the exotic dyes. It has been used since very early times as a hair and fingernail dye. It is sold in some pharmacies. Ask for Egyptian powdered henna.

INGREDIENTS
Henna powder (about 1 teaspoon)
Baby oil or mineral oil (about 1 ounce)

POT
Any small metal cup which can be used over heat

CONTAINER
Bottle or jar with lid or stopper

METHOD
1. Heat oil for a few minutes.
2. Enter henna powder and stir until well-mixed.
3. Pour into jar and cover.

NOTE: This is an aromatic, deep golden-brownish, oily mixture. I cannot claim that it adds sex appeal, but it made me feel bright as a button. Shake well before using.

EGYPTIAN HENNA HAIR RINSE OR PACK

For hair rinse:

INGREDIENTS
Henna powder (1 tablespoon)

WATER
Tap (1 quart, hot)

POT
Bowl

METHOD
1. Wash and rinse hair.
2. Mix henna into hot water.
3. Soak hair in rinse for 15 minutes. If mixture is kept fairly hot, the results will be more pronounced.
4. Rinse out the henna from the hair.

For hair pack:

INGREDIENT
Henna powder (3 ounces)

WATER
Tap (1 cup, hot)

POT
Bowl

METHOD
1. Wash and rinse hair.
2. Stir henna into hot water until thoroughly mixed.
3. Apply paste to hair, covering all areas.
4. Wrap hair with old towel or wear closely-fitting shower cap.
5. Leave henna pack on for from several minutes to 1 hour, according to desired results. *Please experiment conservatively unless you*

want orange colored hair!

6. Rinse hair thoroughly.

NOTE: Long hair requires larger amounts of henna.

TEA HAIR RINSE OR POMADE

It is more difficult to darken light hair by natural means than it is to yellow or redden it. It is reported that American Indians used several plant sources for hair dye. Indigo was used in India as a hair dye. I have been told that a hair dye was made from a walnut leaf mixture much like the walnut recipe in this book. The hair was soaked in a very warm dye liquor for half an hour or so. Tannin-rich substances can stain skin as well as hair.

INGREDIENTS
Black tea (4 ounces)

H.E.C. base for *pomade only* (about ¾ ounce)

Vinegar (1 cup)

WATER
4 quarts

POTS
Step I
Nonreacting

Step II
Iron

METHOD
Step I
1. Cover tea with water and simmer.
2. This liquor is a dark tea color and can be used as a hair rinse by soaking the hair in it. Cool a little before using.
3. *For a blackish pomade:* Proceed to Step II.

Step II
1. Strain tea leaves out.
2. Combine tea liquor and vinegar in iron pot.
3. Simmer slowly until about 3 tablespoons of dye liquor remain.
4. Cool.
5. Stir dye concentrate into H.E.C. base, mixing a little liquid in at a

time until all is used up. This blackish cream is the pomade.

NOTES: H.E.C. base—Haydens Emulsifying Cream base—is a "hydrophylic" cream. It can take up liquid equal to its own weight. It can be purchased in small amounts from a pharmacy. □ A black jell can be made, instead of a pomade, by omitting the base. Prepare a jell by cooking up either psyllium seed or flax seed in water. Strain and use as a jell base with the dye concentrate. (It is difficult to strain the seeds out of the jell.) □ Anhydrous lanolin, a fatty substance, can also be used as a pomade base. □ Neither the pomade or jell actually dye the hair. They simply act as a temporary blackener. They are a bit messy, but can be applied with a brush for "touch up."

CHAMOMILE HAIR RINSE OR PACK

Various flowers have been used since antiquity for hair yellowing. Mullein flowers, marigold, and chamomile are examples. Two methods are given—the rinse and the pack. The latter has a more pronounced effect. Only blonde or silvery gray hair are affected. Flower rinses tend to have a drying effect on the hair.

Rinse
INGREDIENT
Chamomile flowers, dried (use twice as much if fresh) (about ¾ ounce)

WATER
Tap (2 quarts)

POT
Basin or bowl

METHOD
1. Wash and rinse hair.
2. Cover flowers with water.
3. Simmer for 20 minutes.

4. Cool to a comfortable temperature.
5. Dip hair in dye for 15 to 30 minutes.
6. Rinse hair.

Pack
INGREDIENTS
Chamomile flowers, dried (about 1 ounce)

WATER
Tap (about 1 quart)

POT
Nonreacting

METHOD
1. Combine flowers and water.
2. Simmer for 30 minutes.
3. Cool to a comfortable temperature.
4. Apply flower mixture to hair.
5. Wrap hair with old towel or close-fitting shower cap.
6. Leave pack on for ½ hour.
7. Rinse hair thoroughly.

FACE COLOR CREAM
INGREDIENTS
Beet juice from fresh beets (about 3 tablespoons)

Cream base, like H.E.C., obtainable at a pharmacy (about ¾ ounce)

CONTAINER
Jar with lid

METHOD
1. Simmer beets gently and reserve juice.
2. Cool.
3. Stir juice into cream base a little at a time until all liquid is absorbed.
4. Spoon into jar and cover.

NOTES: Almost any color body "paint" can be prepared in this way. Edible berries and fruits for reds and purples; grape juice for blue! Experiment. □ Anhydrous lanolin can also be used as a base for cosmetics and salves. It is a fatty substance. □ Remember to consult your physician before applying substances to the face and body.

TOILET VINEGAR AND INSECT REPELLENT?
Here is an old-fashioned approach to toilet water. It is said to be a skin refresher on hot days and an insect repeller (hopefully).

INGREDIENTS
Apple cider vinegar (about ½ cup)

Fragrant, nonpoisonous flowers or herbs, such as chamomile, lavender, or sweet woodruff (½ pound)

WATER
Tap (to cover)

POT
Nonreacting, with lid

CONTAINER
Jar with stopper

METHOD
1. Cover plant material with water and simmer gently for ½ hour in covered pot.
2. Cool.
3. Strain plants out.
4. Mix vinegar and plant water.
5. Pour into jar and stopper.

NOTE: Be sure you are using nonpoisonous, nonallergenic plants and natural vinegar.

Sources of chemicals, dyes, fleece, plants, seeds, yarn, and books

Following are listed some suppliers of chemicals, exotic dyes, fibers, seed, seedlings, dye wood, and yarn. Most of the suppliers listed below accept mail orders. Price lists or catalogs are available upon request. It is not a complete list, but may prove to be useful. It is hoped that the home dyer may discover sources convenient to her location. Investigate the Yellow Pages of your local telephone book. Look for listings of chemicals, handweaving supplies, school supplies. Ask your pharmacist if he knows of a supplier of technical grade chemicals. These are cheaper than the pharmaceutical grade. Either quality of the necessary chemical can be used in dyeing.

C. F. BAILEY
St. Aubyn, 15 Dutton Street
Bankstoun, New South Wales 2200,
Australia
Dyes, fibers, yarn/Price list, Wool samples $1.50

CLAUDE A. BARR
Prairie Gem Ranch
Smithwick, South Dakota 57782
Native plants, seeds

BRIGGS AND LITTLE'S WOOLEN
MILL LTD.
Harvey Station
New Brunswick, Canada
Yarn

BRYANT LABORATORY INC.
880 Jones Street
Berkeley, California 94710
Chemicals, mordants/Mail order ($10.00 minimum), List the chemicals you want and ask for price list, Sold by the pound

CAMBRIDGE WOOLS LTD.
Box 2572, Auckland, New Zealand
Fleece/Free catalog

COLONIAL TEXTILES
2604 Cranbrook
Ann Arbor, Michigan 48104
Dyes, fleece/Free price list

COMAK CHEMICALS LTD.
Dept. MCG/p, Swinton Works,
Moon Street
London N1, England
Dyes, chemicals

WM. CONDON & SONS LTD.
65 Queen Street, P. O. Box 129
Prince Edward Island, Canada
Yarns/Sample card

DHARMA TRADING CO.
1952 University Avenue, P. O. Box 1288
Berkeley, California 94701
Dyes, yarns

DOMINION HERB DISTRIBUTORS, INC.
61 St. Catherine Street West
Montreal 18, Canada
Botanicals, chemicals, dyes/Catalog

GREENE HERB GARDENS
Greene, Rhode Island 02827
Seeds (including: chamomile, fennel, mullein, tansy, weld, woad, and yarrow)/Catalog

HILLTOP HERB FARM
Box 866
Cleveland, Texas 77327
Herb plants

KEM CHEMICAL CO.
545 S. Fulton Street
Mt. Vernon, New York 10550
Chemicals/Catalog

KIEHL PHARMACY
109 Third Avenue
New York, New York 10003
Chemicals

LAMB'S NURSERIES
101 E. Sharp Avenue
Spokane, Washington 99202
Seeds of wild flowers / Price list

LESLIE'S WILDFLOWER NURSERY
30 Summer Street
Methuen, Massachusetts 01844
Seeds of wild flowers / Price list

JOHN MCINDOE
51 Crawford Street
Dunidin, New Zealand
Dyes / Catalog $.90

MERRY GARDENS
Camden, Maine 04843
Herbs, plants / Price list

MIDWEST WILDFLOWERS
Box 664B
Rockton, Illinois 61702
Seeds of wild flowers

NICHOL'S GARDEN NURSERY
1190 North Pacific Highway
Albany, Oregon 97321
Herbs, plants, seeds / Price list

NATURE'S FIBRES
109 Tinker Street
Woodstock, New York 12498
Chemicals, dyes, yarns / Price list

NATURE'S HERB CO.
281 Ellis Street
San Francisco, California 94102
Botanicals, dyes / Booklet

THEODORE PAYNE FOUNDATION
10459 Tusford Street
Sun Valley, California 91352
Plants, seeds

CLYDE ROBIN
P. O. Box 2091
Castro Valley, California 94546
*Seeds of wild flowers and trees / Catalog
$.50*

THE SHEEP VILLAGE
2005 Bridgeway
Sausalito, California 94965
Chemicals, dyes, fibers, yarns / Price list

SISKIYOU RARE PLANT NURSERY
522 Franquette
Medford, Oregon 97501
Native plants, seeds

SEMTON PRODUCTS
P. O. Box 932
Woodstock, Ontario, Canada
*Fibers, (including nylon, Orlon; and
rayon)*

GEORGE SHERMAN
9317 Guadalupe Trail N.W.
Albuquerque, New Mexico 87114
Dyes, mordants

BOB STOCKSDALE, WOOD CRAFTSMAN
2147 Oregon Street
Berkeley, California 94705
*Exotic wood, dye wood (including canary
wood, coralline, Osage, padauk, pernambuco) Trimmings: $.50 per pound (post-
age extra), By the piece: $1.00 per pound
(postage extra), Shavings: $5.00 per
pound (postage extra) / Prepaid orders
only, No price list*

SUNNYBROOK FARMS NURSERY
9448 Mayfield Road
Chesterland, Ohio 44026
Herb plants

WORLD-WIDE HERBS
11 St. Catherine East
Montreal, Canada
Botanicals, dyes, mordants / Free catalog

THE YARN DEPOT
545 Sutter Street
San Francisco, California 94102
Dyes, fleece, mordants, yarn

MAIL ORDER TEXTILE ARTS BOOKS

ROBIN & RUSS HANDWEAVERS
533 North Adams Street
McMinnville, Oregon 97128
Book list, fleece, Fibers, yarns / Price list

Selected Bibliography

ADROSKO, RITA J. *Natural Dyes and Home Dyeing.* New York: Dover Publications, Inc., 1971.

AMSDEN, CHARLES AVERY. *Navaho Weaving.* Albuquerque: University of New Mexico Press, 1949.

BAILEY, LIBERTY H. *Manual of Cultivated Plants.* New York: Macmillan Publishing Co., 1968.

BAYER, HERBERT; GROPIUS, WALTER; and GROPIUS, ISE; eds. *Bauhaus 1919–1928.* New York: The Museum of Modern Art, 1938.

BENNETT, H., ed. *Formulas for Profit.* Cleveland and New York: World Publishing Co., 1943.

BRONSON, J. and R. *The Domestic Manufacturer's Assistant, and Family Directory, in the Arts of Weaving and Dyeing.* Utica, New York: 1817. Reprinted 1949, Charles T. Branford Co.

BRYAN, NONABAH and YOUNG, STELLA. *Navajo Native Dyes.* Lawrence, Kansas: Bureau of Indian Affairs, Publications Service, Haskell Institute, 1940.

BÜHLER, A. "Primitive Dyeing Methods," in *Ciba Review,* No. 68, June 1948, pp. 2845–2500.

BÜHLER, A. "Indigo Dyeing Among Primitive Races," in *Ciba Review,* No. 85, April 1951, pp. 3088–3091.

Cahiers des arts et techniques d'Afrique du nord. Paris: No. 1, 1951–52.

CARMEN, JEAN K. "Dyeing—An Exercise in Patience," in *The Australian Handweaver and Spinner,* Vol. XXIV, No. 1, May 1972, pp. 8, 9.

CARMAN, JEAN K. "Vegetable Dyes from Australian Eucalyptus," in *Australian Plants,* Vol. 6, No. 49, December 1971, pp. 212, 213.

COLTON, MARY RUSSELL. *Hopi Dyes.* Flagstaff: The Museum of Northern Arizona, 1965.

CROOKES, WILLIAM. *Dyeing and Calico-Printing.* London: Longmans, Green, and Co., 1874.

DAVENPORT, ELSIE G. *Yarn Dyeing.* London: Sylvan Press, 1955.

DAVENPORT, ELSIE G. *Your Handspinning.* Big Sur, California: Craft and Hobby Book Service, 1964.

EATON, ALLEN H. *Handicrafts of the Southern Highlands.* New York: Russell Sage Foundation, 1937.

ELMORE, FRANCIS H. *Ethnobotany of the Navajo.* Albuquerque: The University of New Mexico Press, 1944.

FORBES, R. J. *Studies in Ancient Technology,* Vol. IV. Leiden: E. J. Bull, 1956.

GERBER, WILLI and FRED. "Cochineal as a Domestic Dyestuff," in *Handweaver and Craftsman,* Vol. 23, No. 6, November/December 1972, pp. 16–21.

GRIEVE, M. *A Modern Herbal.* New York: Dover Publications, Inc., 1971.

HUMMEL, J. J. *The Dyeing of Textile Fabrics.* London: Cassell and Co., Ltd., 1885.

HUTCHENS, ALMA R. *Indian Herbology of North America.* Kumbakonam, India: Homeo House Press, 1970.

KIERSTEAD, SALLIE PEASE. *Natural Dyes.* Boston: Bruce Humphries, Inc., 1950.

KIRK, DONALD R. *Wild Edible Plants of the Western United States.* Healdsburg, California: Naturegraph Publishers, 1970.

LEGETT, WILLIAM F. *Ancient and Medieval Dyes.* Brooklyn, New York: Chemical Publishing Co., 1944.

McKENZIE, HOWARD L. *Mealybugs of California.* Berkeley and Los Angeles: University of California Press, 1967.

MAERZ, A. and PAUL, M. REA. *A Dictionary of Color.* New York: McGraw-Hill Book Co., Inc., 1930.

MATHEWS, J. MERRITT. *Application of Dyestuffs.* New York: John Wiley & Sons, Inc., 1920.

MEDSGER, OLIVER PERRY. *Edible Wild Plants.* New York: Macmillan Publishing Co., 1967.

MEYER, JOSEPH E. *The Herbalist.* Privately published, printed by Rand McNally Co., Conkey Division: 1960.

MOHOLY-NAGY, LASZLO. *The New Vision.* New York: Wittenborn, Schultz, 1947.

MUENSCHER, W. C. *Weeds.* New York: Macmillan Publishing Co., 1955.

MURPHY, EDITH VAN ALLEN. *Indian Uses of Native Plants.* Fort Bragg, California: Mendocino County Historical Society, 1950.

PELLEW, CHARLES E. *Dyes and Dyeing.* New York: McBride, Nast, and Co., 1913.

ROBBINS, W. W.; BELLUE, M. K.; and BALL, W. S. *Weeds of California.* Sacramento: Printing Division, Documents Section, California State Department of Agriculture, n.d.

SCHAEFER, G. "The Cultivation of Madder," in *Ciba Review,* No. 39, May 1941, pp. 1398–1406.

SCHETKY, ETHEL JANE Mc D., ed. *Dye Plants and Dyeing.* Brooklyn, New York: Brooklyn Botanic Garden, 1964.

TERGIT, GABRIELE. *Flowers Through the Ages.* Philadelphia: Dufour Editions, 1962.

THOMAS, V. *Guide Pratique de Teinture Moderne.* Paris: L. Mulo, Libraire-Editeur, 12, Rue Hautefeuille, 12, 1900.

WHITING, ALFRED F. *Ethnobotany of the Hopi.* Flagstaff: Museum of Northern Arizona, 1966.

Color
Index

(References are to Recipe number.)

VARIOUS BLUES

EXOTIC, MINERAL, EARLY / 8, 9, 18, 19, 20, 21, 22, 23
WEEDS AND WILD FLOWERS / 57, 58
GARDEN FLOWERS / 92, 93, 95, 96, 97, 101, 102, 116, 117, 118, 134, 139, 140
WILD SHRUBS / 143, 154
GARDEN SHRUBS / 164, 175, 178, 183
TREES / 223, 224
FOODS AND ASSOCIATED PLANTS / 230, 231, 232, 236, 237, 238
NOTE: Plant sources of blue dye are *very* scarce.

VARIOUS PURPLES, INCLUDING MAUVE AND LAVENDER

EXOTIC, MINERAL, EARLY / 8, 9, 11
LICHENS / 24, 26
GARDEN FLOWERS / 98, 113, 140
WILD SHRUBS / 142, 145, 146, 153
GARDEN SHRUBS / 174, 176, 177, 179
FOODS AND ASSOCIATED PLANTS / 230, 231, 232, 234, 239, 242, 244, 253, 255

VARIOUS REDS, INCLUDING MAGENTA, PINK, AND ROSE

EXOTIC, MINERAL, EARLY / 4, 5, 6, 12, 14, 15, 16, 17
LICHENS / 24, 26, 28
WEEDS AND WILD FLOWERS / 85
GARDEN FLOWERS / 98, 99, 115, 129
TREES / 198, 200, 201, 207, 217, 218, 219, 220, 221
FOODS AND ASSOCIATED PLANTS / 234, 241
NOTE: Plant sources of red dye are scarce. Magenta sources are scarcer.

VARIOUS ORANGES, INCLUDING RUSSET AND TERRA-COTTA

EXOTIC, MINERAL, EARLY / 1, 4, 5, 17
LICHENS / 25, 27
WEEDS AND WILD FLOWERS / 31, 32, 37, 41, 47, 76, 77, 80, 84
GARDEN FLOWERS / 99, 104, 105, 107, 108, 121, 132, 141
WILD SHRUBS / 144
GARDEN SHRUBS / 173, 182
TREES / 194, 195, 196, 198, 199, 200, 206, 207, 214, 228
FOODS AND ASSOCIATED PLANTS / 247, 259, 264

VARIOUS YELLOWS, INCLUDING BRASS, GOLD, AND OCHER

EXOTIC, MINERAL, EARLY / 2, 13, 14
WEEDS AND WILD FLOWERS / 29, 30, 33, 34, 35, 38, 39, 41, 43, 45, 47, 48, 49, 52, 54, 59, 60, 62, 63, 64, 65, 67, 69, 72, 74, 76, 78, 80, 81, 84, 86, 90

GARDEN FLOWERS / 94, 100, 103, 106, 120, 121, 130, 131, 132, 138
WILD SHRUBS / 150, 156, 163
GARDEN SHRUBS / 167
TREES / 189, 193, 205, 213, 214, 216, 227, 228
FOODS AND ASSOCIATED PLANTS / 233, 235, 245, 262
NOTE: There are many more sources of plant yellows than are described in this book. It is the most readily available dye color.

VARIOUS GREENS, INCLUDING CHARTREUSE

WEEDS AND WILD FLOWERS / 33, 36, 40, 42, 44, 47, 48, 49, 50, 53, 55, 56, 59, 61, 62, 63, 65, 66, 67, 68, 70, 71, 72, 73, 79, 82, 83, 87, 88, 89, 90, 91
GARDEN FLOWERS / 92, 93, 94, 96, 100, 101, 109, 110, 111, 119, 120, 121, 122, 123, 124, 127, 128, 131, 133, 134, 135, 136, 137, 138
WILD SHRUBS / 147, 148, 149, 155, 156, 160
GARDEN SHRUBS / 165, 168, 169, 175, 180, 181, 184, 186, 187
TREES / 190, 202, 204, 205, 208, 210, 213, 215, 222, 225, 227
FOODS AND ASSOCIATED PLANTS / 240, 242, 245, 248, 249, 250, 251, 252, 254, 261, 263, 268
NOTE: Plant sources of green dye are said to be *scarce*. I have not found it so. Only *grass green* color is scarce.

VARIOUS BEIGES AND TANS

EXOTIC, MINERAL, EARLY / 3
WEEDS AND WILD FLOWERS / 35, 37, 74
GARDEN FLOWERS / 125, 129
WILD SHRUBS / 151
GARDEN SHRUBS / 171
TREES / 190, 191, 203, 208, 209, 211, 212, 228
FOODS AND ASSOCIATED PLANTS / 256, 259, 264, 265, 268
NOTE: There are many more sources of tan dye than are described in this book. This color is one of the easiest to obtain.

VARIOUS BROWNS

EXOTIC, MINERAL, EARLY / 7
WEEDS AND WILD FLOWERS / 36, 39, 40, 42, 43, 51, 52, 53, 75, 79, 82, 85
GARDEN FLOWERS / 100, 106, 112, 114, 125, 126, 128, 130, 137
WILD SHRUBS / 158, 159, 163
GARDEN SHRUBS / 166, 167, 172, 181, 185
TREES / 189, 192, 197, 210, 211, 212, 228
FOODS AND ASSOCIATED PLANTS / 229, 246, 256, 257, 260, 263, 265, 266, 267

VARIOUS BLACKS AND GRAYS

EXOTIC, MINERAL, EARLY / 3, 10
WEEDS AND WILD FLOWERS / 36, 44, 46, 70
GARDEN FLOWERS / 113
WILD SHRUBS / 157, 161, 162
GARDEN SHRUBS / 168, 170, 188
TREES / 204, 226
FOODS AND ASSOCIATED PLANTS / 243, 252, 257, 258, 266

Dye Plant and Recipe Index

NOTE: This index furnishes a list of dye plants, alphabetized by the main descriptive word in the title. The recipe number, color result, and fiber type are also given. Where several color choices are indicated, the dyer will know that the differences are due to the different mordants and/or fibers used.

An *asterisk* in front of the dye plant name indicates that the recipe uses an *unmordanted* textile (fiber, yarn, or fabric). The letters *w, s, c, l,* and *j* stand for wool, silk, cotton, linen, or jute respectively.

A

ACACIA, flowers/189
(*Acacia* sp.)
Yellow or grayed maize yellow to light golden brown/w

ACACIA, pods/190
(*Acacia* sp.)
Moss green or tan/w

ALTHEA SHRUB or ROSE OF SHARON/164
(*Hibiscus syriacus*)
Medium to dark blue/w

ANEMONE, blue/92
(*Anemone* sp.)
Teal blue or light green/w

B

BARBERRY/165
(*Berberis* sp.)
Olive green/w

BARBERRY, and tin crystals/166
(*Berberis* sp.)
Terra-cotta brown/w

BEANS, dry red/229
(*Phaseolus vulgaris*)
Terra-cotta brown/w

*BEET ROOTS, steeped/15
(*Beta vulgaris*)
Magenta to deep red/w

BLACKBERRIES, in iron pot/230
(*Rubus* sp.)
Purple to blue/w

*BOTTLE BRUSH, flowers/191
(*Callistemon* sp.)
Tan to greenish beige/w

BOTTLE BRUSH, leaves/192
(*Callistemon* sp.)
Cinnamon brown/w

BRASS-BUTTONS/29
(*Cotula coronopifolia*)
Deep brassy gold /w

BUTTERFLY BUSH, flowers/167
(*Buddleia davidii*)
Orange-gold or gold-green or golden brown/j,w

BUTTERFLY BUSH, leaves and stems/169
(*Buddleia davidii*)
Olive green/w

BUTTERFLY BUSH, in iron pot/168
(*Buddleia davidii*)
Various greens or black/c,l,j,w

C

CABBAGE, purple/231
(*Brassica oleracea* var. *capitata*)
Various blues and lavenders/w,c,j

CABBAGE, purple, alternate/232
(*Brassica oleracea* var. *capitata*)
Various blues and lavenders/w,c,j

*CACTUS, purple fruit, steeped/16
(*Opuntia robusta*)
Magenta to rose/w

*CACTUS, ORCHID, red-flowered steeped/17
(*Epiphyllum* sp.)
Orange to rose /w

CAMELLIAS, red, in iron pot/170
(*Camellia* sp.)
Medium gray to dark gray/c,w

*CANARY WOOD, steeped/193
(*Morus mesozygia*)
Maize yellow or turmeric gold/w

CANARY WOOD/194
(*Morus mesozygia*)
Terra-cotta or burnt orange/w

CANARY WOOD, and tin crystals/195
(*Morus mesozygia*)
Pumpkin orange/w

CANTERBURY BELLS, purple/93
(*Campanula medium*)
Medium green or pale blue/w,c

CHAMOMILE/233
(*Anthemis nobilis*)
Various gold-yellows, aromatic/w

CHAMOMILE, fetid, stinkweed, may-
weed/30
(*Anthemis cotula*)
Deep gold or tan-gold/w

CHRYSANTHEMUM, leaves/94
(*Chrysanthemum* spp.)
Gold-yellow or green/w

CHRYSANTHEMUM, maroon/95
(*Chrysanthemum* spp.)
Variations of gray-turquoise/w,c

CINERARIA, dark-blue florist's/96
(*Senecio hybridus*)
Variations of turquoise or variations of
green/w

*CINERARIA, dark-blue florist's and
tin crystals/97
(*Senecio hybridus*)
Medium blue or dark blue/w

*CINERARIA, purple florist's, and tin
crystals/98
(*Senecio hybridus*)
Wine red or purple or lavender/w,l,j

COCHINEAL/6
(*Coccus cacti*)
Crimson/w,s,c

CORALLINE/196
(*Clutia tranvancorica*)
Pale apricot or brilliant orange/c,w

CORALLINE, in iron pot/197
(*Clutia tranvancorica*)
Dark brown/w

CORALLINE, and tin crystals/198
(*Clutia tranvancorica*)
Brilliant orange-red to vermilion or

maroon-orange/w

COREOPSIS/99
(*Coreopsis* spp.)
Neon orange to almost orange-red/w

COREOPSIS/31
(*Coreopsis auriculata* and *Coreopsis
calliopsidea*)
Orange to red-orange/w

COREOPSIS, giant/32
(*Coreopsis gigantea*)
Light orange to deep orange/w

*COREOPSIS, seed heads/100
(*Coreopsis* spp.)
Golden brown or bright olive green or
gold/w

CORN, purple Indian/234
(*Zea mays*)
Dark purple to maroon/w

COTONEASTER BERRIES/171
(*Cotoneaster* sp.)
Rose-tan/w

CROCUS, purple/101
(*Crocus vernus*)
Blue to turquoise or apple green/w

CROCUS, purple, and hyacinth/102
(*Crocus vernus* and *Hyacinthus* sp.)
Medium blue/w

CUDWEED EVERLASTING/39
(*Helichrysum petiolatum*)
Light golden yellow or brown, aro-
matic/w

CUDWEED EVERLASTING, and
cupric sulfate/40
(*Helichrysum petiolatum*)
Khaki green or light brown/w

CUDWEED, in iron pot/33
(*Gnaphalium* spp.)
Yellow or green/w

*CUTCH, catechu/7
(*Acacia catechu*)
Brown/c

D

DAFFODILS, yellow/103
(*Narcissus pseudo-narcissus*)
Bright yellow or deep gold/w

DAHLIA, seed heads/107
(*Dahlia pinnata*)
Bright orange/w

DAHLIA-COREOPSIS, old, bouquet / 105
(*Dahlia* sp. and *Coreopsis* sp.)
Intense yellow-orange to orange / w

DAHLIAS, yellow, and English walnut
leaves / 108
(*Dahlia pinnata* and *Juglans regia*)
Burnt orange / w

DAHLIAS, yellow, and onion skins in iron
pot / 106
(*Dahlia pinnata* and *Allium* sp.)
Maize yellow or golden brown / w

DAHLIA, yellow-red, and ammonia / 104
(*Dahlia pinnata*)
Brilliant burnt orange / w

DAISY, brownish, gloriosa, black-eyed
susan / 110
(*Rudbeckia* sp.)
Bright olive green to dark green / w

DAISY, purple or orange African / 109
(*Arctotis* sp.)
Various greens or olive green / w

DOCK BLOSSOMS / 37
(*Rumex* spp.)
Rose-beige to terra-cotta / w,c

DOCK ROOT / 35
(*Rumex* spp.)
Dark tan to old gold / w,c

*DOCK ROOT, in iron pot or with nails / 36
(*Rumex* spp.)
Dark green to brown or dark gray / w,c

*DOCK ROOT, wild rhubarb, steeped / 34
(*Rumex* spp.)
Pale to deep gold / w,c

DODDER, and bits of pickleweed / 38
(*Cuscuta* sp. and *Salicornia* sp.)
Yellow or ocher / w

E

*ELDERBERRY, blue or black, one-pot and
mordant method / 142
(*Sambucus* spp.)
Mauve / w

*ELDERBERRY, blue or black, one-pot and
mordant method and ammonia / 143
(*Sambucus* spp.)
Gray-blue / w

EUCALYPTUS, blue gum; bark / 202
(*Eucalyptus globulus*)
Variations of dark khaki green / w

*EUCALYPTUS, blue gum; leaves / 203

(*Eucalyptus globulus*)
Deep camel tan / w

EUCALYPTUS, blue gum; leaves in iron
pot / 204
(*Eucalyptus globulus*)
Light to dark green or charcoal gray / w,c

*EUCALYPTUS, mealy or ashy stringy-
bark / 207
(*Eucalyptus cinerea*)
Red-maroon or red-orange / w

*EUCALYPTUS, silver-dollar, and tin
crystals / 199
(*Eucalyptus polyanthemos*)
Various brilliant oranges or light
orange / w

*EUCALYPTUS, silver-dollar, with tin
crystals and chrome / 201
(*Eucalyptus polyanthemos*)
Red to maroon / w

*EUCALYPTUS, silver-dollar vari-
ation / 200
(*Eucalyptus polyanthemos*)
Variations of brilliant red-orange or
orange-red / w

EUCALYPTUS, Tasmanian snow-gum / 205
(*Eucalyptus coccifera*)
Mustard gold or dark olive green / w

*EUCALYPTUS, white-ironbark; leaves
and pods / 206
(*Eucalyptus leucoxylon*)
Deep burnt orange or terra-cotta / w

F

FENNEL / 43
(*Foeniculum vulgare*)
Mustard yellow or golden brown;
aromatic / w

*FILAREE, clocks, one-pot and mor-
dant / 44
(*Erodium* spp.)
Brown-green or green-gray or moss
green / w,c,l,j

*FLAX, New Zealand, flowers / 172
(*Phormium tenax*)
Brown / w

FLAX, New Zealand, seed pods / 173
(*Phormium tenax*)
Bright terra-cotta / w

FLAX, New Zealand, seed pods, and am-
monia / 174
(*Phormium tenax*)
Mauve / w

FOXGLOVE, purple/111
(*Digitalis purpurea*)
Chartreuse/w

G

GERANIUM, red, leaves/113
(*Pelargonium hortorum*)
Dark purple to gray/c

*GERANIUM, red and fish/112
(*Pelargonium hortorum*)
Dark brown or greenish brown/w

GODETIA, farewell to spring, and cupric sulfate/45
(*Clarkia* sp.)
Dark gold/c

GODETIA, farewell to spring, in iron pot/46
(*Clarkia* sp.)
Greenish gray/c

GOLDENROD, in iron pot/47
(*Solidago* spp.)
Mustard color or tan-orange or brown-olive/w

GOOSEFOOT, in unlined copper pot or with cupric sulfate/48
(*Chenopodium* sp.)
Dark green or green-gold/w

GORSE, furze flowers/144
(*Ulex europaeus*)
Orange/w

GRAPE, Concord-type; skins, and ammonia/236
(*Vitis labruscana*)
Dark greenish blue/w

GRAPE, Concord-type; skins, and cupric sulfate/237
(*Vitis labruscana*)
Dark blue/w

GRAPE, Concord-type; skins, and ferrous sulfate/238
(*Vitis labruscana*)
Dark blue/w

*GRAPE, leaves; one-pot and mordant method/235
(*Vitis* spp.)
Intense yellow/w

GRAPE, Oregon, berries/145
(*Mahonia* spp.)
Violet/w

GRAPE, Oregon, berries, and tin crystals/146
(*Mahonia* spp.)
Dark blue-purple/w

GRAPE, Oregon, leaves, and cupric sulfate/147
(*Mahonia* spp.)
Light olive green or medium olive green; aromatic/w

*GRAPE, Oregon, roots/148
(*Mahonia* spp.)
Olive green or light green/w, basketry materials

GUM PLANT, gumweed, grindelia/49
(*Grindelia* sp.)
Yellow and gold or olive green; aromatic/w

H

HAWTHORN, blossoms/210
(*Crataegus* sp.)
Variations of yellow-green or variations of gold-brown/w

HAWTHORN, India/178
(*Raphiolepis indica*)
Dark blue or turquoise/w

HAWTHORN, India, and tin crystals/179
(*Raphiolepis indica*)
Purple/w

HEDGE-NETTLE, betony/50
(*Stachys* sp.)
Chartreuse green/w

HERB ROBERT, wild geranium, red robin/51
(*Geranium robertianum*)
Light golden brown to rich brown/w

HIBISCUS, red, rose mallow/175
(*Hibiscus* spp.)
Various dark blues or various dark greens/w

HIBISCUS, red, and tin/176
(*Hibiscus* spp.)
Purple/w

HOLLYHOCK, red, in iron pot/114
(*Althaea rosea*)
Brown/w

HOLLYHOCK, red, and tin crystals/115
(*Althaea rosea*)
Wine color/w

HONEY BUSH, and tin crystals/177
(*Melianthus major*)
Violet/w

HYACINTH FLOWERS, deep-blue/116
(*Hyacinthus orientalis*)
Powder blue to medium blue/w

I

*INDIGO—AFRICAN METHOD/19
(*Indigofera tinctoria*)
Blue/w,c,l,j

*INDIGO—NORTH AFRICAN, three-hour
method/20
(*Indigofera tinctoria*)
Blue/w,c,l,j

*INDIGO—WEST SUDANESE
METHOD/18
(*Indigofera* sp.)
Blue/w,c,l,j

*INDIGO, blue pot/23
(*Indigofera tinctoria*)
Blue/w,c

*INDIGO, saxon vat/21
(*Indigofera tinctoria*)
Saxon blue/w,c,l,j

INDIGO, urine vat/22
(*Indigofera tinctoria*)
Blue/w,c

IRIS, dark-purple/117
(*Iris* spp.)
Various violet blues/w

IRIS, purple, fleur-de-lis, and tin crystals/118
(*Iris germanica* and other *Iris* spp.)
Various dark to light blues/w

*IRON BUFF/4
(Mineral pigment from scrap iron)
Orange to rusty red/c,l,j

*IRON BUFF/5
(Mineral pigment from ferrous sulfate)
Orange to rusty red/c,l,j

K

KLAMATH WEED, and ammonia/52
(*Hypericum perforatum*)
Mustard gold or raw sienna/w

KLAMATH WEED, and cupric sulfate/53
(*Hypericum perforatum*)
Dark yellow-green or light brown/w

KNOTWEED, doorweed, mat-grass/54
(*Polygonum aviculare*)
Creamy yellow or brighter yellow or
brassy yellow/w

KNOTWEED, in unlined copper pot/55
(*Polygonum aviculare*)
Moss green or brassy moss green/w

L

LADIES' PURSE, yellow/132
(*Calceolaria angustifolia*)
Maize yellow to gold or deep orange/w,j

LAUREL, California, bay tree; flowers/209
(*Umbellularia californica*)
Greenish beige; aromatic/w

LAUREL, California, bay tree; fruit/208
(*Umbellularia californica*)
Rosy beige or khaki green; aromatic/w

*LICHEN, brown rock, oyster lichen/24
(*Umbilicaria* sp.)
Magenta-violet; aromatic/w

*LICHEN, old man's beard/27
(*Usnea barbata*)
Orange/w

*LICHEN, staghorn moss/2
(*Letharia vulpina*)
Greenish yellow/w,s

*LICHEN, on oak trees/25
(*Parmelia perlata*)
Deep orange to russet; aromatic/w

*LICHEN, on oak trees, steeped/26
(*Parmelia perlata*)
Bright pink to magenta/w

*LICHEN, on rocks/28
(*Parmelia sulcata*)
Magenta/w

LILAC, blue California/149
(*Ceanothus* spp.)
Light to medium green; aromatic/w

LILAC, purple/180
(*Syringa* spp.)
Light green or light blue-green/w

*LILAC, purple; leaves, in iron pot/181
(*Syringa* spp.)
Various greens or dark green or dark
brown/w,c,j,l

LILAC, purple, twigs/182
(*Syringa* spp.)
Yellow-orange/w

LOBELIA, blue, in copper pot/119
(*Lobelia erinus*)
Pastel green/w

LOGWOOD CHIPS / 8
(*Haematoxylon campechianum*)
Dark to medium blue / c,w,j

LOGWOOD CHIPS / 9
(*Haematoxylon campechianum*)
Blue / w

LOGWOOD CHIPS / 11
(*Haematoxylon campechianum*)
Purple / c

*LOGWOOD CHIPS, one-pot method / 10
(*Haematoxylon campechianum*)
Black to gray / c

LUPINE, purple / 56
(*Lupinus* spp.)
Bright yellow-green or dulled green / w

LUPINE, yellow bush / 150
(*Lupinus* spp.)
Bright yellow / w

M

MADDER ROOTS / 12
(*Rubia tinctorum*)
Bright to dull red / w,s,c

*MADRONE, bark / 211
(*Arbutus menziesii*)
Variations of warm brown or variations of gold-tan / w

*MADRONE, bark, on cotton and jute / 212
(*Arbutus menziesii*)
Rose-beige or chestnut brown / c,l,j

MALLOW, tree, steeped / 57
(*Malva* sp.)
Medium blue / w

MALLOW, tree, and tin crystals / 58
(*Malva* sp.)
Deep blue / w

MALVA WEED, cheeses, in iron pot / 59
(*Malva* sp.)
Cream color or yellow or khaki green / w

*MANZANITA, leaves / 151
(*Arctostaphylos* spp.)
Deep camel or rose-buff / w,c

MAPLE, red flowering / 183
(*Abutilon hybridum*)
Navy blue / w

MARGUERITES, yellow, Paris daisy / 120
(*Chrysanthemum frutescens*)
Gold or mustard green / w

MARIGOLDS, with tin crystals / 121
(*Tagetes* sp.)
Yellow-orange or gold or dull green / w

MEADOW RUE / 60
(*Thalictrum polycarpon*)
Bright yellow; fragrant / w

MILKWEED, showy, and cupric sulfate or unlined copper pot / 61
(*Asclepias speciosa*)
Moss green or brass green / w

MORNING-GLORY, bindweed / 62
(*Convolvulus arvensis*)
Dull green or khaki green to yellow / w

MUGWORT, California, in iron pot / 63
(*Artemisia* sp.)
Gold or chartreuse and various greens; aromatic / w

MULBERRY, black, tree, berries / 239
(*Morus nigra*)
Intense red-violet to dark purple or purple / w,j, reed

MULBERRY LEAVES, in iron pot / 240
(*Morus nigra*)
Yellow-green / w

MULE EARS / 64
(*Wyethia angustifolia*)
Gold to brass / w

MULLEIN, and ammonia / 65
(*Verbascum thapsus*)
Bright yellow or chartreuse / w

MULLEIN, torches, candlewick, big taper, our lady's flannel, and cupric sulfate / 66
(*Verbascum thapsus*)
Moss green or dark yellow-green / w

MYRTLE, wax, berries (dry) / 152
(*Myrica californica*)
Various gray-browns / w

MYRTLE, wax, berries (dry), and tin crystals / 153
(*Myrica californica*)
Maroon purple / w

N

NICOTIANA, maroon, and cupric sulfate / 122
(*Nicotiana* sp.)
Grayed green / w

NIGHTSHADE / 67
(*Solanum* sp.)
Bright yellow or dull gold or various khaki greens / w

NIGHTSHADE, and cupric sulfate/68
(*Solanum* sp.)
Chartreuse or deeper chartreuse/w

O

OLEANDER, dark pink/184
(*Nerium oleander*)
Light gray-green or medium gray-green/w

OLIVE TREE, leaves, in iron pot/245
(*Olea europaea*)
Bright yellow or olive green/w

OLIVES, raw/241
(*Olea europaea*)
Variations of maroon/w

OLIVES, raw skin/242
(*Olea europaea*)
Variations of blue-green or variations of lavender/w

OLIVES, raw skin, and cupric sulfate/243
(*Olea europaea*)
Blue-gray or black/w

OLIVES, raw whole, in aluminum pot on jute/244
(*Olea europaea*)
Deep purple/j

ONION, red, skins/14
(*Allium* sp.)
Gold to henna red to maroon/w,c

ONION, red, skins, and tin crystals/248
(*Allium* sp.)
Khaki to olive green/w,c

ONION, yellow skins, in iron pot/246
(*Allium* sp.)
Yellow-brown/w,c

ONION, yellow skins, and tin crystals/247
(*Allium* sp.)
Tan-orange/w,c,j

OSAGE ORANGE/214
(*Maclura pomifera*)
Intense greenish yellow or deep burnt orange/w

OSAGE ORANGE, in iron pot/215
(*Maclura pomifera*)
Khaki green/w

OSAGE ORANGE, on jute and cotton/216
(*Maclura pomifera*)
Intense green-gold or yellow/j,c

*OWL'S CLOVER/69
(*Orthocarpus* spp.)

Lemon yellow or mustard or ocher/w,c

OWL'S CLOVER, in iron pot/70
(*Orthocarpus* spp.)
Yellowish gray or brass greens to khaki greens/c,w

P

PADAUK/217
(*Pterocarpus dalbergioides*)
Salmon pink/w

PADAUK, and cupric sulfate/218
(*Pterocarpus dalbergioides*)
Deep terra-cotta red/w

PANSY, dark-blue, steeped/124
(*Viola tricolor*)
Blue-greens/w

PANSY, hearts-ease, and cupric sulfate/123
(*Viola tricolor*)
Variations of deep yellow-green/w

PEARLY EVERLASTING/41
(*Anaphalis margaritacea*)
Yellow-gold or orange-gold/w

PEARLY EVERLASTING, and cupric sulfate/42
(*Anaphalis margaritacea*)
Light olive green or light brown/w

*PENSTEMON, red, one-pot and mordant method/125
(*Penstemon* sp.)
Tan to golden brown/w

PENSTEMON, red, with cupric sulfate/126
(*Penstemon* sp.)
Medium brown/w

PERNAMBUCO, brazilwood/219
(*Caesalpinia echinata*)
Blood red/w

PERNAMBUCO, and cupric sulfate/220
(*Caesalpinia echinata*)
Wine red/w

PERNAMBUCO, and tin crystals/221
(*Caesalpinia echinata*)
Vermilion/w

PETUNIAS, purple, and English walnut leaves/127
(*Petunia hybrida* and *Juglans regia*)
Light khaki green/w

PETUNIAS, red, and marigolds/128
(*Petunia* sp. and *Tagetes* sp.)
Various dark greens to brown/w

PICKLEWEED, glasswort, samphire, in
iron pot/71
(*Salicornia* sp.)
Gray-green/w

PIGWEED/72
(*Amaranthus* sp.)
Moss green or brass or pale yellow/w

PIGWEED, in iron pot/73
(*Amaranthus* sp.)
Forest green or khaki green/w

PINE NEEDLES, in iron pot/222
(*Pinus* sp.)
Olive green; aromatic/w,c

PITTOSPORUM, seeds/223
(*Pittosporum crassifolium*)
Dark blue/w

PITTOSPORUM, seeds, steeped/224
(*Pittosporum crassifolium*)
Dark blue/w

PLANTAIN/74
(*Plantago lanceolata*)
Dull gold or dark camel/w

PLANTAIN, old ooze/75
(*Plantago lanceolata*)
Brown/w

PLUM, green, leaves, and cupric sul-
fate/249
(*Prunus* sp.)
Light green or yellow-green/w

PLUM, green, leaves, in iron pot/250
(*Prunus* sp.)
Yellow-green/w

PLUM, red, fruit, and ammonia/251
(*Prunus* sp.)
Variations of dark olive green/w

PLUM, red, fruit, in iron pot/252
(*Prunus* sp.)
Variations of dark gray-green to dark
gray/w

PLUM, red, fruit, and tin crystals/253
(*Prunus* sp.)
Violet/w

*PLUM, dark-red, leaves, one-pot
method/254
(*Prunus* sp.)
Olive green/w

PLUM, dark-red, leaves, and tin crys-
tals/255
(*Prunus* sp.)

Violet to purple or lavender/w,c,j,l

POINSETTIA, leaves/185
(*Euphorbia pulcherrima*)
Greenish brown/w

*POMEGRANATE, flowers/256
(*Punica granatum*)
Coppery brown or tan/w,c

*POMEGRANATE, ooze/258
(*Punica granatum*)
Black/w,c,j,s

*POMEGRANATE, raw, skin, and seeds,
steeped/259
(*Punica granatum*)
Beige to apricot/w

*POMEGRANATE, skins, quantity rec-
ipe/257
(*Punica granatum*)
Dark brown or black or gray/w,c

*POMEGRANATE, skins, North African
one-pot method/260
(*Punica granatum*)
Dark brown/w

POPPY, Iceland, pods/130
(*Papaver nudicaule*)
Mustard yellow or copper brown or light
brown/w,c

POPPY, red Iceland/129
(*Papaver nudicaule*)
Light brick red or beige/w

PRIMROSE, dark-red, in iron pot/131
(*Primula* sp.)
Greenish yellow or bright avocado
green/w

PRIVET, berries, in aluminum pot/225
(*Ligustrum* sp.)
Grass green/w

PRIVET, berries, in iron pot/226
(*Ligustrum* sp.)
Dark blue-gray/w

PRIVET, leaves/227
(*Ligustrum* sp.)
Yellow or dark khaki green/w

R

RABBIT BRUSH/76
(*Chrysothamnus* sp.)
Lemon yellow or gold-copper/w

RABBIT BRUSH, and tin crystals/77
(*Chrysothamnus* sp.)
Yellow-orange or pumpkin orange/w

RAGWORT, tansy-ragwort, stinking
willie/78
(*Senecio jacobaea*)
Bright yellow or brassy gold/w

RAGWORT, tansy-ragwort, and cupric
sulfate/79
(*Senecio jacobaea*)
Chartreuse or mustard-brown/w

RAGWORT, tansy-ragwort, and tin crys-
tals/80
(*Senecio jacobaea*)
Orange or light burnt orange or pale
yellow/w,c

REDWOOD, California, bark/228
(*Sequoia* spp.)
Tan or light golden brown to terra-
cotta/w

RHODODENDRON, leapes, in iron pot/186
(*Rhododendron* spp.)
Gray-green/w

ROSEMARY/261
(*Rosmarinus officinalis*)
Various yellow-greens/w

RUDBECKIA/133
(*Rudbeckia* sp.)
Bright chartreuse to dark green/w

S

SAGEBRUSH/81
(*Artemisia tridentata*)
Various tan-golds or brilliant yellow or
yellow/w,s,c,l,j

SAGEBRUSH, in iron pot/82
(*Artemisia tridentata*)
Variations of dark green or sage green or
brown/w, raffia

SAGEBRUSH, overdye on scabiosa
green/135
(*Artemisia tridentata* and *Scabiosa
atropurpurea*)
Dark avocado green/w

SAINT-JOHNS-WORT/141
(*Hypericum calycinum*)
Yellow-orange or pumpkin/w

*SALAL, berries/154
(*Gaultheria shallon*)
Dark blue/w

*SALAL, berries, and cupric sulfate/155
(*Gaultheria shallon*)
Various dark greens/w

SANDBAR WILLOW, in iron pot/156
(*Salix hindsiana*)

Pale yellow or gold or avocado or deep
mustard green/w

SANTOLINA, lavender cotton, french
lavender/262
(*Santolina chamaecyparissus*)
Sienna gold or yellow/w

SANTOLINA, and cupric sulfate/263
(*Santolina chamaecyparissus*)
Pea green or green-brown/w

SCABIOSA, purplish, pincushion
flower/134
(*Scabiosa atropurpurea*)
Bright green or dull dark blue/w,c

SCABIOSA, purplish, and walnut
leaves/136
(*Scabiosa atropurpurea* and *Juglans* spp.)
Avocado green or dark gray-green/w,j,l

SELF HEAL, heal-all/83
(*Prunella vulgaris*)
Bright olive green/w

*SILK OAK/213
(*Grevillea robusta*)
Intense canary yellow or olive green/w

SILK TASSEL SHRUB, fruits/157
(*Garrya elliptica*)
Gray to black/w

*SNAPDRAGON, dark-reddish/137
(*Antirrhinum majus*)
Light green or dark green or brown/w

SNAPDRAGON, dark-reddish, on plant
fibers/138
(*Antirrhinum majus*)
Pale green or tannish gold/c,l,j

SOUR GRASS, yellow oxalis, wood sor-
rel/84
(*Oxalis corniculata*)
Maize yellow to neon orange/j,c,w

SOUR GRASS, wood sorrel, and tin
crystals/85
(*Oxalis corniculata*)
Deep orange-red to brown/w

SPICE BUSH, and cupric sulfate/158
(*Calycanthus occidentalis*)
Light brown/w

STOCK, purple/139
(*Matthiola incana*)
Blue or turquoise/w

STOCK, purple, and tin crystals/140
(*Matthiola incana*)
Dark blue or purple/w

T

TARWEED/86
(*Hemizonia luzulaefolia*)
Golden yellow or light yellow; aromatic/w,c,j

TARWEED, in iron pot/87
(*Hemizonia luzulaefolia*)
Dark brassy green; aromatic/w,c

*TEA, black/3
(*Thea sinensis*)
Rose-tan or gray or black/w,c,l,j

TEA, red-flowered New Zealand, tree/187
(*Leptospermum scoparium*)
Medium yellow-green/w

TEA, red-flowered New Zealand, tree, in iron pot/188
(*Leptospermum scoparium*)
Greenish-black/w

TEA, sassafras, bark (purchased)/264
(*Sassafras albidum*)
Light terra-cotta to orange-tan/w

TOYON, Christmas berry/159
(*Heteromeles arbutifolia*)
Golden brown/w

TOYON, Christmas berry, berries and leaves in iron pot/160
(*Heteromeles arbutifolia*)
Dark olive green/w

TOYON, Christmas berry, berries and leaves, steeped/161
(*Heteromeles arbutifolia*)
Black/w

*TURMERIC SPICE/1
(*Curcuma longa*)
Bright golden orange/w,c,l,j

TWINBERRIES, and tin crystals/162
(*Lonicera involucrata*)
Gray/w

V

VETCH, hairy vetch, winter vetch/88
(*Vicia benghalensis*)
Variations of deep turquoise-green/w

VETCH, and cupric sulfate/89
(*Vicia benghalensis*)
Variations of bright yellow-green/w

W

*WALNUT BLACK, leaves/265
(*Juglans nigra*)
Cinnamon to dark brown or tan to brown/w,c,j

*WALNUT BLACK, leaves, steeped/266
(*Juglans nigra*)
Almost black or light brown or brown/w,c,j

*WALNUT CATKINS, English/267
(*Juglans regia*)
Light golden brown/w

*WELD, one-pot method/13
(*Reseda luteola*)
Yellow/s,w,c

WOODRUFF, sweet/268
(*Asperula odorata*)
Soft tan or gray-green/w

WOOLLY-ASTER, seaside/163
(*Eriophyllum staechadifolium*)
Bronze-gold to golden brown/w

Y

YARROW/90
(*Achillea millefolium* and spp.)
Yellow to maize or dark green/w

YARROW, in copper pot/91
(*Achillea millefolium* and spp.)
Chartreuse to tan-greens/w

Subject Index

(References are to page number.)

A

Acid rinse / 41
Acidity / 201
After-mordanting / 35, 40, 41
  alum / 40
  chrome / 40
  chrome-alum / 40
  cupric sulfate / 41
  cupric sulfate stock solution / 41
  dunging / 54
  ferrous sulfate / 40
  tin / 41, 45, 61
Algae / 17
Alkaline rinse / 41, 42, 67
Alkalinity / 11, 27, 41, 42, 55, 62
Alum / 4, 6, 25, 27, 51, 53, 55
  after-mordanting / 40
  bath / 39
  pre-mordanting / 37, 40, 53
Alum, native / 51, 53
Alum root / 48, 51, 52, 53
Ammonia / 26, 41, 42, 45, 47, 62, 67, 72
Amsden, C. A. / 24
Annato / 6, 33
Aroma / 17, 80, 82, 85, 109, 124, 166, 176, 187
Artificial dyes / 6, 7, 44

B

Baking soda / 26, 201
Barberry / 33
Bark / 16, 17, 19, 52, 62
  madrone / 17
  oak / 19
Bauhaus school / 71
Bedstraw (Galium verum) / 14, 23
Beetles / 7, 9, 10, 12
  Kermes / 7, 9
  Lac / 7
Beets / 2, 20, 49, 206
Berries / 1, 2, 20, 33, 43, 44, 46, 62, 71
  blackberry / 2, 20, 44, 46
  blueberry / 20, 44
  elderberry / 20
  huckleberry / 44
  mulberry / 2, 20
  strawberry / 2
Black / 4, 7, 28, 53

Blue / 7, 8, 9, 13, 16, 17, 20, 33, 43, 45, 48, 55, 56, 61, 62, 71
Body stain / 1, 2, 8, 44, 177
Brown / 19, 41, 44, 45, 50, 54, 62
Bühler, H. / 24, 51, 57, 58
Burr clover / 17

C

Cabbage, purple / 45, 46
Cactus / 9, 10, 12, 33
  soaking / 48
  steeping / 49, 56, 57
Chamomile / 22, 44, 205
Chartreuse / 17
Cheese weed / 17
Cherry leaves / 17
Chrome / 6, 25, 37, 40
  after-mordanting / 40
  pre-mordanting / 37
Chrome-alum after-mordanting / 40
Clay / 1, 2, 16, 53, 71
Cleavers / 14, 23
Clubmoss / 51
Cochineal / 7, 8, 9, 10, 12, 18
Coffee / 10, 44, 46
Cold bath dyeing method / 49, 51
Color
  expectations / 76, 77
  experiments / 1, 2
  fastness (see Lightfast; Wash fastness)
  rubbing / 1
Color relationships / 72
  similarity and difference / 72, 73
Color relativity / 72, 73
Color texture / 70, 71, 72, 73, 76
Copper / 6, 25
  after-mordanting with / 41
  salts / 24
  sulfate after-bath / 41
  sulfate stock solution / 41
Coral bells / 52
Coralline wood / 19
Cordage / 45
Coreopsis / 16, 19, 41
Corn, purple / 44
Cosmetics / 1, 2, 8, 55, 124, 155, 204, 205
Cotton / 8, 24, 27, 28, 30, 33, 44, 45, 46, 53, 54, 61, 63, 71, 200
Cream of tartar / 25, 26, 33, 35, 38, 64
Crochet yarn / 45, 46
Crocus / 16, 43, 49, 77
Crude alum / 53
Cupric sulfate / 41, 64

D

Dahlias / 16, 22, 117
Dandelion root / 20, 21, 49
Dates / 58, 59, 60
Delphiniums / 33
Direct dye class / 6
Direct dyeing / 1, 6, 33, 44, 51, 55

Scientific Name Index

(References are to page number.)

A

Abutilon hydridum / 155
Acacia sp. / 159
Acacia catechu / 12
Achillea filipendulina / 111
Achillea millefolium and spp. / 111, 112
Adenostoma sp. / 18
Allium sp. / 46, 181, 182
Althaea officinalis / 146
Althaea rosea / 122, 123
Amaranthus sp. 21, 102, 103
Amaryllis / 46
Anaphalis margaritacea / 86, 87
Anemone / 113
Anthemis cotula / 80
Anthemis nobilis / 176
Antirrhinum majus / 133, 134
Arbutus menziesii / 167
Arctostaphylos spp. / 139
Arctotis sp. / 120
Artemisia sp. / 98
Artemisia tridentata / 107, 132
Asclepias speciosa / 97
Asperula odorata / 23, 189

B

Berberis sp. / 146, 148
Berberis canadensis / 147
Berberis vulgaris / 146
Beta vulgaris / 56
Bixa orellana / 6, 33
Brassica oleracea var. capitata / 175, 176
Buddleia davidii / 148, 149

C

Caesalpinia echinata / 170
Calceolaria angustifolia / 130
Callistemon sp. / 159, 160
Calycanthus occidentalis / 143
Camellia sp. / 149
Campanula medium / 113
Ceanothus spp. / 138
Ceanothus americanus / 138
Chenopodium sp. / 89
Chrysanthemum spp. / 114
Chrysanthemum frutescens / 125
Chrysothamnus sp. / 105

Clarkia

Clarkia sp. / 89
Clutia tranvancorica / 161, 162
Coccus cacti / 12
Convolvulus arvensis / 97
Coreopsis sp. / 116, 118
Coreopsis spp. / 115
Coreopsis auriculata / 80
Coreopsis calliopsidea / 68, 80
Coreopsis gigantea / 82
Cotoneaster sp. / 150
Cotula coronopifolia / 80
Crataegus sp. / 164
Crocus sativus / 16, 43
Crocus vernus / 116
Curcuma longa / 3
Cuscuta sp. / 84

D

Dactylopius spp. / 18
Dahlia sp. / 118
Dahlia pinnata / 117, 118, 119, 120
Digitalis purpurea / 121

E

Epiphyllum sp. / 57
Eriococcus sp. / 18
Eriophyllum staechadifolium / 145
Erodium spp. / 88
Eucalyptus cinerea / 165
Eucalyptus coccifera / 164
Eucalyptus globulus / 163, 164
Eucalyptus leucoxylon / 165
Eucalyptus polyanthemos / 162, 163
Euphorbia pulcherrima / 156

F

Foeniculum vulgare / 87
Fucus / 17

G

Galium aparine / 14, 23
Galium boreale / 14
Galium verum / 14, 23
Garrya elliptica / 142
Gaultheria shallon / 141
Geranium spp. / 69
Geranium dissectum / 121
Geranium maculatum / 121
Geranium robertianum / 91
Gnaphalium spp. / 82
Grevillea robusta / 167
Grindelia sp. / 90

H

Haematoxylon campechianum / 13, 14
Helichrysum petiolatum / 85, 86
Hemizonia luzulaefolia / 109, 110

Heteromeles arbutifolia / 144
Heuchera / 51, 53
Heuchera americana / 52
Heuchera cylindrica glabella / 51
Heuchera micrantha / 51
Heuchera sanguinea / 52
Hibiscus spp. / 152
Hibiscus syriacus / 146
Hyacinthus orientalis / 123
Hypericum calycinum / 135
Hypericum perforatum / 92, 93

I

Indigofera sp. / 57
Indigofera tinctoria / 57, 58, 59
Iris spp. / 124
Iris germanica / 124
Iris pallida / 124
Isatis tinctoria / 8, 17

J

Juglans spp. / 133
Juglans nigra / 188
Juglans regia / 120, 129, 189

K

Kermes sp. / 18

L

Larrea sp. / 18
Leptospermum scoparium / 157
Letharia vulpina / 4, 6, 51, 69
Ligustrum sp. / 172, 173
Lobelia erinus / 125
Lonicera involucrata / 145
Lupinus spp. / 94
Lupinus arboreus / 139
Lycopodiaceae / 51

M

Maclura pomifera / 168, 169
Mahonia spp. / 137, 138
Malva sp. / 95
Matthiola incana / 134
Melianthus major / 152
Morus mesozygia / 160, 161
Morus nigra / 178, 179
Myrica californica / 140

N

Narcissus pseudo-narcissus / 117
Nerium oleander / 156
Nicotiana sp. / 126

O

Olea europaea / 179, 180, 181
Opuntia robusta / 56
Orthocarpus spp. / 101, 102
Oxalis corniculata / 16, 19, 108, 109

P

Papaver nudicaule / 129, 130
Parmelia molluscula / 52
Parmelia perlata / 78
Parmelia sulcata / 50, 79
Pelargonium hortorum / 121, 122
Penstemon sp. / 99, 128
Petunia sp. / 129
Petunia hybrida / 129
Phaseolus vulgaris / 175
Phormium tenax / 150, 151, 152
Pinus sp. / 171
Pittosporum crassifolium / 171
Plantago lanceolata / 104
Polygonum aviculare / 93, 94
Primula sp. / 130
Prunella vulgaris / 108
Prunus sp. / 182, 183, 184
Pterocarpus dalbergioides / 169
Punica granatum / 185, 186

R

Ranunculus sp. / 113
Raphiolepis indica / 153, 154
Reseda luteola / 14, 22
Reseda odorata / 22
Rhododendron spp. / 156
Rosmarinus officinalis / 186
Rubia tinctorum / 10, 14
Rubus sp. / 175
Rudbeckia sp. / 121, 131
Rumex spp. / 83, 84

S

Salicornia sp. / 84, 102
Salix hindsiana / 142
Sambucus spp. / 136
Santolina chamaecyparissus / 17, 187
Sassafras albidum / 188
Scabiosa atropurpurea / 132, 133
Senecio cruentus / 114, 115
Senecio hybridus / 114, 115
Senecio jacobea / 106, 108
Sequoia spp. / 173
Sherardia arvensis L. / 14
Solanum sp. / 100, 101
Solidago spp. / 89
Stachys sp. / 90
Symplocos / 51
Syringa spp. / 154, 155

T

Tachardiella spp. / 18

Tagetes *sp.* / 125, 129
Thalictrum polycarpum / 96
Thea sinensis / 4

U

Ulex europaeus / 136
Umbellularia californica / 165, 166
Umbilicaria *sp.* / 78
Usnea barbata / 79

V

Verbascum thapsus / 99, 100
Vicia bengalensis / 110
Viola tricolor / 127, 128
Vitis *spp.* / 177
Vitis labruscana / 177, 178

W

Wyethia augustifolia / 98

Z

Zea mays / 177